UNDERSTANDING REPEATED SELF-INJURY

Understanding Repeated Self-Injury

A Multidisciplinary Approach

Digby Tantam
Nick Huband

palgrave
macmillan

First published 2009 by
PALGRAVE MACMILLAN

Palgrave Macmillan in the UK is an imprint of Macmillan Publishers Limited, registered in England, company number 785998, of Houndmills, Basingstoke, Hampshire RG21 6XS.

Palgrave Macmillan in the US is a division of St Martin's Press LLC, 175 Fifth Avenue, New York, NY 10010.

Palgrave Macmillan is the global academic imprint of the above companies and has companies and representatives throughout the world.

Palgrave® and Macmillan® are registered trademarks in the United States, the United Kingdom, Europe and other countries

ISBN-13: 978-0-230-57939-2   hardback
ISBN-10: 0-230-57939-6   hardback
ISBN-13: 978-1-4039-3696-7   paperback
ISBN-10: 1-4039-3696-X   paperback

This book is printed on paper suitable for recycling and made from fully managed and sustained forest sources. Logging, pulping and manufacturing processes are expected to conform to the environmental regulations of the country of origin.

A catalogue record for this book is available from the British Library.

A catalog record for this book is available from the Library of Congress.

10 9 8 7 6 5 4 3 2 1
18 17 16 15 14 13 12 11 10 09

Printed in China

Contents

Figures and Tables

Text Boxes

Preface

This book is based on our experiences as a nurse and a doctor and as counsellors in looking after people who repeatedly injure themselves. In writing it we have also drawn on published research of repeated self-injury, including research carried out by ourselves.

Our main findings were that self-injury is ubiquitous and universal, although it is not always problematic. In fact, it is often considered unexceptional when it is carried out in public, and when people injure themselves to gain culturally approved ends. We concluded that

■ Problematic self-injury is almost always carried out in private and attempts are made to hide the behaviour. It is usually performed by one person (or by one person and a few assistants) and its scars are also concealed.

■ There is a resistance to all kinds of self-injury which we term the 'safety-catch'. However, this safety-catch can be subverted. We consider how in Chapter 3.

■ Self-injury is repeated because it is a means of changing how a person feels. A particular part of self-injury can therefore be 'triggered' by something that arouses unpleasant and unmanageable feelings. These feelings may be distressing because of a person's earlier experience.

■ In our research we often found that the trigger had to be reapplied frequently before self-injury resulted. This most commonly expressed itself as rising tension, like a winding spring or like squeezing the trigger on a water pistol to build up the pressure. We called this the 'spring' pathway to self-injury. In Chapter 3 we examine what emotions constitute the trigger, why they get wound-up like a spring, and why the skin provides a way of discharging them.

■ Self-injury is closely linked to 'dissociation', a term applied to the partial or complete loss of awareness of an action or a perception. In dissociation a person can seem to others to be acting with full awareness and yet have no awareness themselves. Our research found that the people who repeat-edly self-injure and who also dissociate are as likely to 'switch' suddenly into hurting themselves, as they are to follow the 'spring' pathway. We called this the 'switch' pathway because a person who has no thoughts of self-injury (and who may have no or a low level of craving to do so) can rapidly switch into doing so almost without thinking. In the switch pathway, the trigger is more likely to be a reminder of self-injury, such as finding a razor blade in a drawer or catching sight of someone's scars.

- In Chapter 4 we examine what it is like for someone to have these tendencies to self-injure. Since a person is particularly likely to injure her or himself at times of personal transition or crisis, we find it useful to consider self-injury in relation to personal identity. In this chapter we address one particular element of personal identity – the boundary of the self-image. We suggest that the skin becomes a testing ground for this boundary for people who injure themselves.

- Our final research endeavour was to investigate what treatments and interventions were helpful to people who repeatedly self-injure. We used surveys of professionals, feedback from people who injured themselves, and an analysis of the postings to web-based discussion forums to get a picture of what people who repeatedly injure themselves want and what most helps those who want to change this pattern of behaviour. We use the survey data as the starting point for Chapters 6, 7 and 8 which concern how professionals and other carers can help in the process of recovery.

- Self-injury is carried out in private, but sooner or later other people come to know about it. It can have a profoundly upsetting effect. In Chapter 6 we consider the burden on others and how their reactions can help or hinder people who injure themselves to change if they want to. We also examine the effects of this burden on professional carers in this chapter, and its effects on the self-injurer.

During the course of our research we became aware of how much informa-tion and support many people who injure themselves give to each other. This kind of help is important because it often addresses what a person can do to help themselves. Self-help of this kind is also valued by carers who often want to know what are the dos and don'ts of supporting someone who self-injures. It may be available via the Internet as well as through meetings or support groups. We have included some of the best of this advice within Chapter 8.

Chapter 7 concerns short-term crisis management and the initial profes-sional response to self-injury, whereas Chapter 8 focuses on longer-term interventions and recovery. Chapter 9 summarises the key themes developed throughout the book. We conclude that one of the biggest single problems for people who injure themselves – and for their carers – is the emotional impact of the injury. This may range from fascination through to sheer horror, disgust, anger or fear. Most of these reactions make it hard for people to be rational about self-injury, or to see the person and not the injury. However, working through these emotions can allow more thoughtful consideration of the difficulties faced by a person who has resorted to hurting themselves in this way. One way of achieving this is for all parties to question the assumption that self-injury is extreme behaviour, or that is rare and therefore suggestive of a high degree of personal disturbance.

A NOTE ON LANGUAGE

Self-injury may provoke even reasonable, caring people into harsh, judgemental responses. We suggest that this is because all of us have a 'safety-catch' preventing self-harm which is vicariously engaged when we observe others who harm themselves. One consequence of what people who harm themselves may experience as the bigotry of other people is that people who harm themselves are unusually sensitive to slighting or alienating language. There are good reasons for this. Naming something is one of the ways that we dispose of it. Names can cut off our sympathy for others or increase it. Words are power. Choosing our words and having that choice accepted by others is one way of increasing power and social influence, but conversely having words applied to us reduces our autonomy and alienates us from power.

One example is the use of the word 'deliberate' in the commonly used umbrella term 'deliberate self-harm' (or DSH). We think that the inclusion of the word 'deliberate' distorts the motives of self-injury as much as does lumping self-poisoning and self-injury together. Deliberateness seems to us to suggest that there is a choice about self-injury, perhaps the pursuit of the 'secondary gain' that has been assumed to be a motive since it was first proposed by Freud (1914). When people who injure themselves have been able to describe their experience to us, it is that they injure themselves defensively as a means of survival, and not offensively as a covert means of coercing others. We agree with Taylor (2003) that to call this 'deliberate' self-harm connotes blame. We shall therefore refer to 'self-injury' or 'self-harm' throughout this book, and not 'deliberate' self-harm.

Believing that people who injure themselves can choose not to is one of the attitudes which we have called a 'firm' management style. A firm management style may be a way of creating an emotional distance from a person who self-injures. Other terms that do this include 'manipulative', 'attention seeking' and, sometimes, 'personality disorder'. They all attribute self-injury to a failing in the person who self-injures and this can, we think, create a slippery path to insensitive treatment. We do not think that terms like 'manipulative' and 'attention seeking' add anything useful to understanding. We all manipulate others, but most people have the power to do it without sacrificing themselves. A tragedy for many people who self-injure is that they lack that important social effectiveness. The attention that a person gets from harming themselves is often negative: it is difficult to see how that could be the aim of self-harm.

We will try in this book not to use these and other terms which we consider unhelpful, but we do not want to be precious about this. We know that our language will be influenced by our own background and professional training. There is no 'right' language, and all of us bring preconceptions to the topic of self-injury which are embedded in the language we use. However, we hope that we do not use language to imply that there can be no disagreement with what we say, as professionals sometimes do. Helping people always involves dialogue, and we hope that our readers will feel that they are entering into a dialogue with us, rather than either having to accept or reject what we write without reservation.

Acknowledgements

The authors wish to thank Elsevier for permission to reproduce Figure 9.1 from Spender Q (2005). Assessment of adolescent self-harm. Current Paediatrics, 15, 120–6.

Every effort has been made to trace rights holders, but if any have been inadvertently overlooked the publishers would be pleased to make the necessary arrangements at the first opportunity.

We are very grateful to Professor Emmy van Deurzen and Professor Conor Duggan for their support and encouragement. We would also like to thank sincerely those patients and clients we have worked with clinically over the years who have regularly injured themselves and have taught us so much about their experiences. Many have offered valuable insights of their own into the phenomenon of self-injury as well as practical ideas about how people who self-injure might be better helped. Some of the work reported in these pages was carried out in partial fulfilment of the degree of PhD at the University of Sheffield, and NH gratefully acknowledges the Smith & Nephew Foundation for the award of a research fellowship which greatly assisted the completion of this.

In writing this book we have included a number of illustrative case vignettes. These have been amalgamated from several different cases with any identifying features altered. They are true to life but any correspondence to an actual person is accidental and none of the cases should be taken to be of a particular person.

Chapter 1

The Basic Facts about Self-Injury

This book focuses on people who repeatedly injure themselves by cutting, burning or otherwise damaging their skin and its underlying tissue. This 'self-injury' is one of the two main types of self-harm, the other being self-poisoning with household or agricultural chemicals or with medication. Self-injury and self-poisoning are often regarded as sufficiently similar to be considered as two facets of one problem. This fits with the observation that many of those who cut themselves also take overdoses, but it is not consistent with the very different cultural and psychological roots of self-injury and of self-poisoning. We argue that it is important to consider self-injury in its own right, as we do in this book.

Self-injury remains poorly understood despite being a powerful emotional trigger. Put another way, self-injury is a strong 'emotor'. Its emotive power is certainly relevant to health, but it is also made use of by the fashion industry, by religion and in social rituals marking the transition to adulthood. It has an emotional impact on others that is correspondingly intense. In our view this is because there is an emotional 'safety-catch' that prevents careless self-injury. People who are able to cut or burn their skin intentionally must therefore be able to switch off this safety-catch. We think that evidence of this safety-catch being switched off creates for the onlooker a feeling of danger, in much the same sense as does being around someone with a gun that is ready to fire, and that this is the main reason why self-inflicted injuries are upsetting to other people.

Contrary to popular misconception, self-injury is often carried out in secret and does not usually lead to a demand for attention. Medical care is rarely sought and even when it is, is often not taken up. In a recent unpublished study in Sheffield (Baston, Cross, Thompson and Hockley, personal communication) 45% of those who harmed themselves and for whom an ambulance

I

was called did not travel to hospital, and 17% of those who did go to hospital did not stay in the emergency room long enough to be assessed. Those who injured themselves were more likely than those who poisoned themselves to be in the non-travelling and non-assessed groups.

It is the very private nature of the self-injury that we will be considering in this book. The knowledge that others would disapprove differentiates it from socially sanctioned self-injury,[1] which is mostly religiously inspired. Private self-injury and religious self-injury differ in two main ways. First, private self-injury is secretive and usually hidden from others. In contrast, religious self-injury takes place in cultural rituals and therefore in public (although we are aware that some behaviours, such as self-flagellation, may also be carried out in private as a penance). Second, private self-injury is associated with stigma when discovered and often with shame. By contrast, religiously inspired self-mortification is so often associated with pride that devotees often have to be counselled against this as being a sin.

PRIVATE SELF-INJURY

The key features of 'private self-injury' are as follows:

- Self-inflicted damage to the skin and to underlying tissue.
- Anticipation, either with craving to self-injure, or with mounting tension associated with a struggle to avoid self-injury.
- Thoughts of the consequences of the injury are not entertained or are set aside. People who repeatedly self-injure commonly do so without consideration of the gain or punishment that might follow.
- The goals of the action are wound(s), pain, bleeding or a combination of these. There is no wish to bring about any significant anatomical change and no clear suicidal intent, although death may sometimes follow as a result of recklessness. The act of self-injury appears to be an end in itself.
- Private self-injury may occur in a dissociated state, in which case the person may not be aware of their control over the action. However, it is not the result of command hallucinations, or feeling controlled by an alien presence or in response to a delusional threat as sometimes occurs in people who are psychotic and injure themselves.
- Following the act there is often a temporary feeling of relief, which may sometimes (but not always) be associated with specific thoughts associated with the outflow of blood or with feeling more 'real'.
- There is often reluctance to seek relief from the subsequent pain and trauma; medical care may only be sought after a delay, if at all.

Many individuals who privately injure themselves will do so only occasionally. They may return to it, perhaps as a last resort, at times of overwhelming distress or when they feel unable to cope in any other way. Others find that self-injury can be very difficult to give up once started. Their cutting or burning becomes more frequent and more entrenched as time goes by. As such, it resembles other habit disorders like binge eating, smoking, gambling or Internet addiction. Indeed, many report feeling as if they have become addicted to the behaviour. Even in the absence of any distress, they find themselves developing a strong craving for the next injury. Sometimes, very little time elapses between finishing one cut and thinking about the next, and cutting becomes the dominant theme of a person's life.

Self-injury does not always become entrenched, but when it does it is often accompanied by an escalation of psychological and physical problems. Wound care becomes increasingly challenging, and this in turn can exacerbate interpersonal difficulties. This kind of 'repeated' self-injury is the type that most often leads to a person seeking help, and that most often attracts a psychiatric diagnosis such as 'borderline personality disorder'.

Repetition is often associated with increasing depletion of coping resources, so that cutting that persists over many years often leads to increased anxiety and sensitivity to emotional precipitants. Chronic self-injurers are often significantly less able to cope with emotional stress. Their range of coping resources steadily reduces, and self-wounding itself becomes less effective as a coping mechanism over time. Life becomes very difficult when reduced resilience is combined with impoverished coping resources, plus (as with many addictive behaviours) a diminished return from the one thing that had seemed to help.

Self-injury that continues to be repeated despite therapeutic intervention often results in a particular kind of hopelessness in carers, too. People who repeatedly harm themselves are perceived as requiring a disproportionate amount of health care, perhaps because each episode is often so emotionally draining for all concerned (including the person who injures themselves).

We focus on this kind of repeated, private self-injury in this book because it is the kind that is often most troubling to carers, and because we think that much more can be done to help people who repeatedly wound themselves than many professional carers believe.

PREVALENCE OF SELF-INJURY

Many people injure themselves and it has been estimated that at least 1 in 600 adults wound themselves sufficiently to receive hospital treatment (Tantam & Whittaker, 1992). In one survey of 440 adolescents, 13.9% reported having injured themselves (Ross & Heath, 2002); here self-cutting was the most common behaviour, followed by self-hitting, pinching, scratching, biting and then burning. Young people whose psychological difficulties are severe enough to have led to hospitalization are even more likely to injure themselves, with estimates of the proportion of young people having done so ranging from 40% (Darche, 1990) to 61% (DiClemente et al., 1991).

Teenagers in the UK injure themselves about twice as often as poisoning themselves (Hawton et al., 2002). However a much higher proportion of people who poison themselves end up in hospital with 80%–90% of all hospital admissions for self-harm being for self-poisoning and the remainder being for self-injury. For example, one study in 1997 found that 16% of 934 admissions to one hospital in Central England for self harm were for self-injury, with 10% for wrist-cutting (Dennis, 1997). More recently, Horrocks (2003) found that 21.2% of all attendances to general hospitals in Leeds for self-harm were for self-injury.

SELF-INJURY IS ON THE INCREASE

Private self-injury appears to be on the increase (Nada-Raja et al., 2003), along with self-harm in general. Hawton and colleagues found hospital attendances in Oxford for self-harm rose each year from 1990 to 1997, and the rate of repetition increased significantly during the study period (Hawton et al., 2003).

Some of this increase may be due to better ascertainment with people becoming more willing to admit to self-injury, but this is unlikely to be the whole explanation. Alternative explanations include the social acceptance of tattooing and skin piercing (which we believe can weaken the 'safety-catch' against self-injury); a generally greater tolerance of non-socialized violence (i.e. violence committed outside of socially sanctioned circumstances such as war); and 'copy-cat' or 'modelling' leading to teenagers injuring themselves in emulation of friends and acquaintances.

SELF-INJURY AND GENDER

Findings from community studies are inconsistent about whether self-injury is more common in boys than girls (Hawton et al., 1996) or vice versa (Ross & Heath, 2002). Self-injury certainly affects both genders although, until recently, most attention appears to have been focused on women. Its prevalence is probably similar for both men and women in the general population

(Briere & Gil, 1998; Klonsky et al., 2003) and two studies within Casualty departments in the UK found that over half those who had injured themselves were male (Robinson & Duffy, 1989; Hawton & Catalan, 1987). However, men are more reluctant to seek treatment and so their self-injury may only come to light when it is particularly severe. There is some evidence that self-injury is becoming more common in men. In contrast, rates of reported self-harm (which includes both self-injury and self-poisoning) are higher in women in the UK and throughout Europe (Hawton, 2000).

SELF-INJURY AND YOUNG PEOPLE

It has been estimated that as many as one teenager in ten self-harms in the UK, and a significant proportion of this self-harm appears to be self-injury in the form of skin cutting and, to a lesser extent, burning. A revealing study of 6020 adolescents in English schools found 6.9% had harmed themselves in the previous year and 13.2% reported harming themselves at least once at some time: the proportion was much higher in girls than boys. Many of the reported incidents were by self-cutting, but only 12% resulted in hospital attendance (Hawton et al., 2002). Figures from Australia are not dissimilar: in one study, 5.1% of a large community sample of adolescents reported having self-harmed, the most common methods being self-cutting and deliberate recklessness, although true suicide attempts were only reported by 0.5% (Patton et al., 1997). In a similar study, Martin et al. (1995) found 8.9% of an adolescent sample group reported self-harm, with a similar rate for males and females.

Self-injury often begins in teenage years or even earlier in some cases. In Arnold's (1995) survey of 76 women in the UK, 30% reported that they began injuring themselves before 12 years of age. Similarly, Favazza and Conterio (1989) found 14 years to be the most common age of onset in a study of 240 US residents.

More recent investigations confirm that a significant proportion of young people are injuring themselves at least once, with superficial self-cutting reported in one-fifth of a sample of Turkish high-school students (Zoroglu et al., 2003), and in more than one-third of a sample of Canadian female undergraduates (Paivio & McCulloch, 2004).

Young people often repeat self-injury. The Mental Health Foundation considers 1 in 10 adolescents who have harmed themselves will do so on more than one occasion (Donnellan, 2000, p. 7). In the Oxford self-report study, more than half of those who self-harmed had done so more than once (Hawton et al., 2002), and a survey of female adolescent drug abusers found 29%

of those who self-injured reported cutting themselves only once or twice, while 36% had done so at least six times (Schwartz et al., 1989).

Little information is available on self-injury in older people, but the behaviour does seem to decline with age. This may be due in part to under-reporting, possibly because the shame associated with self-injury is felt more keenly as one grows older. However, as Crowe (1997) observes 'it is quite common to find that in their 30s and 40s many patients who had previously harmed themselves are now no longer doing so'. Older people who do harm themselves are thought to be at higher suicide risk than are younger patients, and are more likely than younger people to be assessed by a mental health professional in the accident and emergency department following self-harm, and are more likely to be offered aftercare (Marriott et al., 2003).

SELF-INJURY AND CULTURE

Self-injury, in the general sense of the term, is certainly not confined to Western culture. In fact, in many parts of the world 'public' self-injury is commonly associated with religious festivals, and in these it is usually young men who injure themselves. For example, self-injury is an integral part of the Shi'ite festival Muharram to mourn the death of Ali, and of various Hindu festivals honouring Shiva or his son Murakan. Religiously inspired, public self-injury of this kind is rare in the West. Indeed, it might be considered obscene.

Suicide rates vary across the world, and may be particularly high in some cultures, such as Sri Lanka and China, but the reasons for this are unclear and may be connected to self-harm with agricultural chemicals and more recently dowsing oneself with paraffin (kerosene) and then setting fire to it. Statistics on private self-injury have not been collected in many of these countries, but in the 13-country WHO/EURO study of parasuicide (Schmidtke et al., 1996) there were very large differences in age-standardized rates of self-harm, with low rates in southern European areas and high rates in the north of Europe.

SELF-INJURY AND ADVERSITY

A considerable number of studies have indicated a strong association between a history of childhood adversity and self-injury later in life. Types of adversity include separation and loss (Walsh & Rosen, 1988) and parental neglect, plus traumatic childhood experiences that includes incest (De Young, 1982): childhood abuse (van der Kolk et al., 1991): sexual abuse (Briere & Gil, 1998): bullying at school (Matsumoto et al., 2004): and witnessing domestic violence

(Boyle et al., 2006). Connors summarizes this body of research by noting that in the history of people who self-injure 'there appears to be a working consensus that one or more childhood trauma and loss experiences exist', although she also observes that some studies have not found any correlation between self-injury and trauma (Connors, 2000, p. 39), and the same statement could probably be made of depression.

The frequency with which mental health professionals see people who have experienced childhood adversity can give a false impression that self-injury is always preceded by a history of difficulties in early life. Self-injury can also be precipitated by adversity in teenage years, by rape in adult life (Greenspan & Samuel, 1989; Zlotnick et al., 1997), by combat experience (Pitman, 1990) and by domestic abuse (Arnold, 1995).

SELF-INJURY AND DISADVANTAGE

Private self-injury occurs in people from all walks of life, but may be more likely in those who are disadvantaged socially or financially. A study of the 2828 individuals who sought hospital treatment in Oxford after self-harm between 1988 and 1996 found rates much higher in those from lower social groups (Hawton et al., 2001). Socio-economic deprivation was closely associated with rates of self-harm among both genders, but was particularly marked in young men even when the effect of social fragmentation was taken into account. Unfortunately the data were not analysed for the sub-group of self-injurers in this study. Ayton et al. (2003) report similar findings in East Yorkshire where socio-economic deprivation was associated with self-poisoning and self-injury.

Of course, people of all social classes do injure themselves and social stress is not confined to the economically disadvantaged. The pressure to succeed may also lead to self-injury (Babiker & Arnold, 1997), as may transgenerational conflict in first-generation children of immigrants. Marginalization may also be the explanation for the high risk of self-injury in gay teenagers, which emerged in a recent survey carried out in the UK by the Lesbian and Gay Foundation.

SELF-INJURY AND MOOD DISORDERS

Self-injury has a complex relationship with mood disorder. A person who cuts their throat for the first time in their 60s after the unexpected death of their wife would be suspected of having a depressive disorder until proven otherwise. If they had other signs and symptoms of depression, it would be the depressive disorder that would be the main diagnosis. The depression would be seen to be the main problem, and the self-injury merely a symptom of that. On the other hand, a person who has been in a social group where tattooing and piercing were the norm may become depressed for the first time when moving into another social group where such skin decorations are looked down on, and lead to stigmatization. This depression may still need treating, but here it is not the cause of the self-injury, but its consequence. Finally, a young woman who is being abused by a partner may become low in her mood in consequence and find that cutting herself actually heightens her mood. In this case the self-injury is a kind of treatment for low mood.

Depressed mood rarely occurs in the absence of anxiety and anger, especially in young people. The complex relationships between self-injury and mood are even more difficult to keep straight when anxiety is included in the picture. Mounting tension with elements of anxiety and irritability often precedes self-injury. Trying not to injure oneself adds to this tension, but other sources of anxiety or frustration do too. Repeated self-injury, like repeated sedation with alcohol or drugs, may actually kindle anxiety. The short-term anxiety relief that immediately follows self-injury may be more than offset by a greater susceptibility to anxiety in the longer-term because the repeated sedation has lowered the threshold at which anxiety develops.

Stigma and social rejection following the discovery of past self-injury may also lead to anxiety and depression, and this may lead to people who self-injure seeking treatment for a mood disorder. Finally, low self-esteem or – as Scheff points out, the frequent experience of shame that is the emotional experience that psychologists have attributed to a deficiency in a hypothetical psychic fuel called self-esteem – may be sufficiently severe as to amount to a depressive disorder. So adolescent mood disorder may sometimes pave the way for self-injury, which may then become self-sustaining.

Psychiatry, as a branch of medicine, has its roots in applied biology. Psychiatric approaches to self-injury have therefore understandably been biased in favour of biological explanations. A simple explanation for the links between self-injury and mood disorder is that self-injury is a symptom of mood disorder that may be more or less obvious, but which is always due to an underlying alteration of brain chemistry. Since the medical treatment of mood disorder has been one of the success stories of modern psychiatry, it should follow that one of the drugs that has been shown to be effective in the treatment of depression and anxiety should be effective in preventing self-injury, too. Regrettably, this has not proved to be the case. The failure to find a drug that effectively prevents self-injury is a further reminder that self-injury is not merely a behaviour – it is an expression of a wish or a desire, and not just a bodily malfunction.

If there is sufficient evidence of a clinically significant mood disorder, independent of the severity or frequency of the self-injury or other self-harm, then offering a treatment for the mood disorder will be appropriate. In fact, the treatment that would normally be given if these symptoms occurred in the absence of self-injury should not be withheld simply because self-injury is also present. An antidepressant may, for example, be indicated in someone who has developed early morning waking, low mood, reduced appetite with weight loss, or some of the other biological symptoms of depression. But even if the antidepressants are effective in treating the low mood, they are unlikely to abolish the self-injury.

SELF-INJURY AND OTHER DISORDERS

People who cut or burn themselves often experience depression, anxiety and panic. Self-injury has also been associated with dissociative identity disorder (Putnam et al., 1986). Self-injury is often (but not always) associated with other forms of self-harm such as misuse of alcohol, committing offences, substance misuse as well as over-dosing on prescribed and over-the-counter medication. The relationship between self-injury and being diagnosed as having certain personality disorders is well-established, although there has been disagreement about whether such a diagnosis is helpful. A history of repeated acts of self-harm is sufficient to satisfy one of the criteria for borderline personality disorder (BPD), and it has been estimated that 70–80% of patients meeting DSM-IV criteria for BPD self-injure (Bohus et al., 2000).

People who injure themselves are more likely to have an eating disorder and vice versa. In single studies, repeated self-cutting has been reported in 40% of a bulimic sample (Mitchell et al., 1986) and in 35% of an anorexic sample (Jacobs & Isaacs, 1986). Using prevalence data from many studies, Sansone & Levitt (2002) estimated remarkably similar rates of self-injury among bulimic outpatients (25%), bulimic inpatients (25%), and anorectic outpatients (23%).

Possible explanations of the association include shared adverse childhood experience, or a common biological substrate of impulsivity (Lacey & Evans, 1986). It has also been suggested, more fancifully, that both eating disorders and self-injury often involve purgation although this seems to assume that the aim of self-injury is not so much to create a wound but to let blood flow (Warren et al., 1998).

SELF-INJURY IS ESPECIALLY COMMON IN PRISONS

Prisons in the UK vary in their recording of incidents of self-harm, and may not distinguish between hanging and self-strangulation with suicidal intent from the kind of self-injury we are discussing in this book. However, in 2001 an improved method of recording self-harm was initiated as a pilot in 10 British prisons to address these difficulties and provide more accurate information. Data from the first six months of this study showed that the overall rate of self-injury was surprisingly high at 840 incidents per 1000 prisoners. More than half the recorded incidents were attributed to self-cutting or scratching, and more than 40% of those who self-harmed did so at least twice in the 6-month period (Howard League, 2003, p. 7). The risk may be higher in those held 'on remand' than in sentenced offenders. Furthermore, in the eight years from 1991 to 1999 there was a 142% rise in the number of prisoners who were self-harming compared with an increase of only 42% in the overall prison population over the same period (Howard League, 1999, p. 8).

Most self-injury in UK prisons is carried out by men, but male prisoners outnumber female inmates by 17:1. The Directorate of Prison Health Care in 1997–8 found rates of self-harm 5.5 times higher among female prisoners than their male counterparts, although a separate study by the Office for National Statistics in 1997 (which excluded suicide attempts) found self-injury affected 7% of sentenced male prisoners and 10% of sentenced female prisoners in their current prison terms (ONS, 1997). This is comparable to the widely quoted figure of 6.5% for male prisoners reported in Toch's earlier study in North America (Toch, 1975). A more recent survey of prisoners in the UK found 23% of women who had spent more than 2 years in prison had self-harmed during their current sentence (Melzer et al., 1999).

In prisons, as in the outside community, there is a strong association with youth. Young prisoners of both sexes appear particularly vulnerable to repeated self-injury and it has been suggested that young people have greater difficulty in adjusting to prison life than those who are older (Liebling, 1998). In fact, concern in 1997 about the extremely high levels of 'cutting up' among female prisoners under 18 years (and summarized in a report by the Howard League) culminated in a change in the law such that teenage girls are no longer sent to adult prisons in the UK.

Self-injury is also more common in other residential institutions, like hospitals and care homes, especially where there is a lack of social stimulus. Solitary confinement is a particular risk (Cullen, 1985). Social isolation may be the common factor in all of these situations (Simeon & Favazza, 2001).

METHODS OF SELF-INJURY

Skin cutting appears to be the most common type of self-injury, but many other methods are used depending on circumstances and individual preference (see Text Box 1.1).

Text Box 1.1 Common methods of private self-injury

Cuts – often made with a blade or glass shard; a cut is usually classed as an incision if its length is greater than its depth. Cuts are often described incorrectly as lacerations, which strictly speaking, are tears arising from blunt force injury.

Puncture injuries – made by a pointed object inserted at right angles to the surface and then withdrawn, or inserted at an angle and then left under the skin. An injury is usually classed as a puncture if its depth is greater than it length.

Dry burns – by contact with a flame or hot object (e.g. iron, cigarette); electrical burns.

Scalds – by contact with hot liquid or steam: external (e.g. via kettle, bath) or internal (e.g. over-hot drinks).

Chemical burns – by contact with caustic substances (e.g. bleach, oven cleaner).

Other presentations – re-opened injures; bruising (potential for fractures) following wall punching, head banging or self-hitting; tissue damage arising from ligaturing an appendage; injures caused by abrading or scouring the skin; internal damage from reversible insertions (typically urethral, rectal or vaginal); injecting contaminants into the skin or deliberately contaminating wounds.

TARGET AREAS FOR SELF-INJURY

Individuals who self-injure often have two or three preferred sites and tend to concentrate most of their cutting or burning at those locations. One study of women who cut themselves by Favazza and Conterio (1989) found the areas most frequently damaged were the arms and wrists (74%), followed by the legs (44%), abdomen (25%), head (23%), chest (18%) and genital area (8%). Another survey of 128 self-inflicted injuries in a sample of adolescents and young adults confirmed the arms as the most popular site (62%), but found the wrists less frequently targeted (23%) (Rosen & Heard, 1995). Choice of location may be determined by convenience (for example, the left forearm is preferred by right-handed individuals), by attraction to areas where a deep injury could be fatal (as with wrist cutting) or by the ease with which the injury can be concealed with clothing. There may also be symbolic factors: for example, Smith and colleagues found that many of the women they talked to had concentrated on areas such as the face, breasts and genitals that were associated with their female identity or were connected with the experience of being sexually abused (Smith et al., 1998, p. 10).

SELF-INJURY CAN LEAD TO DEATH

It is sometimes suggested that people who cut or injure themselves repeatedly are at no particular risk of dying through suicide. This may arise because of enthusiasm, especially among community groups, to teach that repeated self-injury is very different from attempted suicide. We acknowledge that making this distinction is helpful when getting others to understand the behaviour – indeed, we have included lack of clear suicidal intent in our definition of self-injury. At the same time it is essential to be aware that the repetition of self-injury does not indicate that the risk of suicide is low, or that it will remain low. Those who attempt suicide and those who self-injure do not form mutually exclusive groups – the two populations often overlap. Statistically, a history of self-harm increases the risk of suicide by up to a 100 fold (Morgan & Owen, 1990), and follow-up studies of people who self-injure have found suicide rates of 13% (Reilly, 1983) and 16% (Nelson & Grunebaum, 1971).

Risk of suicide is hard to assess since self-injury is varyingly reckless. Sometimes there is very little risk, other times it is major. In addition, the chance of a fatal outcome when indulging in risky behaviour is likely to increase when the individual is ambivalent about living and dying and makes less of an effort to keep safe. The situation is further compounded if cutting takes place while in a dissociated state. Individuals who find they tend to cut themselves 'on automatic pilot' are at risk of doing serious damage without realizing this at the time.

Suicide may be a kind of surrender. Sometimes death may even seem inviting as if it offers warmth or at least relief. Surrendering becomes more likely if a person feels hopeless or if everyone else thinks that they should stop fighting on.

SELF-INJURY AND RELUCTANCE TO SEEK HELP

In community settings, individuals who self-injure vary enormously in the degree to which they seek and accept professional help. This seems to be the case in both physical and psychological domains. Contrary to popular belief, however, most do not seek to draw attention to self-inflicted injuries. The kind of self-injury we consider in this book is a normally performed in private (hence our term 'private' self-injury) and the wounds are hidden from others, perhaps because of feelings of shame. Assistance is not always welcomed, and may even be rejected angrily.

People who self-injure are considered less likely to seek medical help than those who self-poison, particularly young people (Hawton et al., 2002). This may be because the majority of self-inflicted wounds are relatively minor, and even those that warrant attendance at Casualty departments are not usually seen as potentially life-threatening. When assistance from the health care profession is sought, it is often from services that are not hospital-based. One recent study of young adults in New Zealand who presented after self-harm (including self-injury) found that family practitioners, psychologists and counsellors were the commonest sources of help (Nada-Raja et al., 2003).

Older adolescents and young adults have the most difficulty asking for help. A recent survey of over 3000 young adults in the UK found a widespread reluctance to seek help when experiencing mental distress, especially among young males (Biddle et al., 2004). It is also known that many acts of self-harm in adolescents do not come to the attention of their families (Melzer et al., 2002).

Women are more likely than men to seek help for both physical and psychological difficulties, and are more likely to remain engaged in treatment when it is offered. Many studies have reported a well-defined trend of men delaying seeking professional help when they become ill. When they do seek help, physical symptoms appear to be the defining factor, with men less likely to report distress or psychosocial problems as an additional reason for consulting a professional (Galdas et al., 2005). This certainly seems to be the case for self-injury. One possibility, suggested by Taylor (2003, p. 83), is that self-harm is seen in western society as essentially a female behaviour and that this causes men who self-injure to feel ashamed and further marginalized by being men, rather than women. There may be fear that for a man to seek help for self-inflicted injuries is to appear neurotic.

Cultural differences in seeking help among those who self-injure may also be significant, although this topic seems to have attracted little research. One study found that South Asian women in Manchester who self-harmed tended to access services only 'at a point of desperation', rather than prior to the crisis (Chew et al., 2002).

DO EMOTIONAL RESPONSES TO SELF-INJURY HINDER DECISION MAKING?

Self-inflicted cutting, burning or other injury is often distressing to the person who does it as well as for other people who witness the results. It may or may not be associated with suicidal thoughts or intent, but whatever the aim there can be little doubt that self-inflicted damage to the skin is remarkably emotive for all who become involved. It is not unusual for people who self-injure to experience shame and self-loathing. Those who attempt to provide care often find themselves engulfed by strong emotions such as anger, frustration and disgust.

This may be one reason why professionals are often so divided about how to respond to particular clients. This is not helped by the skimpy evidence on what does help. The most studied interventions, for which there is most evidence of efficacy, are often the most complex, the most costly and the least available because extensive training may be required.

People who self-injure can be difficult to understand and manage, and self-injury exerts a powerful impact whether the people injuring themselves intend this or not. Partners, family and close friends often feel out of their depth. GPs, psychiatrists, nurses, social workers and other professionals may also struggle to cope, for the behaviour can powerfully challenge their skills, competency and role.

Although this book is intended for health care professionals, we hope that it will also be useful for those people who repeatedly injure themselves and those who are about them and who wish to become more involved in, and knowledgeable about, therapy.

Chapter 2

Understanding the Person Who Self-Injures

ACTIONS AND BEHAVIOUR

Self-injury is a behaviour. An animal can injure itself inadvertently, for example in its struggle to escape from a trap. But it is also an action when it is carried out by a person. It has a meaning or, rather, it can have many meanings. So Simone Weil, a spiritual writer who died of inanition in a British hospital in 1943, was hailed by some as a saint whose self-starvation was an inspiring identification with the world's poor and suffering, but by others (including the Catholic authorities) as a sufferer from anorexia nervosa. What her death meant was not fixed but a matter of argument which has yet to be resolved. Actions like self-injury do not have fixed meanings, but are open to interpretation and re-interpretation. To write off self-injury as merely a behaviour – as the US term 'self-injurious behaviour' (or SIB) seems to do – is an interpretation, but only an interpretation. It is the interpretation that we place on an action, the meaning that we assign to it, that determines our response and therefore the psychological and social consequences of that action.

Approaching self-injury as a behaviour often leads to it being considered as a symptom of some disorder. Approaching it as an action allows for the possibility that self-injury may be rational, but it may have a downside, too. We hold people to be responsible for their actions. So if we think that self-injury is an action, it is appropriate to assume that a person could stop injuring themselves if they decided that it was in their own interests to do so. We will see later that this is the view taken by many practitioners who have what we will term a 'firm' management style. In contrast, people who consider that self-injury is merely a behaviour do not hold the person responsible for it. They argue that behaviour can be intrinsic, or learned, or conditioned, but is not chosen.

Taking self-injury as a behaviour might seem to be the more attractive option, since it acknowledges that the people who injure themselves may suffer at least as much from their behaviour as everyone else. This is the step often involved in 'medicalizing' self-injury. But there is a downside to this, too. It assumes that self-injury is literally meaningless. This seems to trivialize what for many people who self-injure seems to be a dangerous but important, even transformative, undertaking. People who injure themselves privately may not yet know how they are trying to transform themselves, but they do know that harming oneself is not lightly done, and certainly that it is not merely a habit, nor just a copycat behaviour.

We think that the practitioner who wants to help a person who is self-injuring has to be able to keep both perspectives in mind. People who injure themselves rarely have a simple, straightforward reason that makes them do it. Self-injury usually seems caused, like a behaviour, rather than planned like an action. But afterwards, a person may be able to find many reasons for the self-injury that make them want to claim it as a significant act and not just a thoughtless reflex. So it is rarely helpful to ask why people have injured themselves, but it may be useful to ask what triggered the self-injury or what led up to it. It can also be helpful to ask what having injured themselves means now that they have done it.

We define private self-injury in Text Box 2.1 below.

Text Box 2.1   Definition of private self-injury

Self-inflicted damage to the skin and underlying tissues which tends to be recurrent and in which there is no clear suicidal intent; a tendency to exacerbate or prolong the pain or suffering caused by the injury; and an indifference to any final anatomical change. The wound and the bleeding are the goals of the injury, and the act is usually carried out in private.

WHAT IS IT LIKE TO LIVE WITH SELF-INJURY?

It turns out that people who injure themselves also think of what they do as both behaviours and as actions. Which is chosen depends on how they feel about themselves, who they are speaking to, and whether they are viewing self-injury in prospective or retrospective terms. Many attempts have been made to capture the inner experiences of people who self-injure, including the classic study by Liebenluft and colleagues (1987). We too have tried to capture some of the essentials, and also some of the variation between people who self-injure, in two vignettes. These vignettes, though hypothetical, are drawn from our clinical experience of clients who self-injure.

Mary's story

Mary is 23 years old. She lives in a flat in her hometown and works as an administrative assistant at the local college. Looking back on her life, Mary feels that she got on reasonably well with her parents, although she remembers becoming very distressed when she was nine after her father had left home. She has not seen her father since. Mary has a supportive partner who lives close by. He sometimes stays with her overnight, but always returns to his own flat when she wants to be alone. Mary has no psychiatric history. Last year she asked her GP to refer her to a counsellor because she felt she needed some additional help in dealing with her emotions.

Initial episode – she made a series of shallow cuts to her left forearm with a penknife when she was 15 years old. Mary recalls that this was in response to intense feelings after being rejected by a boyfriend.

Repetition – Mary has been cutting her left forearm and the upper surfaces of both thighs for about eight years. She often cuts every day, but will occasionally go several weeks without hurting herself. Her normal practice is to dismantle a disposable razor and extract the blade from its plastic surround. She then cuts herself, dresses the wounds and throws the blade away.

Cycle – Mary describes a cycle that usually starts when she suddenly finds herself 'winding up' (her words). She finds this state rather hard to describe, but uses phrases like 'something building up inside' and 'feeling crap'. Mary feels herself increasingly in danger of losing control as these unwelcome feelings intensify. She is particularly worried that, unless she acts to defuse the situation, she could lose control completely and may end up seriously harming herself. She feels a great need to calm her emotions in some way, and knows that cutting will achieve this. At other times, however, Mary just finds she has a strong craving to cut that seems to come from nowhere. This sudden desire to hurt herself is not obviously dependent on her mood – Mary finds that she doesn't have to feel angry, depressed or upset for it to occur.

During each episode, Mary cuts her skin lightly and repeatedly in a criss-cross pattern. She normally feels no pain when she does this. She observes her blood flowing as she cuts. As it flows, the intense and unpleasant feelings within her begin to subside. Mary reports losing track of time while cutting, and often enters into a dream-like state that is in pleasant contrast to her previous discomfort. She tends to finish the episode with one definitive and deeper incision, although she is not always aware of doing this at the time. This last wound is the one that causes her the most problems – her other cuts are shallow and heal quickly with little scarring.

Mary generally feels considerable relief after cutting, although she often experiences guilt and shame about what she has done to herself. She has mixed feelings about her scars. Sometimes they take on a positive symbolic meaning, each scar a sign that she has dealt with yet another wave of unpleasant feelings and has managed to survive. At other times, she finds that her scars remind her of her losses. She has noticed that other people usually react strongly if they catch sight of them, and so is very careful to keep them hidden.

Mary dresses her own wounds. Her choice of site means that other people will be quite unaware of her cutting unless she wears short-sleeved tops or goes swimming or sunbathing. Her deeper cuts often bleed rather more than she likes, and can take a long time to heal. They usually leave significant scars. Mary has found that sometimes the bleeding does not stop, which she finds very frightening. Her wounds occasionally get infected even though she is always very careful to avoid dirt. Whenever these situations occur, Mary forces herself to go to the Casualty department in her local hospital, but she does not like doing this and avoids it if she can. She doesn't like drawing attention to herself and feels ashamed of what she has done.

Who knows – her partner, her counsellor, Casualty staff and her GP.

Mary's view about why she started – Mary is puzzled about this, but remembers that there was something very significant about the loss of her first boyfriend when she was 15. The thought of cutting herself first entered her head while she sat crying and alone in her bedroom. At the time she had found the feelings of rejection overwhelming and recalls thinking to herself that 'crying just isn't enough'. She had not considered hurting herself before then, but was suddenly tempted by the idea of cutting her skin and seeing her blood drip. This seemed like a profound way of demonstrating how she really felt. She recalls wanting to demonstrate this to herself – but not to others. She had decided at that time not to tell anyone about her cutting, and it was several years before she did so.

Mary's view about why she continues – Mary now finds herself returning to cutting whenever difficult emotions surface. She feels she has so far been unable to find any other method of coping. She is frightened that (a) her cutting is starting to lose its effectiveness at calming her emotions, and (b) alternative methods of coping would work too slowly, leaving her at risk of serious damage by her own hand.

Views of her carers – Mary's partner is indeed supportive, but finds himself horrified by the appearance of her wounds which he prefers not to see. He is also angry that her cutting seems to indicate a preoccupation with a past boyfriend, which he thinks she should be over by now. If he is honest, he blames Mary for not putting more of an effort into getting over that relationship.

Mary's counsellor works psychodynamically, but is struggling to get Mary to see many links to her past before the break-up with her first boyfriend. The counsellor knows that she could offer Mary a number of interpretations regarding her self-injury, but is unsure if this would be helpful. Like Mary, she is actually quite concerned that her patient's cutting could escalate and become life-threatening. The counsellor is also aware that Mary is beginning to behave as if she is addicted to cutting, and is unsure what therapeutic options are available for someone whose cutting has become so very entrenched.

Several of the Casualty nurses at the local hospital also have mixed feelings about Mary. She comes across as a pleasant, co-operative young woman who does not demand immediate attention. However, she only ever presents with partially healed wounds that are badly infected, or difficult to suture, or both. She always takes up quite a bit of their time, which some of the nurses feel might better be spent on patients whose injuries result from accidental rather than intentional action.

John's story

John is 22 years old and lives alone in a small flat. He does not work and is claiming sickness benefit. John's childhood was unhappy. His alcoholic father regularly beat his mother. John avoided school whenever he could and left home when he was 16. For as long as he can remember, John has always been preoccupied with his short stature and slight build, seeing himself as 'skinny' and 'weak'. As a child he sought out macho cinema icons for his heroes, but then became distressed at the contrast between those images and his view of himself. John's poor self-esteem has become chronic, and he now feels that others invariably see him as both weak and as a failure. John has little social contact. He tends to stay in his flat, only emerging at night when he is least likely to be seen.

Initial episode – he began burning and cutting the skin on his arms when, at 12 years of age, he discovered his alcoholic father physically abusing his mother and felt unable to protect her.

Repetition – John burns his arms and legs most days with lighted cigarettes, and cannot remember a day when he hasn't done it. However, he now cuts himself only rarely. He has never sought treatment for any of his wounds and feels that he would never do so. He says he is embarrassed by them.

Cycle – John experiences an unbearable impulse to self-harm whenever anything reinforces his view of himself as a weak person. This impulse can emerge for apparently trivial reasons – John can be triggered into self-injury simply by catching sight of someone taller than him, or by hearing a woman shouting in a TV programme. He then becomes overwhelmed by feelings of impotence. John has a strong desire to punish himself for not doing more over the years to make himself a stronger person. He feels unable to resist and quickly gives in to the impulse, usually by holding a lighted cigarette against his skin. This is always very painful, but he finds that the pain helps blot out the feelings.

After a few minutes, John starts to feel numb inside. His emotions become less troublesome. However, he cannot relax for long before he is troubled by feelings of disgust and shame. These seem to arise partly because he has failed again and proved incapable of resisting the impulse to self-injure, and partly because he always considered self-injury to be something women do – which only adds to his feelings of inadequacy.

John sometimes finds it difficult to burn himself, wincing before applying the cigarette to his skin. This reinforces his feeling that he is weak and inadequate. He can solve this difficulty by getting drunk. Alcohol helps numb his revulsion at hurting himself, but further increases his shame when he recalls his father's alcoholism.

Who knows – his consultant psychiatrist, his community psychiatric nurse, and his GP (although John never goes to see him).

John's view about why he started – John vividly recalls first burning himself after feeling distressed by being unable to protect his mother. He also recalls seeing his movie heroes as 'tough' when they walked proud but injured from burning wreckage, and thinks that as a child he probably wanted to see himself in the same way.

John's view about why he continues – John knows that his burning allows him to cope with the way he hates his own stature and his inability to be a strong person. He sometimes finds that the appearance of his scarred arms makes him feel tough and strong when he catches sight of himself in the mirror, but that feeling is soon replaced by shame that he has let this happen to himself and that he is too weak to resist the impulses. John finds this experience of feeling ashamed very difficult to handle; he says he has often resorted to burning himself as a means of coping with it, and is all too aware that he is describing a self-perpetuating cycle. He says he'd like to stop burning his skin with cigarettes, but feels it is unlikely that he ever will.

Views of his carers – His consultant psychiatrist finds that John rarely attends his appointments and that John says very little when he does turn up. He considers John to be suffering mild clinical depression and has prescribed various antidepressants, apparently to little effect. He is unsure what else to offer him as John is unwilling to engage in any counselling or other psychological therapy, and has no interest in increasing his social contact. Concerned about John's social isolation, the consultant psychiatrist asked a community nurse to make regular home visits.

As a result, the community nurse now visits John every week. She agrees that he is low in mood at times, but is not convinced that the suicide risk is significant. She does not see John as having serious mental health problems, and finds it hard to empathize with him. John sometimes becomes angry at her, accusing her of not understanding how badly he feels. On several occasions he has burnt himself in front of her, apparently to make a point, which she finds very disturbing.

Themes

There are common themes in these two examples. It is clear that both Mary and John have found self-injury to be a very effective means for getting relief from difficult feelings. In both cases, however, the relief is short-lived and the behaviour seems to have become entrenched. Clear suicidal intent is absent in both cases. There is a degree of secrecy and a reluctance to seek physical help, although John is sometimes able to hurt himself in front of his nurse to demonstrate how distressed he feels. Both individuals experience shame as a result of their self-injury, and this can add to tension and even trigger further self-harm. Both would probably welcome an effective alternative way of coping, but neither is convinced that this is achievable at present and Mary is concerned that it could be dangerous to try.

There are also differences. Mary feels no pain, whereas John cuts to experience pain and uses it to help blot out his feelings. Mary has little difficulty cutting herself, because she has effectively managed to switch off the restraint most people feel against hurting themselves. John, however, is not always in this position; he sometimes needs the effect of alcohol to dull that restraint so that he can allow himself to burn his skin. Finally, Mary can get strong cravings to cut in the absence of any clear trigger, whereas John does not report this.

People in close contact with Mary and John also experience difficult emotions. Mary's partner feels horror and anger; her counsellor feels anxiety and frustration; and some of the hospital nurses feel intolerant and misused. John's doctor feels cut off and impotent to help him, while his community nurse finds herself lacking in empathy and disturbed by his behaviour.

INTEGRATING PERSONAL AND BEHAVIOURAL PERSPECTIVES

Mental health professionals often feel torn between focussing on symptoms or focussing on the person 'behind' the symptoms. To arrive at a balanced view of both means combining the behavioural (or symptomatic) and the intentional (or personal) perspective. This is particularly challenging when we consider those disorders that are often called 'habit disorders' in which the symptom of the disorder is an action like gambling, drug taking, or self-starvation, but where that action seems to have escaped from deliberate control so that a person might say, 'I would stop if I could, but I can't. I'm addicted'. We consider that repeated self-injury is a kind of habit disorder, or an addiction.

Many professionals take a behavioural perspective. Thinking of self-injury as a behaviour reduces the level of emotional engagement, and may make it possible to deal with the person who self-injures as if they are a victim and not an agent. Behavioural accounts are strongest when based on populations and not on individuals. They therefore aid the professional who wants to generalize from previous experience of similar 'cases'.

Informal carers and people who self-injure may find behavioural accounts upsetting. They seem to strip an individual of their individuality. They pathologize. They seem to deny the possibility of change. They create, too, a difference between the professional who is presenting themselves as healthy and the person or 'patient' who self-injures as unhealthy. More subtly, they can be pseudo-scientific. For example, explaining that a person often does things without thinking by saying that they are 'impulsive'. Is that a useful explanation, or is it circular? Does 'impulsivity' mean any thing more than a tendency to do things without thinking?

We agree with all of these strictures. We, too, find behavioural descriptions to be sometimes inhuman and potentially inhumane. But we do not think that we can simply rely on a purely intentional account of self-injury, either. As our accounts of John and Mary showed, people who injure themselves are themselves unsure or mixed about the motives of their actions. In one study (Haas & Popp, 2006), 120 individuals who injured themselves without suicidal intent answered 154 questions designed to assess the function of their self-injury in the short term. The authors carried out a factor analysis which revealed no less than 12 factors: 'self-punishment', 'coping with emotions', 'extreme rage', 'vitality', 'dissociation', 'changed perception', 'control over body', 'uniqueness', 'interaction', 'addiction', 'coping with sexuality' and 'expression of sexuality'.

We all account for our actions after the fact, rather than before (Tantam, 2002) and so do other people. Our own accounts are not as privileged as we sometimes claim. They may vary, be inconsistent, be poorly thought through, or be transparently inadequate justifications. We cannot ignore each other's accounts – to do so is inhumane – but we can challenge them, and sometimes defeat them. Defeating another person's account though is not a step to be taken lightly, and certainly does not mean that a person is left with no account to give.

DISPOSITION AND ACCOUNTING

One way of combining both a behavioural and an intentional account is derived from Aristotle who suggested that we act out of habit, particularly when we are stressed or have to act as a matter of urgency, but that those habits are built up from actions we have chosen to take in the past. Deidre's story illustrates this.

> Deirdre had been cutting herself since the age of 12, often several times a week. She cut herself so often that she had persistent iron deficiency anaemia. She did not know why she harmed herself (she also took overdoses, too), only that it kept her from thinking and feeling too deeply. Then she got pregnant. She was passionately concerned about the welfare of her child, and decided that she had to stop cutting herself while she was carrying the baby, since she knew that her anaemia could affect the baby's development. Taking overdoses was also out of the question, because of the welfare of the foetus. Deirdre's began to experience feelings that she had not felt before, and desperately wanted to get rid of them in her old manner. But after one or two crises during which she struggled for hours looking at a blade, she found that she could tolerate some of these unwanted feelings and even began to find other ways of dealing with them.
>
> Deirdre was beginning to develop new habits and therefore change her disposition to self-harm in response to certain kinds of tension. Her progress was not steady – no one's is when changing an ingrained habit. There was at least one occasion when Deirdre found herself cutting her arm without even remembering finding a blade and starting to cut. Fortunately, she 'came to' before the cut became deep enough to cause significant blood loss.

Deirdre had developed a disposition to cut herself through having repeatedly cut herself in the past. A behavioural account provides a good way of explaining this disposition, we think, and we will summarize some of the evidence in this chapter. But Deirdre's disposition could be changed, gradually and by small steps as we suggest, by a change in her values. Before she became pregnant, one of her values had been that she was worth little and that punishing herself was therefore good. Once she became pregnant, this value was trumped by the value she placed on the health of her baby. This new and dominant value (by value, we mean a combination of belief with passion or emotional commitment) made Deirdre reject any account of her actions which might be construed as to the detriment of her baby's health. Since self-harm could only be construed as being to the detriment of the baby she was carrying, Deirdre had to give it up to hold on to the account of herself as a good mother, which she considered to be more fundamental than any account of herself as a good or bad person.

IF ONLY PSYCHOLOGY WERE MORE PHENOMENOLOGICAL

Our analysis of Deirdre is consistent with a 'phenomenological' approach (Graumann, 2002). It is based on a careful description, checking of that description with subjective experience (ours in this case, since we are imagining Deirdre, but in clinical practice we would be checking with an actual 'Deirdre') and then reformulation, trying to dispense with as many prior assumptions as possible – a process that is known as phenomenological reduction.

Our reduction demonstrates that there are at least two distinct dispositions to Deirdre harming herself. There is an inner, unpleasant tension that Deirdre knows can be relieved by cutting herself (we call this 'the spring'), and there is a disposition of which she is unaware which leads to her cutting herself without intending to (we call this 'the switch'). There is another factor, too, which opposes the disposition to self-injury. Although we did not bring out how it played out in Deirdre's life, we have mentioned it in connection with self-injury by other people, and called it 'the safety-catch'.

Scientific and medical research into self-injury has not made these phenomenological distinctions, but has been based on categories of self-harm or types of people. However, unlike some phenomenologists, we do not think that quantitative research of this kind should simply be dispensed with. We do however think that it needs an additional interpretative step to make it applicable to particular people. This additional step depends on the intuitions of those making it, just as the rightness of phenomenological reduction depends on the ability of the phenomenologist to bracket out their own assumptions and prejudices.

Our phenomenological reduction of the scientific evidence is considered in the next chapter.

IS SELF-INJURY ALWAYS PATHOLOGICAL?

Some readers may feel that more effort should be made to write about the value of self-injury, and that authors of books such as this spend too much time pathologizing it. In fact, we do recognize that self-injury has often been socially commended, and that some still is.[1] Even self-injury that meets our definition of private self-injury is highly regarded by some when it is pursuant of religious self-discipline. Arguably this is self-injury pursued as a means to a desired end, and not as an end in itself. But this is not really a helpful distinction, since all self-injury can be presented as an action with a goal in mind.

Some people say that they cut themselves because that is the only effective means that they have to 'cope'. Not cutting themselves would be worse, or so they say. Others say that cutting themselves may be a kind of memorial of some momentous event in their lives, or that it marks a transition (Favazza uses the term 'liminal' power) to bring them into a more spiritual understanding.

We are not in a position to gainsay any of this. Nor can we completely defend ourselves against the complaint that any objection that we may have is simply an emotional response produced by our own safety-catches against self-injury being vicariously jammed on. We do however think there is a kind of innate value in the idea of bodily integrity which, of course, self-injury goes against.

Having said that, we do not wish to foist help or even diagnosis on people who injure themselves as a life-style choice. This book is not about them, but about the many people for whom self-injury becomes a trap. For them it is the type of trap which does not augment their wellbeing, but restricts it. To those who want to be allowed to injure themselves without the intrusion of other people wanting to stop them, we would counsel awareness that cutting oneself is a powerful move in human relations because of the intrinsic motive power of the emotions that it arouses. We believe that taking power over others is unethical unless they benefit as well as oneself. This applies as much to people who cut themselves in their relations to their friends and carers, as it does to mental health professionals in their relationships with their patients – including their patients who injure themselves.

Chapter 3

A Unifying Model Based on the Phenomenology of Self-Injury

BACKGROUND FACTORS

Most of us feel fear, resentment and impotence at times, but we usually manage to contain these feelings or find a way of managing them. We have argued that one reason why a person who self-injures cannot contain these and other feelings is that they become like a spring that winds itself up. Put another way, they are like the trigger on a water pistol that pumps up the pressure in the water until something has to be released.

We find this 'water-pistol' analogy useful in several ways. It illustrates how these uncontainable feelings often have to be re-experienced frequently before someone finally resorts to cutting or burning their skin. Whereas the first few experiences of distressing emotions may have little effect (as with the first few squeezes on the trigger of a water pistol), when experienced again and again they act progressively to build up the internal pressure. This pressure then builds until something has to be released.

We can imagine several possible factors that could affect emotional processing, and make some people more susceptible to feeling such triggering emotions and therefore to inflict self-injury. We suggest four possibilities here. First, the circumstances in which people find themselves could be so aggravating that their emotions become too intense to be contained. Second, other people might prevent them from expressing their emotions so that they find themselves getting wound-up more than other people normally do. Third, there are no interpersonal opportunities open to them for dealing with the emotion in any way other than through self-harm. Fourth, they may lack the capacity for dealing with emotions generally or lack the capacity to deal with triggering emotions specifically.

There appears to be a strong match between early experience and such emotional triggers. For example, Martin and Waite (1994) found that adolescents who assigned their parents to the 'affectionless control' quadrant of the Parental Bonding Index had a 3-fold increase in relative risk of self-harm compared to those who did not, and our own study of a small group of self-injuring women also revealed a strong tendency to rate early care giving figures as cold and controlling. Arguably, the experience of early care as cold and overprotective corresponds to the triggering emotions of resentment and neediness, and of feeling unhappy, friendless, afraid and powerless.

PAIN AND ANALGESIA IN SELF-INJURY

It has often been observed than many people who cut their skin report little or no pain at the time their cuts are made. Some studies have suggested that this occurs in at least half of those who self-harm in this way, and that those affected tend to show an increased threshold for pain perception even in the absence of distress (Bohus et al., 2000). The cause of the analgesia is unclear. Explanations include physiological factors, such as increased endorphin secretion, psychological factors and cognitive impairment in distinguishing painful from mildly painful situations (Russ et al., 1992). Numbing of the skin can also be a symptom of dissociation, and this alone may be sufficient to ensure that subsequent cutting is painless.

The potential for pain arising from a self-inflicted burn is considerably greater than from a self-inflicted cut (unless the burn is full-thickness and damages sensory nerves), and the anticipation of pain arising from a burn is usually significant. Those who are able to burn themselves repeatedly may be better protected against extreme pain at the time they do it, and the ability to dissociate is one means by which this could occur. Self-burning is poorly researched in comparison with self-cutting, although one study of a sample of delinquent Japanese adolescents showed that those who burnt their skin in addition to cutting it scored higher on a measure of dissociative experiences compared to did those who only cut themselves, but did not self-burn (Matsumoto et al., 2005).

There will be important implications for an individual if numbing of the skin occurs regularly and reliably. Local analgesia is likely to make the act of self-cutting or self-burning considerably easier and will have a significant weakening effect on the safety-catch. Furthermore, previous experience of analgesia is likely to give confidence that self-injury will not hurt too much if circumstances arise when the individual feels the need to injure him or herself again.

It would be a mistake, however, to over-generalize and assume that this is always the case, or that analgesia at the time of cutting implies that sutures can be inserted painlessly without local anaesthetic some hours later. Many people who cut themselves (and particularly those who self-burn) will say they do so in order to experience pain, and a desire to self-punish is frequently reported (Briere & Gil, 1998; Rodham et al., 2004). We know that pain has potential to control, modify or maintain arousal states (Jones, 1982) and so it is perhaps unsurprising that some people who self-injure report using physical pain as way of controlling emotional pain. Some will use pain to interrupt a downward spiralling chain of thoughts, or to provide a release from feeling trapped in distressing memories. Pain from a self-inflicted cut or burn can provide a concrete physical focus, providing distraction from inner psychic pain or symbolically converting it into something that feels more tangible. Self-induced pain may also provide the sufferer with important evidence that he or she is alive. It can also offer punishment for sexual desire and thereby relieve sexual guilt (Daldin, 1988), which may be a particular difficulty for those who were horrified to find themselves becoming unwillingly sexually aroused during an abusive act.

DOES SELF-INJURY ALWAYS HAVE A CLEAR CAUSE AND FUNCTION?

Self-injury can serve a remarkably wide range of functions. These have been reviewed very efficiently elsewhere (for example, Suyemoto, 1998; Klonsky, 2007) and a comprehensive synopsis is not attempted here. The list is extensive and includes:

- Self-punishment
- Regulation of strong unpleasant feelings
- Anti-suicide
- Control of dissociation
- Assertion of agency
- Subconscious means of resolving conflict over sexuality

- Redirected social aggression
- Control of others
- Systemic interaction
- Atonement for shame
- Sensation-seeking
- Communication and expression
- Repair of faulty boundaries
- Biologic or organic explanations

Attempting to match a specific function to a particular person's self-injury is, however, unlikely to be of much help in a clinical setting. There are several reasons for this. One is that self-injury can serve several functions simultaneously (and so is often described by psychologists as 'over-determined'). Another is that the meaning of self-injury for a particular person may yet be undetermined.

We conclude that a reductionist view can be useful when searching for causal and maintenance factors, but it may be over-simplistic in situations where it is not possible to attribute a meaning to behaviour. We believe there are some circumstances in which there are many reasons for injuring oneself – most, if not all, of which one only comes up with after the event, and there are other circumstances where it is not possible to define any clear reason for injuring oneself. Put simply, self-injury can take place with 'meaning unknown'. This is a state of affairs which people who self-injure are often quite happy to acknowledge, but which some therapists appear to find rather difficult to tolerate.

It is important to be clear that here 'meaning unknown' does not imply anything casual or frivolous about the behaviour. Cutting may be extremely important for the person who does it, but at the same time completely lack any easily defined purpose or meaning. It just 'is' from the client's point of view. This resonates with Laplanche's idea of 'empty signifiers' that cannot yet be defined, but which have the potential to attract signification in time.

It is suggested here that self-injury may still be an empty signifier for some who do it. They will therefore be unable to suggest what it means them. As time goes by their self-injury may come to attract a specific meaning, and hence may inspire new affects which cannot yet be predicted. This can have clinical implications. Attempting to help the client by suggesting likely reasons for his or her self-harm may sometimes be useful, but it can be counter-productive to insist that a specific meaning applies, like saying 'I think that you cut yourself because you are angry with your father', when it does not.

MAINTENANCE FACTORS

It is not always possible to separate out causal and maintenance factors, and several of the theories we have mentioned describe how the behaviour might be maintained as well as its aetiology and function. A behavioural model based on learning theory is frequently invoked to explain how self-injury is maintained. According to this, an individual will adjust his or her behaviour in response to changes in the immediate environment. The concept of reinforcement as a form of operant conditioning is central to this approach, and here the environment can be internal as well as external, and the reinforcement can be positive as well as negative.

Table 3.1 Possible maintenance factors for self-injury

Persistence of the original circumstances that led to initiation of self-injury – such as an abusive relationship, confinement, social isolation or repeated rejection by significant others.

Conviction about self-injury – such as believing that survival is impossible unless one remains in a injured state, that one deserves punishment, that cutting is the only way to reduce unpleasant feelings and that overt action is always necessary to communicate feelings to others.

Emotional response from others – such as concern about injuries expressed by friends and family. Reinforcement is external and positive when self-injury becomes associated with some welcome response. The medical profession's ethical requirement to treat injuries and provide medical or nursing care may also be perceived as closeness and affection and so provide further positive reinforcement, albeit unintentionally.

Social aspects – as with 'secondary gain' from having friends who cut, or from acquisition of social status ('the worst cutter on the ward'; 'the hardest man in the prison'). The social benefits of self-injury can be learned through vicarious reinforcement; observing how the environment can respond positively to other self-injurers can lead to copying and experimentation to explore whether the response can be enhanced.

Atrophy of coping skills – such as occurs when the individual increasingly relies on cutting as the preferred means of coping with difficult feelings and difficult situations.

Reliable respite from dysphoria – negative reinforcement is said to occur when self-injury reliably relieves distressing emotional states; the process can be powerful enough to maintain a cycle of tension build-up and relief via self-injury, even without any additional external effects.

Addictive aspects – as may occur with short-lived euphoriant effects (reported by some individuals, apparently in response to the effects of endogenous endorphins released following injury), coupled with the transient nature of any respite from distressing emotion.

We can suggest a number of likely maintenance factors (see Table 3.1), many of which can be seen as exerting their influence through some degree of positive or negative reinforcement.

RESISTANCE TO GETTING INJURED – THE 'SAFETY-CATCH'

There is no lack of examples of self-injury even in the world of children. Older children become aware of tattoos and piercings as they observe the people around them. They know, sometimes from their own experience, that people may bang their heads or hit themselves when they are extremely distressed. In some cultures, people still tear out their hair in grief. Young teenagers in the West are likely to have at least one friend or acquaintance who has scratched him or herself.

Most adults have an innate resistance to getting hurt or injured. There is an obvious risk to health, and even life, when living flesh is damaged and we are normally very reluctant to act in a way that increases the chance of becoming infected, disabled or pained. It is as though each person has his or her own safety-catch against personal injury (see Text Box 3.1), even though this may be stronger in some people than in others. If the safety-catch provides automatic protection, it follows that it must somehow be relaxed or bypassed in order for a self-inflicted injury to take place.

Text Box 3.1   Features of the 'safety-catch'
■ Innate and/or internalized from early caregivers
■ Self-protective function, normally automatic
■ Maintained by three factors: disgust, fear and anticipated pain
■ Safety-catch must be bypassed for self-injury to occur
■ Failure of safety-catch often seen as abnormal
■ Individuals who can bypass the safety-catch are prone to stigmatization

The concept of a safety-catch seems also to apply in other areas. Many people would say they feel restrained against, for example, engaging in perverse sexual practices, taking part in dangerous sports, eating certain foods or living in direct contact with dangerous animals like snakes and scorpions. Because these types of safety-catches are almost universal, individuals who are able to bypass them tend to be noticed. Some get seen by others as exceptional and gain a place in the record books – as with the woman from Thailand who recently set a record for living for 32 days with over three thousand scorpions, or Evel Knievel, the dare-devil motorcyclist who succeeded in jumping over nineteen cars. Others are viewed as abnormal and find that what they do stigmatizes them. There seems no clear way to predict what will be admired and what will be abhorred, although the cultural context is likely to be very significant.

There are other domains where the restraint is less universal – for example, starting fights, driving recklessly as well as bingeing on food or alcohol. The safety-catch is domain-specific, and so there will be one form that restrains against injury to the self and another that restrains against injuring someone else. An individual who regularly cuts will have a weak safety-catch operating with respect to self-injury, but may have a strong restraint against hitting another person ('*I could never hurt anyone*'). In contrast, someone who never cuts has a safety-catch for self-injury that is stuck firmly in the 'on' position ('*I could never cut my own skin*'), but may have few qualms about punching someone who provokes them. This is one way of explaining why impulsive aggression can be expressed in very different ways in different people.

The desire for self-preservation is often viewed as innate, since a naturally squeamish reaction to blood and deformity is seen almost universally in humans, chimpanzees and in several other species (Marks, 1988). Horror at seeing one's own wounds and blood might confer a selection advantage by reducing the chance of early death, thus allowing greater time for offspring to become independent and survive. A similar explanation was proposed by the English naturalist and evolutionist Alfred Russel Wallace to rationalize the existence of pain in the higher, more complex life forms. Wallace argued that pain acts as an aid to self-preservation until reproduction has taken place, but that this is less significant for lower forms of life that tend to reproduce their kind more rapidly (Wallace, 1910). An alternative view is that positive attitudes to self-care and self-protection are derived from internalizing the caring and protective functions of parents (Khantzian & Mack, 1983). Resistance to self-injury appears to be lacking in the very young – for example, head banging has been shown to occur in up to 15% of normal children aged 9–18 months, reducing to 10% at 3 years and zero at 5 years (De Lissoroy, 1961).

Our clinical experience is that disgust, fear and anticipated pain are what mainly constitute the safety-catch. The sight of open injuries or bleeding generates disgust in many people, and recent studies have shown that this response may protect individuals from disease, and that women and children experience it more strongly than men do (Curtis et al., 2004). Extreme disgust can lead to nausea and fainting (Page, 2003), and is the basis of 'blood-injury phobia' in which a person avoids any situation where they may be exposed to blood or wounds.

It is not clear how deep a wound really is from simple inspection. So even a superficial injury may induce anxiety that it will result in loss of function or in death. If we think about cutting into ourselves, we often think of what we might do to vital structures under the skin. We also think of the pain, too. Fear and pain interact and may combine together to produce 'horror'. Seeing another person's injury (or worse, to witness them cutting their skin) makes us cringe with disgust or feel sick with horror partly because it makes us disgusted or frightened, but also because we have some intimation of the pain that such an injury would cause us.

WEAKENING THE SAFETY-CATCH

Injuring oneself deliberately means first overcoming the safety-catch against self-injury, much as bungee jumping means first overcoming the safety-catch against throwing oneself from a high place. Although there is no research that has explicitly been about overcoming the safety-catch, there is a considerable amount of research on the factors leading to occasional self-injury which we can use. Some of these factors are summarized in Text Box 3.2.

Text Box 3.2   Factors that allow the safety-catch to be turned off

- constitutional factors such as impulsivity
- intoxication
- religious or spiritual ecstasy
- grief
- social norms and social influence
- habituation and hardening
- dissociation

Constitution

There may be constitutional differences in the safety-catch, possibly associated with serotonin metabolism or serotonergic receptor types, and the efficiency of serotonergic transmission (Arango et al., 2003). A particular allele of the tryptophan hydroxylase gene has been identified as more common in self-harm subjects than in controls (Pooley et al., 2003), and an allelic variation in the serotonin transporter gene appears to contribute to the expression of anxiety symptoms in individuals who self-harm (Evans et al., 1997).

Impulsivity

One element of the safety-catch – anticipated pain – requires imagination and the power of the imagination of future consequences to inhibit present behaviour. The term 'impulsive' is often applied to people in whom this power is weaker, and a number of studies have found a strong association between self-injury and impulsiveness (for example, Herpertz et al., 1997 and Simeon et al., 1992). For this reason it has been suggested that private self-injury can, in many cases, legitimately be classified as a specific medical disorder (i.e. under 'Impulse-Control Disorder – Not Otherwise Specified' within Axis 1 of DSM-IV).

Religious and other ecstasies

Ecstasy has similarities to trance, and to hypnoid states, following hypnosis (Butler et al., 1996). Religious ceremony may induce trance, particularly when accompanied by repetitive stimulation like drumming or chanting. This kind of trance, or religious ecstasy, may be a means to achieve a state of religious exaltation, and self-injury may then become an indicator to others that a person has achieved this. It is sometimes referred to as controlled dissociation, controlled because the effects are regulated by the social influence of others participating in the ceremony. Historical examples of religious ecstasy associated with self-harm are the Bacchantes who celebrated Bacchus at the festival of Bendis by wild dancing, drinking, orgiastic sexuality and self-injury; and the flagellants, pilgrims seeking escape from the bubonic plague who wore thorns and scourged themselves in memory of Christ's scourging on the way to Golgotha. We discuss dissociation later because it plays an important part in the switch pathway to self-injury as well as in turning off the safety-catch. We will be mainly concerned there with uncontrolled dissociation, which occurs during private self-injury, and is most often associated with emotional difficulties (Negro et al., 2002).

Research into the practices of the more extreme religious and spiritual cults has demonstrated how new members can be inducted using aggressive and potentially damaging hypnotic and dissociative techniques (Dubrow-Eichel & Dubrow-Eichel, 1985). They include suggestion, meditation, distraction, singing, monotonous chanting or drumming, overloading the person with more new information than they can process at any given time, as well as asking the subject to divide their attention between two or more sources of information input or between two or more channels of sensory input. Most of these techniques are executed within the context of intense group activity or while isolating the person in new and unfamiliar surroundings which can itself increase hypnotic susceptibility (Barabasz, 1984). Reports suggest that members can spontaneously re-enter dissociative states following such 'conversion', and some can experience periodic episodes of unwanted trance even after leaving the cult (Dubrow-Eichel & Dubrow-Eichel, 1985).

We have considered trance-like states and religious ecstasy, but there is also the ecstasy of grief, as illustrated by the following example.

> Carrie had been a devoted mother to her only son who had survived a very difficult birth only to develop leukaemia in his early childhood. She had nursed him patiently as he endured seemingly endless rounds of treatment in hospital. Finally, at the age of 12, the doctors declared the lad was finally free of the illness. It was therefore a tragedy when, just the following week, he was hit by a car while crossing the road outside their house and died of his injuries. Carrie's grief was intense. She was inconsolable. Carrie was so overwhelmed that she began banging her head and followed this by punching the wall with her bare fist, which she did three or four times in quick succession. For Carrie, the intensity of her grief completely overcame her natural aversion to damaging herself in this way. She afterwards said that she felt virtually no pain at the time and was not in the least concerned about the long-term consequences of her actions. It was only later that she came to realize how painful and debilitating a bruised hand could be.
>
> Carrie was in an ecstasy of grief, which led to her becoming as we say, beside herself. Being beside oneself is a kind of dissociation (we discuss this later), which has the consequence of reducing the awareness of pain or of the consequences of injury. As a consequence, the safety-catch to injury can become turned off, as it did in Carrie.

Intoxication

Alcohol or drug intoxication provides some degree of anaesthesia, as well as dulling the imagination and blunting emotional response. Sometimes intoxication may lead to unusually severe self-injury. Intoxication may inactivate the safety-catch by inducing dissociation, like trance or religious ecstasy (Langeland et al., 2002) and indeed many religious rituals may require celebrants to drink intoxicants or to inhale smoke from burning them, suggesting that the influence of the drug and of the ritual are synergistic.

There are reports of dissociative symptoms developing after drinking alcohol (Seedat et al., 2003) and following the use of a variety of illicit drugs (Medford et al., 2003) including cannabis (Matthew et al., 1993), d-methamphetamine (Davison, 1964), 'Ecstasy' (Wodarz & Boning, 1993) and ketamine (Morgan et al., 2004). Dissociative experiences may also occur as an unwanted side effect of certain prescription drugs including indomethacin and other non-steroidal anti-inflammatories; brief dissociative episodes can result following rapid withdrawal of certain antidepressants (Mourad et al., 1998). Benzodiazepines can increase the propensity to dissociate and there have been reports of fugue states linked to diazepam and flunitrazepam (Simmer, 1999; Tang et al., 1996). In certain cases dissociative symptoms can be exacerbated by caffeine (Stein & Uhde, 1989) and be induced by fasting (Demitrack et al., 1990).

Other psychological situations

Certain psychological situations are capable of inducing dissociation and therefore potentially inactivating the safety-catch. Both unusually low and unusually high arousal can have this effect. Examples of unusually low arousal include the transient depersonalization observed in healthy individuals during sensory deprivation as a consequence of relaxation (Fewtrell, 1984; Fitzgerald & Gonzalez, 1994), and rarely, following meditation (Castillo, 1990). High emotional arousal can also induce dissociation, particularly the type called 'depersonalization' (we consider this in more detail later). Nearly a third of those exposed to life-threatening danger experience depersonalization (Noyes et al., 1977).

Persistent dissociation following an adverse event is associated with a failure to move on emotionally from it, a condition often termed post-traumatic stress disorder. Post-traumatic stress disorder may be associated with a higher risk of self-injury. This is not so much because of inactivation of the safety-catch, but more because of a different and more persistent dissociation from the traumatic event, which becomes 'compartmentalized'. We discuss the significance of compartmentalization for the switch pathway to self-injury later in this chapter.

SOCIAL NORMS AND SOCIAL INFLUENCE

Self-injury may occur in a context that is culturally sanctioned and thus in keeping with the social norms that prevail. The members of certain tribes in Africa, for example, live in a society where self-inflicted scarring is a normal and relatively common practice, perhaps carried out for decoration or as a sign of passage into maturity. In such circumstances the tribal members are likely to find their resistance against engaging in that specific type of decorative self-harm to be very weak. The social acceptability of both the procedure and its result appears to counter any natural aversion.

Similarly, a college student in current western society who wishes to keep up with current fashion may have little compunction about having her ears, tongue, nose, nipples, or labia pierced. Brenda is one such:

Like many of her fellow students, Brenda wanted another ear stud and was planning to visit a local body shop and pay someone to carry out the simple piercing procedure. On finding there was a queue (and also that she was short of money) she decided to take the 'do-it-yourself' option, piercing her own ear lobe with a needle and inserting the new stud herself. Brenda admits that she would probably not have thought about doing this herself before learning that several of her friends had done the same.

When it actually came to doing it, Brenda found that the most difficult barrier to overcome was the pain she anticipated feeling when inserting the needle; the other factors pertaining to her safety-catch (fear, disgust) were already minimized because she perceived multiple piercing as the prevailing social norm and she knew of friends that had self-pierced in the past. Any aversive aspects appeared to be negated by the behaviour of her peers and by the desirability of the result. Brenda felt that the means justified the end, and although grimacing when preparing to insert the needle, she was able to complete the task. She had managed, briefly, to bypass her innate safety-catch against self-injury. The bypass itself was short-lived, but it allowed her to carry out this simple procedure and she felt no shame in doing so.

Carl's safety-catch was subverted, too, by his sub-cultural expectations, although these were different to those operating on Brenda:

Carl was doing his first prison stretch. He discovered that 'cutting up' was seen as a reasonable – and almost commonplace – method of coping with feelings of anger against the confining system, and a method of demonstrating toughness for some of the inmates. Self-cutting was a behaviour accepted by his peers in these circumstances and Carl gradually aligned himself with a new set of social norms. He found himself bored and then slowly becoming curious to the point where eventually he started to consider the possible advantages of cutting himself.

In time Carl found himself wanting to emulate the behaviour of those who seemed to be strong or to be respected by other prisoners. As the weeks went by he found he felt more and more as if he could cut his skin as a means of gaining some sort of relief – especially when he felt angry. In effect he sensed that his safety-catch was becoming weaker. His initial disgust at the sight of slashed and scarred arms on other prisoners gradually lost its aversive power. Carl's fear of being rejected by his peers if he were to cut also disappeared as he came to realize that some of the inmates regarded heavily scarred forearms as a sign of a 'hard' man who deserved respect. With a little practice, he found that he was even able to suspend his anticipation of how painful it might be to cut himself as they did.

CELEBRITY AND PUBLICITY

Publicity about self-harming is followed by an increase in incidence, suggesting that publicity can also act as a model. Publicity coupled with celebrity may be particularly influential (Strong, 1998). In a television interview in 1995, Princess Diana, the wife of the Prince of Wales and therefore the person who would have become the Queen of the United Kingdom had Queen Elizabeth II died or abdicated, admitted before millions of viewers that she had intentionally cut her arms and legs. Diana had thrown herself into a glass cabinet at Kensington Palace, slashed at her wrists with a razor blade and cut herself with the serrated edge of a lemon slicer (Morton, 1997). At the time of this revelation it was not unusual to witness comments like: 'Lady Di does it … and she's a nice person … so maybe what I do to myself isn't so bad after all.' It is also interesting to note that in the week following Diana's death, reported rates of self-harm increased (Hawton et al., 2000).

HABITUATION AND 'HARDENING'

We suggested at the start of this chapter that there are three principal components that maintain the safety-catch: disgust, fear and anticipation of pain. These would have to weaken for the restraint to be relaxed. Each may be weakened by habituation. Many nursing and medical students effectively use self-exposure to harden themselves when witnessing or executing procedures that involve wounds and injuries. Exposure and response prevention can be an effective means of treating blood-injury phobia. Similarly, in the case of self-injury, repetition may weaken the catch so that 'once the threshold is crossed it is easier to act again' (Gardner, 2001, p. 26).

Habituation through repetition can be augmented by 'hardening' or the adoption of beliefs that justify wounding. Soldiers are trained to suspend their disgust of killing a person by thinking that it is 'the enemy'. A man might feel less restrained about punishing his errant son with a severe beating if he thinks 'it's the only way he'll learn, so I'm really doing it for his own good'. Disgust at the prospect of cutting one's own skin may be suspended by thinking 'Cutting will calm me and stop me from doing something bad to someone else, so it's OK'.

TRIGGERS, TENSION AND THE SPRING

Overcoming the safety-catch begins with small steps, which are hardly self-injury at all. For example, a curious teenager may scratch her forearm lightly with a brooch pin, perhaps just to see what it is like. Each repetition of the scratch will make the safety-catch easier to surmount and the cut deeper. Eventually, he or she will be able to use a blade to cut into the skin.

But why should he or she do so? The only possible explanation is that the self-injury does more than satisfy curiosity (probably accomplished by doing it just once), but that it provides some additional benefit. In this section, we consider the second element of our model, which is that self-injury has an effect on emotional states that is perceived as beneficial, or at least needed.

Repeated use of this method of relieving feelings leads to more overt injury. It also leads to spending more time thinking about injuring oneself, and (importantly) the development both of wanting to injure and being reluctant to self-injure. This conflict leads to mounting tension composed of an unpleasant mixture of depression, anxiety and anger (Gardner & Cowdry, 1985a) which is sometimes referred to as 'dysphoria'. We find it useful to view the build up of this tension as analogous to the winding up of a spring. Self-injury can offer a rapid and powerful reduction in this internal tension. In our analogy, it unwinds the 'spring' of tension. We discuss the 'spring' pathway to self-injury in the following section.

Many of the things that we do that are bad for us, we do to assuage bad feelings. They are sometimes called comfort behaviours. We prefer the term, 'relief habits' because comfort suggests an actively pleasant feeling which rarely, in fact, accompanies doing what is bad for us. We eat too much, or we eat foods that are 'naughty but nice' to pick ourselves up. Drinking, taking drugs, watching television, slumping on the sofa are all examples of relief habits: things that we do when we lack the energy to do things that we know will enhance our wellbeing but which are, somehow, a bit too challenging.

Private self-injury has similarities to grooming, another comfort behaviour, and certainly fits into the category of things that a person does to get rid of feeling bad. So we should expect that the emotional states that people who self-injure want to change are unpleasant ones, and that self-injury is motivated by – we shall call it triggered by – feeling bad.

EVIDENCE FOR TWO PATHWAYS TO SELF-INJURY – THE 'SPRING' AND THE 'SWITCH'

Our model of self-injury involves three elements: 'safety-catch', 'spring' and 'switch'. We have already discussed the operation of the safety-catch earlier in this chapter. It is now time to consider the possible pathways, or routes, to self-injury.

Table 3.2 Descriptions of experiences prior to self-injury in a female sample

Theme	Examples
Winding up	Feeling wound-up; feeling as if tension and pressure are building up inside
Effort to resist	Struggling to resist the urge to cut
Cueing tension	Reference to something that can start the process off again
Premeditation	Making a decision to cut; deciding that a cut is now inevitable and just has to be done
Recollection	Reliving the past; remembering past self-harm
Switching on	Perception of something switching on and off; finding that a cut happens in an instant
Triggering	Perception of something acting as 'the final straw'; knowing that one was bound to self-injure following a particular experience
Craving	Feeling a strong desire or need to cut; wanting desperately to cut
Involuntary action	Feeling like someone else has taken over; the experience of another hand holding the blade; the experience of being on automatic pilot
Rumination	Unable to get thoughts or memories out of one's head; going over thoughts of doing cutting

We have been able to identify not one but two pathways, based partly on collecting and analysing reports from women of their emotional states before injuring themselves. For convenience, we term one the 'spring' pathway and the other the 'switch'. In one study (Huband & Tantam, 2004), we identified ten key 'themes' (see Table 3.2). The experiences recalled were a mix of the 'spring' phenomenon in which the trigger pumps up the tension (themes of winding up, cueing tension, triggering and effort to resist) and the 'switch' phenomenon (themes of switching on, craving and involuntary action). Some women reported experiencing both types of phenomena ('pathways' to self-injury); they recalled, for example, times when they felt tension building and a desire to cut which they were trying very hard to resist – and then suddenly finding they had cut themselves, apparently without realizing it.

The 'spring' pathway aligns with the tension-reduction model summarized by Brain et al. (1998) and apparently substantiated by a number of recent studies (e.g. Kamphuis et al., 2007; Kleindienst et al., 2008). Here self-injury allows the individual to reduce internal tension and regain control over difficult feelings. The 'switch' path has similarities with what some have described as 'impulsive self-injury', although we do not find the concept of impulsive self-harm particularly useful, partly because impulsivity is such a broad concept. Viewing self-injury as an essentially impulsive act makes it difficult to account for times when there is a protracted struggle to resist.

In addition, we found some evidence of rumination in nearly a third of these messages. This adds support to the idea that cognitive rehearsal of past experience can play an important part in the build-up to an act of self-injury.

We also examined these reports for any reference to emotions that appeared to have potential to act as triggers for self-injury. It emerged that the emotional triggers were similar for both the spring and the switch scenarios. There was, however, a difference in the women who used the switch pathway; they tended to be older, to have cut more and to have cut deeply more often or frequently. Those who used the switch pathway also tended to have more frequent dissociative experiences as indicated by higher scores on the Dissociative Experiences Scale (Bernstein & Putnam, 1986) compared to those who did not.

These negative precursors of self-injury may be classified into three broad categories – feeling trapped, feeling neglected and feeling anger (at others for the current situation or at oneself for failing to resolve the difficulty). It seems likely that the combination of being both trapped and neglected significantly increases the risk of self-harm as is seen in the caged primate, the prisoner in solitary confinement or the adolescent trapped within a disturbed family (Tantam & Whittaker, 1992).

WHAT MIGHT TRIGGER SELF-INJURY?

Potential triggers

People who self-injure often use the term 'triggering' to mean something more restricted than the triggering that we have considered up to now. They are referring to descriptions, which might induce the emotions that immediately precede the urge to self-injure. When talking to others who also self-injure – and particularly when writing letters, emails or contributing to Internet discussion groups – they are usually very careful to give warning if concerned that what they say or write could trigger a reader to self-harm. Being someone who self-injures means that one is sensitive to what might trigger others to self-injure. A convention has emerged in recent years among both formal and informal groups of self-harmers whereby it is expected that the writer will insert a 'spoiler' (a warning sentence) into the text before any potentially triggering passage. Typically, such a 'spoiler' would take the form >>> *Warning – the following material may be triggery* <<<, or perhaps >>>*Following message 'spoilered' for mention of blades and blood* <<<.

'Spoilers' are written by people who self-injure to warn others that their message may inadvertently prompt a reader to cut herself or himself. Examples can be seen in the specialist newsletters and self-help literature often circulated by people who self-injure among themselves, and also in messages posted publicly on the Internet on the numerous websites that offer informal support to those who self-harm.

Examination of messages that have been marked in this way provides valuable information about what can trigger self-injury in people who are predisposed to doing so. In one study, we examined the messages posted over a month on three publicly accessible bulletin boards that focused on self-injury and where contributors posted their messages anonymously. Over a four week period, a total of 276 messages were identified that contained warnings or 'spoilers' about the content. The most common reason for inserting a warning into a message was that it contained some description of the actual act of cutting, and this occurred in 30% of the 'spoilered' messages.

Reading a detailed account of cutting (particularly if the account is graphic) may unintentionally lead to a self-injury episode by putting the reader into the state of mind that leads to cutting, much as alcoholics may find themselves craving a drink after watching a beer advertisement on the television. This is an example of the switching that we will consider in the next section.

Other themes that were 'spoilered' were (in order of frequency) despair or misery (16%), suicide or death (13%), abuse or rape (8%), self-hate or feeling unlovable or unworthy (8%), eating or weight or body image (7%), swearing or strong language (5%), medical health or treatment (4%), family relationships or childhood memories (4%), sex (2%) and religion (2%). These percentages need to be interpreted with caution since the figures will partly reflect the frequency with which specific issues were raised and presented in the ongoing discussion. It is clear, however, that most of the 'spoilered' themes were either descriptions of emotions, or descriptions of experiences that were likely to be emotional for the reader, as well as for the writer.

Emotional triggers

We went on to see whether there were any emotional triggers in common in messages where the writer described events and feelings that led them to anticipate an act of self-injury. The latest edition of Roget's thesaurus was used to assign each emotionally descriptive word or phrase to the superordinate category ascribed by the thesaurus (see Table 3.3).

Feelings of powerlessness, self-dislike, suffering, resentment and fear occurred in a significant proportion of these messages. These are some of the emotions that many people find hard to express and that some try hard to suppress. Our everyday experience indicates that they are, too, the kind of emotions that do not go away until they are dealt with in some

Table 3.3 Discourse themes suggestive of triggering emotions

Theme	Example	Proportion of messages containing this theme
Impotence	Feeling powerless to resist	15%
Dislike (of self)	Hating myself and what I do	15%
Suffering	Feeling very unhappy	11%
Resentment	Feeling anger towards someone	10%
Seclusion	Feeling solitary and friendless	9%
Fear	Feeling scared and frightened	7%
Exertion	Trying hard (usually to cope with distress or to resist self-harm)	5%

way, if only because most of us tend to dwell on, to ruminate about, those experiences in which we have felt impotent or resentful. These are lingering emotions, and we go over past experience in the hope that we can find a way to re-narrate our experience so that the emotion is discharged. If we do not succeed, we may find that the emotion is intensified and that we have an increased disposition to respond with feelings of impotence or resentment. In addition, we found some evidence of rumination in nearly a third of these messages.

Self-injury becomes of benefit if these emotions cannot be dealt with effectively in other ways except by self-injury. Normally the pre-eminent means of dealing with emotions is by naming them, but one study has shown that people who injure themselves have a degree of alexithymia, or inability to put names to emotions (Polk & Liss, 2007). Our study indicated that this was the route to repeated self-injury in those women we studied, despite their attempts to prevent it and the mounting tension or spring that resulted. Other studies have come to similar conclusions. A recent review of 18 such studies concluded that the evidence was strongest for 'affect regulation' as the motive for self-injury compared to 'self-punishment', 'anti-dissociation', 'interpersonal-influence', 'sensation-seeking', 'anti-suicide' and 'interpersonal boundaries' (Klonsky, 2007). The evidence that it was mounting unpleasant emotion that triggered self-injury were given in this review as: '(a) acute negative affect precedes self-injury; (b) decreased negative affect and relief are present after self-injury; (c) most self-injurers identify the desire to alleviate negative affect as a reason for self-injuring; and (d) the performance of proxies for self-injury in the laboratory leads to reductions in negative affect and arousal' (Klonsky, 2007, p. 235). Klonsky also concluded that the other 'functions received modest support' and we consider several of them later in this chapter.

HOW CAN SELF-INJURY CHANGE EMOTIONAL STATE?

Most of the time we only deliberately harm our skin if the skin itself has become uncomfortable. We might rub a bruise, pick at a scab or scratch an itch enough sometimes to make ourselves bleed. Making the skin the target may not be an accurate reflection of what is causing the discomfort. Itchiness can, for example, be an expression of a systemic condition like jaundice, involving the whole body. Even so, scratching may still relieve the symptom at least temporarily. It would be wrong to take the analogy too far but private self-injury is a bit like scratching an itch, or at least scratching angrily and with focussed attention on an unbearable and recalcitrant itch until the skin bleeds. Of course, in self-injury the sensation that one is trying to relieve is not itchiness but some kind of emotional discomfort which we are calling the trigger.

We scratch our skins because that is where the itch seems to be. Indeed, an itch probably does correspond to the release of prostaglandins, histamine and other inflammatory products within the skin itself. But why would we locate an emotion in our skin? Furthermore, why would we think that we might be able to change the emotion by scratching (or burning, or cutting) the skin?

Children are rocked, stroked, tickled and groomed by their mothers and other carers. So are lovers, particularly during the 'bonding' phase. Skin contact is an important means of establishing this bond. Just like scratching an itch, this involves neuropeptides, but long-term genetic changes are also involved, along with alterations in the endogenous opioid (endorphin) mediated reward system. The lack of bonds leads to a feeling of emptiness. It has been hypothesized that the social isolation of people in solitary confinement or in deprivatory institutions might be a reason why people in these situations, who experience a kind of empty apathy, are particularly likely to injure themselves.

Grooming can also be used to counteract the negative feelings induced by contact with others, as well as fill the void left by social isolation. Getting one's hair styled or cut, getting a manicure or a wax, having a massage – all of these are ways of soothing away troubles. Most primates groom much more than human beings, and Dunbar argues that its important role in the social life of other primates has, in humans, been taken over by gossip (Dunbar, 2004). So gossip, too, is a way of restoring one's spirits. Talking to oneself, while it may work to fend off social isolation ('whistling in the dark' as it is often called), does not usually relieve anger or distress. It only works if the talk is of a specific kind, if it is an enactment of a conversation with another person – a conversation with an absent partner or parent, for example – or if one rehearses having it out with the person towards whom one has the bad feeling.

Among primates, dominant animals are groomed more than submissive animals. Being groomed is an indication of social status or, as we would say, of being valued. The reward system that subserves being valued is the one linked to task accomplishment. It is mediated in some of its crucial connections by a particular neurotransmitter – dopamine. It is quite different from the social isolation reward system and is probably only mildly (if at all) stimulated by self-grooming unless in the context of a re-enactment.

Primates in captivity show a number of unusual behaviours that resemble human beings who experience social isolation and a lack of tasks to solve. Some of these, such as stereotypies or repeated behavioural sequences (such as pacing or leaping repeatedly from one part of the cage to another and back again) are reduced in primates by making them have to work to get their food. These stereotypies probably correspond best to the mindless kinds of self-injury that result from comfort behaviours like hair pulling. Other more explicit self-injury behaviours like self-biting (also common in captive primates) do not improve when the animals are moved to an environment that is more cognitively complex (and thus more stimulating). In one study of rhesus monkeys, 14% of the monkeys bit themselves. These monkeys had more stressful events in the first two years of their lives (a period that covers the same span of development as the first five years of a human child) than the monkeys who did not bite themselves. The self-biting monkeys also had more separations from their mother during this period (Novak, 2003). These vulnerable monkeys had the kind of hormonal response to challenge (a blunted cortisol response) that is often associated with vulnerability to stress in human beings. For these monkeys, the self-biting was triggered by aggressive encounters with other monkeys, and sometimes when the keeper had to do things in the cage. These threats increased the vulnerable monkeys' heart rates substantially, but the rate dropped when they bit themselves suggesting that the bite somehow reduced the arousal provoked by the threat.

Cutting, abrading or burning the skin may be an extreme form of grooming behaviour, as these examples suggest. So perhaps the apparent benefits of self-injury are similar to those of grooming. Grooming may be a distraction and self-injury may also have this function, particularly if the injury process is experienced as painful. Some people who injure themselves experience the preceding dysphoria as diffuse and ill-defined, and so find it helpful to have a single wound on which to focus.

Grooming has direct effects on neurochemistry and this may also be true of self-injury. Effects include the release of endorphins, an increase in dopaminergic transmission and changes in 5HT transmission. These effects may be partly synergistic, but exactly where and how the changes in neurotransmitters have their effects in people is unclear. It would also be premature to generalize from animals. For example, either buspirone or fluoxetine is effective at reducing repetitive self-biting in caged rhesus monkeys (Fontenot et al., 2005), but neither of these drugs is consistently effective in reducing self-injury by people. Nor do we know what inner experience corresponds to a change in these transmitters. Endorphins are particularly involved in pain pathways. They are also involved in parts of the brain (the amygdala) in those pathways that mediate security and anxiety proneness. It would however be premature to suppose that self-injury reduces 'mental pain' or that it increases attachment.

RELEVANCE TO HUMAN SELF-INJURY

It is unlikely that low serotonin states will prove to be the final explanation for self-injury, not least because self-injury is not simply a behaviour but is also an action, as we will consider later in this chapter. But there is an association between serotonin and many aspects of self-injury that helps us to understand the disposition to harm the self.

Low serotonin states are linked with impulsive actions (Markowitz & Coccaro, 1995) and with self-injury (Siever et al., 1992). They are also linked with low mood, and therefore with a wish to punish the self, perhaps as a consequence of the lack of assertiveness, with which they are also associated. This leads to anger being displaced on to the self rather than on to others, for fear of their aggression.

Low serotonin states are reminiscent of what Gerald Caplan, a child psychiatrist and psychoanalyst, called 'narcissistic supplies'. His idea was that narcissism or self-love – we might call it self-esteem, but actually it is more properly thought of as the confidence in one's value to others – was a kind of psychic fuel. The original source of this fuel is the love of a carer, and it is the feeling of being cared for that keeps it topped up. Both low levels of circulating serotonin and self-injury are associated with a history of a lack of love and care as a child (Crowell et al., 2008).

Narcissistic supplies are drained by having to counteract negative appraisals by other people. We need supplies not just to feel optimistic about our future projects, but also to feel that we are valued by others, that we have status. When our narcissistic supplies begin to be lowered, the first thing that goes is sometimes our social status. We call this 'humiliation' – it is the combination of a negative valuation of ourselves by others coupled with a loss of status. Once the narcissistic supplies get drained further, we experience a loss of optimism, too. We feel that other people's evaluation of us is correct. We feel we are bad, just as they imply, and moreover that we are of no account. This state of emotional and social inactivation is 'shame'.

We can cover up shame, but we cannot so easily fill up the void that it leaves in our emotional life. Shame is associated with a particular kind of intolerable emptiness that we want to fill with immediate gratification, even if that is derived from shameful activities. In fact, in this state of shame, what is valued by society may become less of value to us, and what is devalued by society becomes paradoxically appealing. Shame is also associated with an intense desire to hide the shame, and to hide the causes of the shame. Self-injury may provide the means to do this. Shame may also explain why people who repeatedly injure themselves may sometimes do so following a pleasurable event, which might normally be expected to leave positive emotions behind, and not the negative emotions that are the triggers of self-harm. Pleasure in someone who is shame-prone can provoke shame at being happy, and turn the positive experience into a negative one.

STIGMATIZATION AND THE DISPOSITION TO SELF-HARM

People who are stigmatized may feel humiliated and this may be what increases their disposition to self-harm. People who are being punished (for example prisoners, and particularly those who are hidden away) may feel shame. People who experience adverse events but feel that they must hide them are among the other groups who are particularly at risk of shame. People who are bullied, or people who are physically or sexually abused, are prime examples. They may feel shame, not because they are in any way to blame for their predicament, but because they cannot own up to it. Importantly, they feel powerless to change the situation.

The pervasive emotional emptiness that makes every day seem like drudgery and takes away hope for the future is recognized to be one of the principal risk factors for self-injury. Indeed emotional emptiness, which can be replaced by short-lived but fleeting emotions, is one of the defining features of 'borderline personality disorder' – a term that is often applied to people who are disposed to self-injury.

DISSOCIATION AND SELF-INJURY

People who self-injure tend to have stronger dissociative traits than those who do not (Zlotnick et al., 1999; Brodsky et al., 1995; Brundle, 1995), and those who engage in frequent cutting tend to report traits that are stronger than do those who cut infrequently (Low et al., 2000). If dissociation is tracked over time in people at risk of self-injury, the level peaks during cutting and decreases thereafter (Kemperman et al., 1997). One possible explanation – and one that has dominated explanations of self-injury in the past – is that people injure themselves to terminate dissociative episodes. Another explanation is the one that we have already considered: that dissociation turns off the safety-catch against self-injury and so makes self-injury more likely.

'Dissociation' means that mental functions that are normally inseparable become split off. In particular, it means that willing something ('volition' or 'intention') becomes split off from being conscious of willing something ('awareness' or 'consciousness'). As a consequence of dissociation, an intentional action or perception may appear to be automatic, reflexive or unconscious.

Everyone has dissociative experiences at one time or another. These include experiences like driving (or walking, or cycling) from one place to another and arriving at the destination only to realize that one has no memory at all of the journey. It also includes people going 'berserk' or 'running amok', when serious violence can be done and a person does not remember doing it after. These two instances involve memory and therefore identity. A person who does not remember driving across London might say, 'it wasn't me doing the driving. I was on autopilot'. A person who hits someone in a blind rage might say afterwards, 'It wasn't me that did the hitting – I'm just not like that'. Or they might say that they could not help themselves for they were triggered into the rage by something that happened – 'like a red rag to a bull' as the expression has it.

These are situations in which a person does not feel fully responsible for what they did because they believe that they were 'not all there' when they did it. The model for this kind of dissociation is the hypnotic trance, and like the trance it is not fully clear who is responsible for a person's actions during dissociation. Stage hypnotists may give hypnotic suggestions to their subjects which lead them to do embarrassing (and occasionally amusing) actions which they would certainly not do if they were not hypnotized. The hypnotized person may argue afterwards that they were acting out of character because they could not help themselves. But hypnotists deny their ability to be able to make a subject do something that they do not want to do, and sometimes, watching a stage act, we do think that the subjects are taking the opportunity of being hypnotized to play act.

When the consequences are more serious, the law takes the view that either (a) someone was responsible, or (b) that their action was an 'automatism'. Automatisms are always abnormal in legal terms, and their occurrence is prima facie evidence of illness. So a person who commits an offence due to an automatism may be sentenced to be detained in a hospital.

SUSCEPTIBILITY TO DISSOCIATION

Dissociative experiences are wide-ranging but are usually only reported as symptoms when inconvenient or distressing. They can be mild and common-place such as daydreaming, occasional forgetfulness, lapses of attention or numbness upon receiving bad news. They can also be profound, as with dis-sociative amnesia where several hours of every day seem to be lost, or deper-sonalization involving disturbing out-of-body experiences. In its most severe presentation, an individual's ability to sustain relationships with others can be affected.

Children (especially young children) often dissociate, and a tendency to fantasy-proneness, daydreaming or even conversing with imaginary friends is usually accepted as a normal part of their development. It has been suggested that the very young tend to use dissociation as a means of dealing with the wide range of new experiences which they need to assimilate, but which they are temporarily unable to process. The child who can dissociate may do so as a normal response to an unfamiliar event. This allows the 'experience' to be held in the episodic memory until it can be processed by thinking it through (or, perhaps, talking it over with oneself). After such processing, the experi-ence is stored as elements in consciously accessible memory. Until then, the episodic memory is not accessible to consciousness and is in fact dissociated from consciousness. An exception is when it is relived as a complete episode, along with the emotions that occurred during the episode. This is the basis of the flashback that occurs in post-traumatic states.

The incidence of dissociative experiences seems to be highest in child-hood, remains significant during adolescence and steadily declines after the late teenage years. In one study, median scores on a widely used self-report measure of dissociative experience were nearly twice as high in 14 year olds and two and a half times as high in 12 year olds in comparison with those for college students with a median age of 24 years (Ross et al., 1989). One possi-bility is that maturity brings with it the capacity to deal more directly with new experiences; another is that the rate at which new experiences present themselves to the growing child reduces as his or her world becomes more familiar.

In adulthood, women report more dissociative experiences than men although, like self-injury, the size of the disparity may be due in part to the tendency for women to seek help and to remain engaged with treatment where this is offered. Findings are not always consistent, however. Dissociation was found to be almost as common in unselected male as in female psychiatric outpatients in one study (Lipschitz et al., 1996).

Some people may be particularly susceptible to dissociative experiences, probably as a result of a hereditary trait (Jang et al., 1998). This is most likely the same one – hypnotizability (Agargun et al., 1998) – that makes some people good hypnotic subjects. Three similarities suggest a close relationship between hypnosis and dissociation: (a) the frequency of dissociative experience and the susceptibility to hypnosis are both correlated with performance on tests of suggestibility; (b) hypnotic trance and dissociative trance have many similar features; and (c) hypnotizability tends in the general population to decline with age at the same rate as dissociability. The closeness of the link has led some people to view dissociation as a kind of self-hypnosis. It has been suggested that hypnotizability can be increased by dissociation (Frischholz et al., 1992) and also that hypnotizability is a diathesis for developing dissociation (Butler et al., 1996). There are reports of depersonalization and dissociated states occurring as side-effects of hypnotherapy raising the possibility that, for some, hypnotic techniques may lower the threshold for dissociation and make the condition worse.

DISSOCIATION AND TRAUMA

It is often stated that dissociation occurs because it is a way of escaping the otherwise inescapable, and that it can have an immediate protective effect against overwhelming stress (even though its persistence may be one of the factors that ensures that any ensuing stress disorder cannot be resolved). Sexual abuse in childhood is often given as a paradigm of this. The child who is being abused by an adult is terrified but lacks the knowledge, physical strength or social status to escape. The sexual stimulation is unpleasant and is experienced as shameful, which makes it doubly unpleasant. So all the child can do is to 'escape inside' into an alternative and better world. Having once done this, it becomes easier to do over and over again until it is happening all the time. Years have often passed. So the child is by this time an adolescent who is now terrified by feeling her or himself slip away into this unreal world. However, self-injury and, perhaps, particularly the flow of blood brings back reality and makes the world real again.

The use of dissociation as a means of escape from trauma is so often asserted (Yates, 2004) that it is puzzling that there is very little evidence for it and some against it. Gershuny and Thayer (1999) concluded from a review of the literature that dissociation is not only a symptom of PTSD, but also that dissociation actually reduces a person's ability to cope with trauma. They also found that people who dissociate a lot have more anxiety and distress over the longer-term than those who dissociate little.

THREE TYPES OF DISSOCIATION

In an earlier section in this chapter, we reported a comparison based on our subjects' scores on the Dissociative Experiences Scale. This self-report instrument is one of the most commonly used scales to measure dissociation traits, but analyses suggest that it may, in fact, measure 1, 3 or 4 separable phenomena (Holmes et al., 2005). The three-factor solution seems to have been the one most often found. That is, in most studies where this scale was used, it was picking up three distinct things: attention, compartmentalization and detachment.

The first – 'attention' – is the kind of dissociation with which we are all familiar, and involves becoming so absorbed in something that we are unaware of our surroundings. This type of dissociation is completely normal and most people experience it most days of their lives.

A second type of dissociation – 'detachment' – leads to experiences like depersonalization (feeling that one's body is not one's own), derealization (where the world around seems unreal and emptied of meaning like a doll's house) and feeling as though one is numb or that one is temporarily unable to discern emotional meaning. The detached person may feel that they are not fully present in the world (depersonalization); that the world around them is unreal and often unimportant (derealization); that time is not flowing correctly so that new experiences feel as if they lack any surprise or interest because they have been seen before (déjà vu) or even lived through before (déjà vécu). The phrase 'spacing out' is sometimes used by self-injurers when they begin to experience depersonalization; others may describe a period of derealization as a time when they had been 'spaced out'. A related type of dissociative experience involves objects appearing abnormally small, distant or altered in size (sometimes termed 'Alice in Wonderland syndrome' after the phenomenon described in Lewis Carroll's 1865 novel *Alice in Wonderland* and believed to have been inspired by Carroll's own migraine experiences). Finally, there is the experience that the person is not located in his or her own physical body, and that their body is functioning like a robot ('out of body experiences').

The third type of dissociation – 'compartmentalization' – is the type that is particular associated with what psychiatrists call borderline personality disorder, with PTSD and also with a past history of sexual abuse. Compartmentalization is so called because people seem to compartmentalize themselves. On one hand, there are all the actions, thoughts and feelings that they own, which they are aware of doing and are therefore able to control. These belong in one compartment; but there is another compartment (or compartments) where actions, thoughts and feelings that are disowned belong (disavowed, warded off, repressed are some of the other terms that have been used). Of course these are not literally compartments; some people have preferred to call them 'states of mind' and others call them 'identities' or 'subpersonalities' or 'alters'.

Dissociative detachment and self-injury

Dissociative experiences reported in the context of self-injury episodes are wideranging. Some examples are given in Table 3.4 based on our own studies of recollections by women of their experiences before, during or after they had cut or burned themselves (Huband & Tantam, 2004). Virtually every type of dissociative detachment symptom is represented, although depersonalization was the most commonly reported. In addition, there were two dissociative symptoms that we consider to be examples of dissociative compartmentalization (not being able to remember cutting, and experiencing self-injury while on 'automatic pilot').

Does dissociation motivate self-injury?

Dissociative detachment is unpleasant for most people and can be very distressing. It has been suggested that a self-inflicted cut or burn is an effective way of reconnecting with the real world, in the same way that children who dissociate learn that a dissociative state can be ended by suddenly jolting the body (Herman, 1992). We agree that self-injury, and particularly making oneself bleed, is often described as an effective way of waking oneself up. But it is not the commonest reason given for self-injury, as we have seen already in this

Table 3.4 Examples of dissociative experiences reported before, during and after self-injury

Detachment

- Feeling as though the cut was happening to someone else's arm
- Feeling that the hand holding the blade is not connected to me
- Feeling emotionally numb
- Feeling physically numb; local analgesia during cutting
- Seeing the world through a mist or fog
- Feeling detached from the self
- Feeling unreal; not feeling alive
- Having out-of-body experiences
- Experiencing flashbacks

Compartmentalization

- Not being able to remembering cutting
- Experience of cutting while on 'automatic pilot'

chapter. Nor do the reasons for the effectiveness of cutting seem convincing. It has been suggested, for example, that seeing the blood flow jolts a person out of their detachment. People are quoted as saying that it made them realize they were alive. Sometimes the passage from Shakespeare's Merchant of Venice is quoted, too, when Shylock says, 'If you prick us, do we not bleed?'.

However, bleeding was not being put forward as a test of being alive by Shylock, but as one of the tests of a common humanity for Jews and Christians. Others included laughing when tickled, dying when poisoned and taking revenge when wronged. We think that bleeding is particularly associated with shame and with sacrifice; hence its use in this passage which is about Shylock taking a pound of flesh from a defaulter on a debt. We do not think that there is any theoretical reason why it should be linked, particularly, with the relief of detachment. Furthermore, it is not unusual for sufferers to describe burning their skin with a lighted cigarette as quite effective in terminating an unpleasant detached state – a process that does not involve any flow of blood.

The risk of detachment increases when a person becomes tense or anxious. We think it more likely that detachment is a consequence of the winding of the spring leading to self-injury. The release of tension after the cut or burn has taken place – the release of the spring – does remove that sense of detachment, but only as a secondary consequence of relieving the tension.

In our study of people who repeatedly injured themselves, 70% reported experiences that were recognizably dissociative ones preceded the injury, but 30% said that these experiences followed the injury. Sutton (2004) reports a similar finding and suggests that self-injury may be used to induce dissociation as well as to terminate it. This is in keeping with the idea that dissociation can be an effective coping mechanism when it allows the individual to 'tune out' distressing or unwanted experience (Kennerley, 1996), and both the above sequences accord with the view that self-injury can toggle dissociation on and off (Connors, 1996), thereby allowing sensation to be regulated.

Dissociative compartmentalization

All of us have some degree of compartmentalization. We may be very different at work than at home. We may act out of our normal character (take on another 'role') once we put on a uniform. But normally we are aware of ourselves in all of these compartments, although we may not be aware of being so different when we are in one or the other.

Compartmentalized dissociation, however, is a bit more like sleepwalking. It is perhaps more like having the kind of blackout that heavy drinkers get when they can carry on doing and talking, but have no memory of what has happened the following morning and may, indeed, deny having done or said the things that they did. Compartmentalization also occurs in some epileptic states and as the result of drugs – like phencyclidine (PCP or 'Angel Dust') – that are termed 'dissociatives'. Hypnotic trance is also, as we have seen, a kind of compartment created in a person – here the compartment is one in which they can be directed by the hypnotist.

Compartmentalization is probably the basis, too, of post-traumatic stress disorder. An adverse experience becomes a trauma because it cannot be processed or rather it is processed by being denied or disavowed rather than being worked through. The model is taken by analogy from the consequences of a penetrating physical wound which, if it does not heal inside, can be walled off by scar tissue. This scar tissue may paradoxically prevent healing, but does allow some return to function because the damaged tissue is separated from the undamaged tissue around it.

Dependence on self-injury
The threshold for dissociation, like that of hypnotic induction, is reduced by previous dissociation or trance. The more a person uses dissociation (perhaps to inactivate the safety-catch so that they can release the tension of their emotional spring by self-injury) the more they will dissociate in the future (Himber, 1994). People who injure themselves are therefore more likely to use compartmentalization as a way of dealing with adverse experience and the more that they use it, the more they will use it.

Compartmentalization reduces the effectiveness of emotional processing. So one consequence of using self-injury for emotional coping is that whatever its short-term benefits, the long-term effect is to reduce and not enhance coping. This paradoxically results in a greater need to fall back on self-injury or, put another way, the development of a kind of addiction to, or dependence on, self-injury.

Psychological compartments are created because a person is not willing to process the information that they contain. As a result, such compartments are independent of the will, and cannot be entered, or left, willingly. In post-traumatic stress disorder, a person may find themselves in a different compartment of being as the result of a sound, a smell or an allusion if these are linked with the traumatic experience.

EMOTIONAL FLAVOURS AND COMPARTMENTALIZATION

Going back to our old school may, suddenly and unexpectedly, make us feel like the child we had been with the same anxieties about walking on the grass or opening the door of the staff room. We find we have temporarily 'switched' into another compartment of our mind, the one where our younger self still lives on. Re-visiting a battlefield, the house where our mother died, the country of our birth if we are exiles – all of these have the same power. Sometimes the experience is pleasant, sometimes unpleasant, but it is always complex, compelling and immediate.

Although we can sometimes make the switch by an effort of the imagination, it is more often an immediate, involuntary experience as if something outside us has thrown a switch. We can find ourselves switching if we put on the identity of that other self, for example if we put on an item of our old school uniform like a hat, cap or scarf. But what normally throws the switch is a shift in our mood to one that was characteristic of that other compartment in ourselves. This is particularly likely to happen if the compartment has a characteristic mood, as in the examples that we have given – the battlefield or the homeland – are likely to have. The mood, or emotional climate, or emotional atmosphere or emotional flavour – all terms for the same thing, although we prefer 'emotional flavour' – is often characteristic because it is made up of both pleasant and unpleasant feelings. The emotional flavour of school may have some elements of fear, for example, but also of fun or friendliness. Emotions do not vanish when we have experienced them but tend to linger. So when we re-experience something emotional (we call this 'an emotor') we may have a different feeling from it, but that gets blended into the former feeling from it, that has lingered. Over time, an emotor may therefore develop a highly complex, unique emotional flavour.

DO NOT READ THE FOLLOWING PARAGRAPH IF YOU REPEATEDLY INJURE YOURSELF

We say that we get a different feeling *from* an emotor because it often feels as if the things that we react to emotionally have an intrinsic emotional power that transmits the emotion to us. Think of something sharp. When we look at it we feel a shudder, a frisson, of something. We do not think of that as being a judgement by us of a neutral object. We experience the thing itself as having some power to cause a frisson, much as the sight of a snake or a spider induces fear, and this is what we call the emotional flavour. So the emotional flavour of a blade is … well, we leave the reader to feel what it is for them. For someone who has repeatedly cut themselves, then the emotional flavour of a blade, or perhaps just the particular kind of blade that has been used, includes elements of relief that the cutting brings. The emotional flavour of the blade may come to be calming, even soothing. Seeing a blade may then switch that person into another compartment of themselves. This may be the compartment that occurs after cutting when they do feel calm, and without knowing what they are doing, they may have cut themselves. This is the reason that we put the warning message at the beginning of the paragraph. We did not want someone to read the paragraph, visualize a blade and as a result switch to self-injury.

THE SWITCH PATHWAY

We have already mentioned the 'switch' pathway to self-injury, and that it is an example of the kind of dissociation that is called compartmentalization, in which a person can change their mood and – almost – their identity, prompted by an emotor with a strong enough flavour: like gunfire to a battle-scarred veteran or their usual blade to someone who has repeatedly cut her or himself. It is worth considering how such a pathway might develop.

If a person repeatedly injures themselves, the state of being in and around the injury can become a compartment of a kind similar to that of the walled off trauma in a person with post-traumatic stress disorder. If they regularly use one method of self-injury, such as a particular blade to cut themselves, this can become associated with that compartment just as the sound of gunfire can alter a Vietnam veteran's awareness so that they find themselves back in Vietnam again, even while walking along a street in Chicago or New York.

We call this process 'switching'. It represents a quite different route to self-injury, but it is a pathway quite as important as the 'spring'. Since switching can lead to sudden self-injury without the precursor of steadily building tension, the person experiencing this pathway is easily misunderstood.

The switch pathway, like the spring pathway, involves dissociation. For convenience, we have summarized the relationships between dissociation and the two pathways in Table 3.5.

IDENTITY

So far in this chapter, we have been considering the habits and circumstances that influence the possibility of a person injuring themselves, i.e. their disposition

Table 3.5 Dissociation and self-injury

- Dissociation inactivates the safety-catch and so enables self-injury
- The winding spring produces dissociation, which is terminated by self-injury
- The winding spring leads to self-injury, which induces dissociation
- Exposure to a reminder of self-injury switches on an act of self-injury without a person willing it

to self-injury. But we call these dispositions and not causes because self-injury is an action and not just a behaviour. It is a person who acts on the disposition. Dispositions can be so strong that the person acting may feel that they have little choice, but over a period of time there is always enough of a margin for the person to resist – if there is reason to do so – and by resisting, alter the strength of the disposition.

Reasons are difficult to pin down. Very often we do not know the reason for doing something till afterwards. We may anyway give a different reason, and even believe that we have a different reason, to different people or at different times. One of us has discussed this at some length previously (Tantam, 2002).

Reasons are tied up with our identity: who or what we are, deep down; what makes us, 'us': our unique distinguishing characteristics; our thumbprint; what others recognize in us as our identity. Some identity is given (for example, our DNA), and some is ascribed (for example, our passport number). But our 'personal' identity is created and maintained by ourselves, even if this is done in collaboration with others. An important means of creating our identity is through our actions and the reasons we give for them. Wanting to maintain a particular identity is one reason for not acting on dispositions that might reveal inconsistencies with that identity.

In considering the 'spring', we wrote that it was wound by the tension between the wish to release bad feelings through self-injury and a resistance to doing so. One kind of resistance is provided by the safety-catch, which as we saw becomes weaker and weaker with the repetition of cutting. Another source of resistance is identity: being a person who injures themselves creates an identity in our own and other people's eyes which can be desirable (see the case of Carl, above), but is most often unwanted.

There are people who are comfortable with having an identity as a self-injurer, but they are in our experience, rare. A smaller number of people have friends or acquaintances who accept this self-injuring identity without demur, and an even smaller number who have partners, parents or children who appreciate their self-injuring identity.

Some might say that this is just stigma or even more simply, that it is an irrational fear traceable back to the safety-catch. But anyone who claims this has to justify it, as we always have to do when it comes to claims about our identity in the face of counter-claims.

Are people who self-injure being manipulative?

This is a very common counter-claim to a self-injuring identity. Its force is heightened by being based on two acknowledged facts: that self-injury has a powerful effect on other people and that people who injure themselves often feel that they lack power. Indeed, as we have seen, the feeling of helplessness is itself a trigger for self-injury. Manipulation may also be presented as 'secondary gain', as 'cutting to get care', or as disguised coercion. Whichever formulation is used the accusation is that the person is trying to gain their own ends without 'owning up' to them, and therefore without giving other people the opportunity to negotiate whatever ends serve the whole group, and not just the person who is self-injuring.

While it is no doubt correct that self-injury does come across as a kind of 'demand with menaces', there is no reason to suppose that it is planned that way very often, if ever. Certainly, people who self-injure normally consider themselves to be victims and not agents. To say someone is manipulating may reveal more about the identity of the person saying that, than of the person about whom it is said. It is a kind of bullying which invalidates another person's intentions rather than exploring them. We agree with Meyer (1984) who suggested that accusations of manipulation from therapists or other professionals flag up the professional's lack of empathy and so increase the chances of further self-harm.

All of us need others to cooperate with us so that we can gain ends that suit us. Being able to persuade other people to go along with us willingly is the most harmonious way of doing this, but in order for us to achieve this harmony we need to own that we are very often self-seeking. Notwithstanding the anti-therapeutic nature of accusations that self-injury is a kind of coercion, we do note that people who are recovering from self-injury often make progress when they recognize that they are no different from everyone else in this matter. Like everyone else, people who self-injure want to get other people to go along with them. Owning this without it being seen as an unacceptable threat to identity is a step towards no longer needing self-injury.

You can't love us if you do this to yourself
Self-injury often begins in adolescence and although it may begin in secret (we consider the effects on identity of secret self-injury in the next section), it is often discovered by family members. Their counter-claim to the legitimacy of the self-injury is often, as the title of this section indicates, that self-injury is an attack on others which could only occur as a lack of love.

It is certainly true that there may be a lack of love in the families of people who injure themselves and we have provided scientific evidence of this in an earlier section. But it is hating oneself and not hating other people that is the trigger to self-injury (see Table 3.3). Having an identity that seems unacceptable to others is what inspires this. Being told, or being given to understand without being told, that one's love is inadequate can lead to identifying oneself as a hateful person and seeking self-injury as an escape from this.

A parent, a partner or even an over-involved therapist may think that the person who injures themselves would not do so if they cared about the people who care for them. The context, however, is usually one of interpersonal conflict and this conflict is not really about love at all, but about control. 'If you really loved me, you would ...' often means 'if you allowed me to control you, I could think that you really loved me'. It may be that a person finds himself or herself locked into a relationship with one or more people who interpret control as love. Not unreasonably, they find they cannot accept the identity of being under the other person's thumb. In this situation, they then have a fight on their hands to establish their own identity in the face of what seems like attempts to undermine it. Self-injury can certainly play a part in this battle.

Abuse, both physical and sexual, might be defined as a relationship between a dominant and a vulnerable person in which control masquerades as love, care, discipline or sexuality. It is not therefore surprising that the experience of abuse may be particularly likely to lead to self-injury.

Establishing identity by wresting control

The skin is, literally, the boundary between a body and its environment. Figuratively, too, it is the boundary between the person and the social world. Although the skin clearly belongs to the body, its coverings belong to the environment. It is less clear-cut whether or not the skin belongs to the person. Its decoration may be determined by society, as we have seen. Its scars may tell of old social obligations. The skin is a transition zone, and sometimes a battleground. Skin that has been touched may be experienced as partly owned by the person doing the touching. Cutting the skin in the touched area may be a means of re-establishing ownership over it (Cavanaugh, 2002).

COPING WITH PAST TRAUMA AND ABUSE

Women who injure themselves have a particularly high incidence of sexual abuse, suggesting that sexual abuse increases the risk of self-injury. Sexual abuse is often described as a trauma, the Greek for 'injure'. Could injuring oneself be a way of undoing being injured by someone else? Psychophysiologically, this may be so. The trauma of sexual abuse may result in secular changes in autonomic reactivity leaving the abused person with long-standing hyperreactivity to stress (McDonagh-Coyle et al., 2001). These changes may be particularly expressed in the skin as many junior doctors have unwittingly experienced when they have tried to take blood from a woman who has been abused, and found that her skin blanches and all the superficial veins squeeze closed as the needle enters the skin. Cutting into the skin may, paradoxically, relieve some of this hyper-reactivity, as we will discuss in the next chapter.

The main link between trauma, abuse and self-injury may however be what Anna Freud called 'identification with the aggressor', and what her father called 'undoing'. More recently, Bandura has obliquely referred to something similar in his theory of self-efficacy. What hurts most about trauma is also what leaves the deepest scars from torture – the experience of being under the control of another person, of lacking in efficacy and of feeling powerless. Identifying with the aggressor and traumatizing oneself in response to being traumatized are ways of regaining some degree of control, as the following example illustrates:

> Maria had been abused by her father and neglected by her mother. She was a wild girl who found it difficult to relate to her peers. She was bullied at school and the bullying became more savage when she went to secondary school. She had a vivid memory of having stones thrown at her when she was about 12 and of one cutting her cheek. She remembered picking it up, scratching her cheek with it herself and feeling a kind of relief. She thought that was when her repeated self-injury began.

The skin in trauma may for a time actually be the representation of another person if it has been taken over by the abuser. This means that it is possible to have a relationship with one's skin that is like having an intimate relationship with another person. The wound is the meeting place: a place where care can be bestowed and hostility ventilated.

Injury is used in rituals and ceremonies as a way of improving the appearance, as a commemoration, as a means of causing pain to be overcome, as a *rite de passage* following which a person becomes an adult or as a means to produce bleeding and the benefits of bleeding. When a particular young person starts to cut themselves we cannot say if he or she knows of any of these particular meanings, but we can assume that he or she does have some sense of the ceremonial nature of self-injury even when carried out in private. Young people who have only once or twice scratched themselves, and then perhaps only mildly, will often describe some thoughtful preparation before doing it, and will go to some lengths to ensure they are not discovered in the act of damaging their skin.

What we are sure is that any person who begins to cut themselves in private will know that they are doing something that others will disapprove of. Even if others do not disapprove of self-injury, they will disapprove of it being done in private. So self-injury is inevitably a secret act against others. That may be enough of a motive, but there is an additional element. Several people may have joint ownership in a particular person's skin. Parents may forbid their children to pierce or tattoo their skin, partners may object to this too and even employers may exercise a right to dictate the appearance of their employee's skin. So marking one's skin may also be to file the claim, '*this is mine to do with what I want*'.

Ownership of the skin is a particular issue in people who have been abused. Emotional abuse may involve disparagement about skin colour, some of it racial but some non-racial. Children can be bullied by their parents or others because their skin is too light and pasty ('*you need to get out more*' is what parents often say) or too dark. Skin and nails might be too dirty or too clean. Hair may be too long, or too short. Skin blemishes may be a source of shame. Physical abuse leads to other kinds of ownership. Children might be forbidden to show their skins in case the bruising, wheals or scars are disclosed to others.

Sexual abuse is perhaps the most invasive of all, since there another person wants to use the abused person's skin for sexual gratification and may imply that the abused person has no right to withhold it. For example, the experience of being raped can lead to feelings of estrangement from the body, almost as if it had become the property of the rapist. Sexual abuse that is repeated, especially when it occurs in childhood, can also lead to profound changes in the way a survivor perceives his or her body and the skin enclosing it. Skin may come to feel alien and disgusting and may temporarily come to represent the hated abuser. It is therefore not surprising that some women who have been raped or sexually abused as children mark their skins in order to reclaim them. But marking can be achieved by a socially directed method, such as getting a tattoo or having a nose stud (of course, we are not implying here that everyone that gets a tattoo or a stud has been abused).

Why do some people prefer to do the marking in private? Doing it in private may make it a more extreme rebellion, or it may be a way of avoiding conflict when a person has not fully escaped from the abuse. But another reason is that this is not an enactment, but a re-enactment. In injuring themselves the person is re-enacting a previous experience, but now they are the director rather than the passive victim. The survivor attempts to take control of a situation that was previously unmanageable, perhaps thinking to herself '*this time I'll be in charge of the pain and decide when it's too much*' (Connors, 1996). Daphne Miller has written about a 'trauma re-enactment syndrome' (Miller, 1994) in which those who survive psychological trauma in their early years begin hurting themselves in adolescence or adulthood (effectively doing to themselves what was done to them in childhood), and there are many published case reports supportive of the re-enactment hypothesis (van der Kolk, 1989). While this hypothesis remains rather difficult to test, clinical experience is often suggestive of there being at least some features of re-enactment in self-injury. The secrecy and the shame that attaches to the self-injury itself are often disproportionate, and one way of explaining this is to say that they actually belong to the abuse, of which the self-injury is a partial re-enactment.

YOU ARE NOT WHO WE THOUGHT YOU WERE

Self-injury in private may, on occasions, remain secret. Although it may still be a way of reasserting control over the skin, the battle is inside the person and not outside, with the people doing the controlling.

Secret self-injury allows a person to have two identities: a public, conformist one and a private one, that of being a self-injurer. Having two identities is made easier by (and itself facilitates) dissociative compartmentalization in which a person has, as it were, two personalities.

Hiding one's 'true' identity may be a reaction to the over-control and lack of affection of family members, but it may also be motivated by having a scary or hateful secret that cannot be shared. It is this secret, and the need to deal with it on one's own without recourse to support from others, that creates the private identity in the first place. The feelings of loneliness that it engenders can be one of the triggers to self-injury. The self-injury then becomes a secret that needs to be concealed as well, further separating the private identity from the public one.

Secrets that are sufficiently powerful to drive a person to create a public identity to conceal them are often associated with social rejection, humiliation, or even worse, shame. They include a sexual orientation that is thought to be unacceptable, having been abused and being bullied. All of these can lead a person to injure themselves, leading to the paradox described by Anna Freud of 'identification with the aggressor'. This is when a person bullies or abuses themselves in order to deal with the insufferable emotions of having been bullied or abused by other people.

Shame and atonement

Shame appears particularly significant in the context of self-injury and it would appear that self-inflicted skin damage (and particularly blood flow) could somehow expiate or atone for shame. Shame is derived from the old German word for wound, and it may be that, in some way, creating one's own injury can reduce the sting of the psychological wound – the shame – that someone else has created.

Shame has three elements: (a) believing that others scoff, mock, disparage or diminish oneself or one's actions; (b) believing that others are justified in doing so; and (c) an urge to hide oneself. People who self-injure are often shame-prone (in the sense that they are easily shamed by others), but are also ashamed of their shame and so are at pains to hide it. Shame is difficult to dispel and hard to endure. It can be sufficiently strong to destroy a person's very sense of identity. Strong feelings of shame commonly precede an episode of cutting or burning, and efforts to cope with shame may be one reason for self-harm (Briere & Runtz, 1993).

Blood and shame have a special association too, at least in Christianity since, to paraphrase Hebrews 9:11, blood washes away sin. It is also worth noting the historical connection between self-sacrifice and well-being. Acts of self-mortification have been viewed as a way of achieving some spiritual grace and appear to be able to offer rapid release from distressing shameful feelings. If self-injury is able to expiate shame directly as this suggests, it is not hard to see why the behaviour effectively becomes the self-help 'treatment of choice' for individuals in emotional crisis, and may help to understand why, in one study of adolescents who self-harmed, half of the female self-cutters reported wanting to punish themselves (Rodham et al., 2004).

Ivanoff et al. (2001, p. 153) describe an interesting study in which high levels of shame (but not other emotions) prior to commencing psychotherapy significantly increased the likelihood of self-injury within the first four months of therapy. The level of shame continued to predict self-harm even when the frequency of self-harm during the previous year and the presence of other negative emotions were controlled for (Brown et al., 1997).

Assertion of agency

For some, feelings of passivity feature particularly strongly as precursors to self-injury. These include feeling powerless, feeling helpless and in the type of 'abject' depression in which a persons feels they lack any ability to act in an assertive or positive way. Shame can also have a passive aspect. Vulnerability to feelings of this sort can arise from experiences in early life – for example, feeling over-protected, abused or repeatedly being told that one is incapable – as well as from experiences in adulthood that include feeling trapped in an abusive relationship or feeling that one has been violated in some way, as in rape.

It may be important here to differentiate shame from guilt. Strictly speaking, shame is a distinct emotion with its own specific behavioural repertoire, such as hanging one's head, blushing or failing to meet another's eyes. Feeling guilty is a type of anxiety, and what distinguishes it from other fears or anxieties is a particular fear, since feeling guilt is feeling fear of punishment. Thus shame is associated with a sense of the self as passive, powerless and the object of disgust. The other person is perceived as able and the source of contempt. A person who feels shame feels unwanted and disliked. In contrast, feeling guilty is associated with the self as having power which it either misuses or fails to use. The self is intact, capable and the source of failure; now it is the other that is injured, hurt or let down (Gilbert et al., 1994). A person who feels guilty feels that he is capable, but that he has done something wrong or has failed to do something that was a duty or a requirement.

The more a person feels in charge of their life, the more they are at risk of feeling guilty, but the less they are likely to feel shame. This is reflected in the fact that guilt cannot be transferred, but shame can. If our colleague commits a misdemeanour we do not thereby become guilty of anything, but we might be ashamed to have had him or her as a colleague. In guilt, we focus on ourselves as an agent. In shame we focus on others' judgements of us. Shame therefore feeds into the helplessness that many people who self-injure experience. It also feeds into their hopelessness because there is no finite price to shame. Unlike guilt, where there may be a tariff of punishments (and punishment is likely to determinate), shame may carry on and on until assuaged or atoned for. Self-injury may be one way of providing that atonement. We think it likely that for many of those who say they harm themselves to experience pain, the pain they seek is probably not directed at shame, but at guilt, by anticipating and perhaps therefore diverting punishment.

Self-injury can be associated with passive feelings in other ways. When a person feels they have lost control in all other situations, the act of self-injury may be one thing over which he or she can exert absolute control; it enables the individual to '*do something*'. Where the effect is uncontrollable anger towards another person, but that anger is experienced passively, control may be regained by channelling it against the self. This may appear as a safer option to directing the anger at another; Menninger (1935) observed that it would be less threatening for children to injure themselves non-fatally than to injure some person with whom they were intensely angry but upon whom their survival depended.

Chapter 4

Overcoming Self-Injury: Working Hard at Recovery

INTRODUCTION

In the last chapter we considered how people who injure themselves experience the accumulation of negative emotions which cannot be worked out interpersonally. We suggested that this accumulation provides increasing tension, which is eventually discharged by self-harm. Why this should work is not known, but we considered many possible explanations. However, there is no doubt that *something* works, since self-injury is so culturally important at times of identity change. We also considered what happens when a person repeatedly injures themselves, and the effect that this has of creating separable emotional states into which a person may switch and, in switching, cut themselves without premeditation. In this chapter we explore what it is like for a person to have these tendencies to injure her or himself. Since a person is particular likely to self-injure at times of personal transition or crisis, we think it helpful to consider self-injury in relation to personal identity. In this chapter we look at one particular element of personal identity – the boundary of the self-image. We suggest that for people who injure themselves, the skin becomes a testing ground for this boundary.

> Christine had been cutting herself and taking repeated overdoses of medication for about 4 years. She came from a privileged background, and she and her twin sister had recently begun to attend University. Her parents seemed as concerned about her self-harm as could be, but why

Christine was harming herself never came out. She herself was desperate that she could not control her actions, which she presented as those of someone else. Family meetings moved from being psycho-educational to becoming much more tense and for a short while her father moved out of the parental home, although this was never explained. Then over a period of a week, Christine took several overdoses and cut herself with increasing frequency. She was seen by her therapist daily, and at the time of the penultimate self-injury episode said that she thought that she was getting over it. But she took an even larger overdose that night and died at home before the ambulance arrived.

Zelda had been cutting herself for well over half her life. She had been abused at home, but never fully broke free. Eventually her parents divorced and a year later Zelda became pregnant for the first time. By this time Zelda was cutting herself several times per week and taking an overdose of medication almost monthly, although she refused any medical treatment for this, and was also misusing prescribed sedatives. She lost so much blood through self-injury that she became chronically anaemic despite receiving iron supplementation. Her self-injury increased in the early weeks of the pregnancy, but then Zelda said that she would have to stop because of the baby. And stop she did. Zelda has rarely injured herself over the subsequent 10 years and has not done so at all recently.

Zelda and Christine both represent an extreme of self-injury in which the behaviour is not at all under their control. In both cases it is associated with self-hatred, which is expressed in moods of despair and overdoses of sedatives, and motivated by a wish to sleep or escape. Both Zelda and Christine had periods of in-patient treatment for their self-injury, too. However, the outcome was very different and, in this chapter, we will consider why.

Zelda and Christine had both become habituated to self-harm in that it was the first solution that presented itself to them among an increasing range of dysphoric emotions or interpersonal problems. Zelda sometimes described having 'come to' after cutting herself – an indication that she may have become addicted in the sense that we discussed in the last chapter. Both were receiving intensive psychotherapeutic treatment, and both had also received milieu therapy, drug therapy and art therapy. But it is difficult, when putting their two histories together, to avoid thinking that it was Zelda's baby that made the difference.

Zelda seemed to rebel against becoming pregnant and her self-injury increased even further during the first few weeks of her pregnancy. But when she decided that she would bring up the child on her own, and that she would have nothing more to do with the father, her attitude changed. She told her therapist that she could not put her child at risk; that she had to, among other things, stop cutting herself so that her haemoglobin could rise.

Zelda and Christine had often said – as do many people do who injure themselves – that their family or their therapist would be better off without them. Tragically, at their last family meeting, Christine's family seemed to agree when Christine said this once again. Her Mum murmured something to the effect that all the stress was getting to her father, and that was why her parents had temporarily split up.

THE DETERMINATION TO RECOVER

'*Are you telling me that I've just got to pull my socks up?*' How often have most mental health professionals, and most parents, heard that? 'Pull your socks up' is the most elementary kind of command to try harder. Its popularity is based on the same observation that we have made: that personal change is usually preceded by an increased determination to change.

The same observation has been formularized in the change model proposed by Prochaska and DiClemente (1983) summarized below in Text Box 4.1. According to this model, when the possibility of changing a habit is suggested, a person might say, '*I'd rather not think about it*' or '*I could change whenever I wanted, but I don't want to right now*' (the *pre-contemplation* stage). However, not everyone says this, and very few people only ever say this.

Text Box 4.1   Stages of change as proposed by Prochaska and DiClemente (1983)

Stage 1 – Pre-contemplation – I am not currently considering change.

Stage 2 – Contemplation – I am ambivalent about change, or I am considering change some time in the future, but not within the next month.

Stage 3 – Preparation – I have some experience with change and I am trying to change. I am planning to act within the next four weeks.

Stage 4 – Action – I have been practicing new behaviour for 3–6 months.

Stage 5 – Maintenance – I have shown my commitment to sustaining new behaviour by continuing it for more than 6 months.

Stage 6 – Relapse tolerance – I have a plan for coping with relapse and I am able to tolerate occasional relapses as part of the overall process of change.

At some stage, most people will say '*I've been wondering whether it's time to move on*' or '*I do need to change, but it's not a good time right now*' (the *contemplation* stage). Change rarely occurs in either of these two stages, and it is counter-productive for therapists to try to pressurize their clients to change. Change, as the saying has it, has to come from within.

Prochaska and DiClemente distinguish between two stages of change: *preparation* and *action*. In recent years, they have added two further stages. The first is *maintenance* (or sticking to abstinence) when the original reasons for giving up seem less cogent. The second is *relapse tolerance* so that when relapse occurs (which they suggest is inevitable) steps are taken to minimize its impact.

Some therapists boast that they can make people change simply by exercising some superior skill or persuasive power. This fiction means that other, more self-critical therapists sometimes feel that they are letting their clients down by not persistently trying to make them give up self-injury. However, pushing someone to change who is not ready to do so puts a considerable strain on the client, who may leave therapy as a result. There is also the very real possibility of an increase in self-injury in response to this type of pressure.

On the other hand, there are no grounds for clinician nihilism. Prochaska and DiClemente's make helpful suggestions about what therapists can do to encourage their clients to move from one stage to another. Even if a client is not ready to consider stopping self-injury, there may be good reasons for psychotherapy or counselling to be provided, and if so it is important that the client is still able to report accurately how often self-injury is occurring. There is a difficult balance for the therapist to strike between spending time talking about self-harm, and spending time talking about the client's actions and reactions that they may be ready to change.

WHAT WEAKENS THE DETERMINATION?

Changing an entrenched habit is a challenge that many people face at some time in their lives. Habits provide us with two benefits: predictability and reward. Some habits persist because they restrict us, and in so doing they reduce the unexpected. They therefore screen us from anxiety-provoking novelty and disturbing potentiality. Perhaps these sorts of habit can better be called routines. Most of us have them. For example, most of us have a routine about when we get to work, and a routine about how we get there. It helps us to know when our bus will stop and where. It also helps us to know how bad the traffic will be or whether we normally get in before our boss. Such habits, or routines, are protection from the type of anxiety that too much novelty provokes – a kind of anxiety that is sometimes called 'existential' because it is a reaction to our smallness in relation to the world. It's the kind of anxiety that '*completely annihilated the brain*' of Trin Tragula's wife in Douglas Adams' fantasy, the Hitchhiker's Guide to the Galaxy. She told her husband, '*Have some sense of proportion*' as often as 38 times a day, and so he built the Total Perspective Vortex 'just to show her'. '*And into one end, he plugged the whole of reality ... and into the other, he plugged his wife: so that when he turned it on she saw in one instant the whole infinity of creation and herself in relation to it.*'

Although self-injury may become routine, this is rare. When it is described as habitual, it is the other sense of habit that is being referred to, the sense that is often called 'a bad habit'. 'Bad habits' are actions that people want to change because they have adverse long-term consequences, but they find that they are unable to change because they are rewarding in the short-term.

These short-term rewards are often described as pleasurable, but in fact the ones that are hard to overcome are not pleasurable in the sense of being gratifying. Instead they are comforting. They are rewards because they reduce unpleasant emotions rather than inducing pleasant ones. They act as a kind of emotional salve, calming emotional hurts and soothing emotional pain. Like the effects of antidepressants, these rewards may seem rather tame, but they are powerful nonetheless. 'Bad habits' are 'bad' for the person with them because often these short-term rewards are counter-balanced by long-term disadvantages. 'Bad' habits may also be disapproved of by others, in which case the 'bad' habit can also be a source of shame, something to be hidden.

In the case of self-injury we have already seen that there is a particular group of emotions which are intolerable to people who injure themselves – we have called these 'trigger emotions' in the last chapter. These are the emotions that the habit of self-injury is particularly effective in relieving. So the determination to overcome self-injury will be weakened by circumstances that increase the trigger emotions, or by those that weaken existing ways of dealing with these triggers. When a person is trying to stop self-injury and is failing to do so, the disappointment and the shame that the failure can induce may, paradoxically, increase the chances of them injuring themselves again. This seems to us a particularly vicious circle. In fact, thinking of 'bad habits' as bad at all can transfer some of the shame or disappointment to the person who fails to change them. This means that they – and other people – start to think not only that the habit is bad, but also that the person who fails to change is a 'bad person'. It is hard to underestimate the negative impact of this on someone who already has a very low opinion of her or himself.

We need a better, less emotionally loaded word. 'Junk' food is the term that is applied to food that can become a bad habit; 'fix' is the term applied to the use of drugs to overcome bad feelings; 'enslavement' or 'addiction' to the acquisition of money; 'quirk', 'thing' or 'bent' to sexual habits; and 'obsession' to eating disorders. All of these terms have negative and pejorative overtones, like the word 'bad'. In this book we have chosen instead to use the term 'relief habit' as the most accurate, and the least dismissive, term.

No one is proud of a relief habit. Determining to give one up is easy, but anyone actually doing so has to grapple with the experience that the more that one tries to change it, the more it asserts itself. Giving up self-injury may be easy to promise oneself when the emotional spring is unwound and life seems fairly untroubled. But then when the spring winds again, or when one thinks seriously about what it will be like when it does, cutting can feel irresistible whatever the arguments for stopping it.

In the last chapter, we introduced the idea of happenings having emotions associated with them. We called happenings that were particularly susceptible to these 'emotors' and noted that we experience emotors as having the capacity to arouse emotions in us. We referred to this capacity as their 'emotional flavour'. Some emotional flavours are capable of absorbing a considerable amount of additional flavour, and even of turning unpalatable flavours into palatable ones. When this happens the flavour may become even more palatable – much as a splash of vinegar, which is sour and virtually undrinkable on its own, can enhance the palatability of a serving of potato fries (or, in Britain, 'chips').

Many relief habits are maintained by the exposure to a strong emotor – one which has a combination or mixture of flavours. Importantly, some of the flavours making up the mix are disgusting on their own, but when blended together with other emotions they enhance our desire to experience the emotion again. The more often the emotor works its magic, the greater the number of different kinds of unpleasant feelings that it can convert into something palatable by blending them with its own emotional flavour. As a result, the more often that we fall back on a relief habit as a way of changing an emotional experience, the more irresistible it becomes.

Repetition therefore weakens determination. But so, paradoxically, does determination itself or, rather, the kind of determination which expresses itself in forcing oneself to change. Forcible suppression of one's feelings leads to further winding of the spring, and sooner or later the tension will overwhelm any resolution, however firmly made. Thus some people with bulimia find that the more determination they put into suppressing the feelings associated with wanting to binge, the less they seem to be able to resist the urge to do so. Some drinkers begin each day with a determination not to allow the emotions that lead them to drink alcohol to overtake them, and then within a few hours are overwhelmed by the need for a drink. Perhaps similarly, the self-injurer who attempts to suppress his or her feelings in a determination to give up cutting may find that this determination almost seems to make matters worse. This is a very significant and unfortunate paradox. It leads to much confusion and misunderstanding. The person who self-injures comes to feel almost as though the harder he (or she) tries not to cut, the more likely it is to happen. Many clients have said to us that they try very hard indeed not to hurt themselves, but have come to the conclusion over the years that often all they can realistically do is delay the inevitable. Those who care for them are also confused. It is hard to appreciate that someone who continues to cut or burn their skin can sometimes be putting in considerable effort to change, and the net result is that the person who self-injures feels very misunderstood.

WHAT DO I HAVE TO DO BEFORE I CAN CHANGE?

Once a person has injured themselves on several occasions, it is likely that a habit has been established and that simple determination to change will not be enough. Many people who do, in spite of this, succeed in changing do so by adopting one of four strategies (see Text Box 4.2).

Text Box 4.2   Four strategies available to people who are trying to change

- Prevent the build up of emotions that trigger self-injury
- Focus on short time periods – take one day at a time
- Decide on something to take the place of self-injury
- Change one's assumptions about self-injury

The first is by reducing the rate of accumulation of triggering emotions. '*Looking after myself better*' is what people often term this. We will consider it in Chapters 7 and 8 when we consider psychological treatments and self-help.

If looking after oneself can be thought of as increasing the energy for change, the second strategy can be thought of as focussing the energy. All of us have experienced being daunted by a task that is facing us. Changing jobs, spring cleaning or moving house: these and many more big tasks can often seem too much unless we can break them down and focus on one step at a time. 'One day at a time' is a key principle of the 12-step programme of Alcoholics Anonymous and has been adopted by many similar approaches to overcoming dependency. But it does not just apply to overcoming this day's craving. It also applies to giving something up for ever. A private passion like self-injury may, at the moment one is thinking of giving it up, seem to have been a wonderful solace and an essential aid in the struggle against collapse. At this moment, the pain of the burn, the embarrassment of people catching a glimpse of the scars on the arms, or even the contempt of ambulance and emergency room staff, all of these unpleasant consequences of self-injury may fade completely. All one can think of is how difficult it will be coping forever without the self-injury. It is useful at these moments to say to oneself that one is not making a decision forever, but only for a day. There will be another day, and another chance to decide.

There is a third thing that has to be in place before there can be a change; this is something to take the place of the self-injury. For many people with a self-harm addiction, some other kind of habitual and ultimately self-harming behaviour is the obvious substitute. Many people who injure themselves turn to alcohol in later life as an alternative to provide comfort from trigger emotions, and the bottle replaces the razor blade as an emotor and a symbol of relief. An alternative is to find some kind of talisman – in other words, some kind of benign, strong emotor – which can provide a more life-enhancing substitute for self-injury. The following extract from a fictionalized story describes this well:

> Tara said, 'I remember taking my prescription and going out to the local chemist's to get my tablets in the evening when it was quiet. I was thinking that once I had a full month's supply, I might just take them all at once and have it over with. However, when I put my hand into my pocket to pay, I didn't feel my purse. My hand touched something else. It was a little stone that my brother had given me when we were young. I always carried it around, but I had sort of forgotten about it. Touching it made me think of him, and his smiling face, the only one I remember from when I was a child. Funnily enough the stone felt warm as if he had just handed it over. I gripped it tight and instead of wanting to die, I wanted to grip on to life, too. Having it in my hand made me stronger. I said to myself, "I'll keep my brother's stone by me always from now on." It feels like my brother is still with me, and looking out for me, even though he got killed over three years ago.'

The stone worked for Tara because some of her brother's emotional flavour had passed into it. Touching it aroused in Tara the same emotions that she would feel with her brother, emotions which were, we presume from the story, the kind of comforting ones which can absorb pain and fear and make them tolerable, much as going into your brother's room in the middle of the night can take away the fear of a bad dream.

The fourth strategy is the most far-reaching. It involves challenging one of the primary assumptions on which self-injury rests, challenging the notion that some emotions simply cannot be entertained or coped with.

WHAT CAN I DO WITH MY EMOTIONS? THEY'RE SO PAINFUL ...

Ask many people why they can't change a relief habit and they will say, '*it takes my mind off things*'. People may indeed argue that their need for relief is particularly or unusually great so that the habit must be resorted to. Alternative ways of coping with unpleasant emotions include trying to suppress them, forcing oneself to relax or engaging in some form of diversion.

Suppressing emotion may be one of the factors that contributes to the spring winding in the first place, and we would not advocate it except as a very short term expedient. Relaxation (we include here the technique of progressive muscle relaxation, sometimes called 'relaxation therapy'), as we found in our survey of professionals (Huband & Tantam, 1999), is one of the more commonly recommended therapeutic interventions but unfortunately it is one of the least valued by people who injure themselves, at least in our study. One reason for this is that relaxation can, by clearing the mind, actually increase the intensity of the desire to self-harm. While the value of relaxation will inevitable vary from person to person, and some people who self-injure report considerable benefit from it, a significant proportion appear to find it very unhelpful.

Diversion works well when the diversion is inadvertent, but it is a difficult trick to pull off for oneself. One way that does work for some people is by having a reminder of why one is giving up self-injury in the first place. This might be a list of reasons, or an image, or an aim. Thinking about one of these can help to divert thoughts and change a feeling of tension into a feeling of hopefulness. Another method that can sometimes work is to concentrate on a series of small, diverting tasks such as solving a relatively easy puzzle, playing a game of solitaire or using a felt tip pen to colour in a benign picture. We discuss these sorts of techniques in more detail in Chapter 7.

Many studies of emotional processing indicate that suppressing emotions actually strengthens them. Indeed, it is often suggested that effective psychotherapy proceeds by making it possible for a person to experience a previously 'warded off' emotion. It is hard to do this on one's own, for it requires considerable courage. Many people need a companion or a source of emotional strength. They may find this in hidden places within themselves, but most often turn to love, religion or community to find it.

One reason why it may be so hard to allow an emotion to surface is that emotions are a call to action, and it is normally through action that our emotions are fulfilled. Relief habits like smoking, over-eating, binge drinking, and self-injury are a kind of action too, but not a fulfilment. They are private actions which are intended to stifle change, often in the service of other people whom change threatens; for example, Christine's life was locked into her family and they did not want to change. Christine either had to school her own emotions, or risk being expelled by the family. She chose the former, and used self-injury as a means of doing so.

Christine's suicide may have followed her realization that others would welcome her death. This is a terrible realization that often seems to presage the ultimate despair and meaninglessness that leads to suicide. We have come across it in people who have been told by their mothers that they tried to abort them. We know of one patient whom we will call Roger who was told this on his 21st birthday. Roger felt that he had been crushed. He said that there was no longer a space for him in the world and his subsequent repeated attempts to kill himself were because he felt that he no longer had the right to exist.

IDENTITY AND SELF-INJURY

If I say that I've lost my identity, it is likely to mean that I'm in a distressed state of uncertainty about who I am. But it doesn't mean that other people won't recognize me. Identity theft means using bank numbers or social security numbers to impersonate someone: if I say that my identity has been stolen, it doesn't mean that I don't know who I am, but it may mean that someone else may no longer recognize me for who I am. Identity therefore has this double aspect. It is both what I think of as what makes up 'me' or 'myself', and it is also made up of the characteristics that enable other people to know who I am – and these can be quite arbitrary characteristics like a driving licence or a passport.

The two aspects of identity are linked. People who have had their identities stolen do experience an unpleasant diminution of their own uniqueness and specialness. People who have a strong personal identity, expressed perhaps in their unique dress or idiosyncratic behaviour, may also be instantly recognizable to other people without any need for cards or documents. The two aspects come together particularly in bodily characteristics, or rather in our perception of our bodily characteristics, our 'body image'. Body image is both integral to who a person considers her or himself to be, and who others think they are.

Stigma – a term originally used to describe injuries to the skin made during the course of a judicial process like branding or, in the case of Jesus Christ, execution – has become a term for the consequences of skin alteration for the psychology of the individual generally, and for their identity in particular (Major & O'Brian, 2005). Stigma increases a person's identifiability, but it may also 'spoil' the sense of who they are because the wound or scar is considered to be a mark of shame. Most people, and we include here many of those who have had burns and scarring to their skin, are able to overcome this. For a few, however, it becomes an enduring vulnerability because too much attention to the stigma can reproduce incapacitating shame. One factor that adds to this shame-proneness is hiding the scar, or the stigma. People who injure themselves almost always target areas of skin that are concealed by clothing. Understandably, they wish to hide their scars, but by doing so they create the possibility of being found out, and so jeopardizing their identity. This forms another vicious circle for people who injure themselves, but because this aspect is rarely discussed or written about, it is rarely anticipated. Realization of the problems associated with concealing and revealing scars may only come after several years of repeated self-injury, and it often comes as a considerable shock.

We often feel that our emotions dominate us at particular times of life when we feel uncertain about our identity, and particularly when we are undergoing a transition from one identity to another. This can be provoked by biological change as during adolescence, or by social change following the breakdown of a relationship for example. Our emotions push us to change our identity to encompass our changed circumstances. However, this is only possible if our circumstances afford the possibility of a change in identity, and if we have the energy to accomplish such a change. Self-injury is more common during such developmental crises and our experience is that this is because it provides a way of dealing with emotion while accommodating restrictions on identity change.

POSSESSION OF THE BODY AND THE BODY IMAGE

The pressure to change may be so intense that a person might feel that their body is no longer their own, and that self-injury – or other kinds of bodily modification, like an eating disorder – is a way of reclaiming their body. The notion of 'reclaiming' one's body might seem strange. After all, our bodies are one of our few possessions that we are born with, that we stay with all of our lives, and that we die with. However our relationship with our body is a relationship with not just with our physical body, but also with what our body *means* to us. This is with what L'Hermitte called *l'image du moi corporel* (L'Hermitte & Tchehrazi, 1937), known in English as 'body image'.

The body image is what we consciously believe about our body. It requires a particular area of the brain to be intact, suggesting that it is not just a story about the body, but a representation stored in the brain. Body image is modified by experience, possibly directly by a process of cognitive inference from repeated pairings of experience (Armel & Ramachandran, 2003), but not by thinking. In fact, although body image can be consciously experienced, it is not created by conscious reflection. We can talk about our body image, but we can only talk about it in the same way that we can talk about, say, a dream that we have had. Our body image – like the dream – is something we know is ours, and yet both have been created outside our awareness. Both are therefore mysterious and, in some way, external to ourselves. Our body image has something of the elusiveness of self-injury itself. Its influence on us is not mediated by meaning, any more than the action of absent-mindedly scratching the skin has a meaning.

Our awareness of our body comes from our body image. It is not something we can change directly, but our actions do have a marked effect on it. For example, eating something sugary increases what people judge their waist measurement to be. Other people's actions, too, can affect our body image. Being told that we look good makes our body look better to ourselves too, and being told we are looking overweight makes us more aware of our flab. It is not therefore surprising that people who have been abused often experience their skins differently, although here the effect may be much more extreme than just feeling a bit more ugly.

The skin is the largest organ of the body and its importance for body image is proportionately large. According to Psychology Today (2006), American men and women spend $10 billion a year on skin care products, presumably because of the importance to body image of having a good image of one's skin. The skin is obviously an important part of the body image for most people. One reason for this is that the skin is the organ which mediates emotional contact between ourselves and other people. Stroking or touching the skin stimulates the brain, and releases transmitters which regulate emotional tone, restoring calm to infants (Weller & Feldman, 2003) – a fact well known to mothers and other comforters of babies. It is perhaps less well known that receiving this kind of comfort regularly in early life results in greater satisfaction with the body image of the skin in later life (Gupta et al., 2004). Clinical experience suggests that the converse is true, and that experiences of being touched aversively – or even of not being touched at all – can lead to disturbances in the skin image up to, and including, the experience of the skin disappearing from the body image because it is 'owned by someone else'. There can be a neurological basis for this, but the phenomenon is most often considered to be a psychological one, which is often termed dissociation.

DISSOCIATION AND IDENTITY

The disappearance of the skin from the body image is only one example of dissociation. Dissociation may also be associated with actions being carried out for which there is afterwards no memory, alterations in perception, as well as other body image changes. There is a close link between dissociation and alteration in identity. Indeed, there is a condition termed 'dissociative identity disorder' (which was previously, and confusingly, termed 'multiple personality disorder') in which a person actually experiences themselves as two or more different people all sharing the same body, and the same mind.

We considered in Chapter 3 the likelihood that a capacity for dissociation increases the risk of self-injury. Here we want to consider the consequences of dissociation for identity and therefore for the ability to overcome repeated self-injury.

Several authors such as Anzieu have supposed that there is a 'psychic skin' that surrounds and protects our identity, much as the skin surrounds and protects our body. We think that this is a helpful metaphor which can help us to think about the link between identity, the body image and self-injury. We wrote in the previous section that people who injure themselves sometimes feel that their skin has disappeared from their body image. If we take Anzieu's analogy further, we could say that the boundary of their body image lies somewhere inside their skin, not at the skin surface itself. We could further imagine that the body image, and a person's identity, becomes fissured by new internal boundaries, new psychic skins or, as some people have called them, envelopes. Put another way, the body image cracks – and may then become fragmented. The extreme conclusion of this would be dissociative identity disorder in which a person actually experiences themselves as being several different people all in one body and mind.

We could also imagine that the mental skin – or skins – sometimes get warped or twisted so that certain personal characteristics, which for most people are important components of their overall identity, get left outside the body image boundary. Perhaps for someone who self-injures, it is their skin image that has been left out. Other things can get left out as well – important bits of our image of the world that contribute to our identity, such as the assumption that we have reliable friends, stable work, supportive family, a good place to live, a just world to live in, and so on.

It is easy to think of processes that create boundaries in this way. Secrets create boundaries within social groups and are causes for inappropriate boundaries to form. Self-deception is an example of an internal boundary, as is dissociation. Shame drives us to hide aspects of our self from public scrutiny, and this too can lead to the creation of disabling internal boundaries to our identity.

SELF-INJURY AS SURVIVAL

Many people describe injuring themselves to break through a barrier. This may be a kind of emotional numbness, or a feeling of not being fully there, or an impotent feeling of rage or helplessness. As we have seen, one way to understand the problematic identity changes that occur when people are restricted in their identity is through development of additional boundaries. If there is indeed a link between the skin – the physical boundary of the body – and these internal boundaries, then self-injury might be a way that people use to try to break through them and get back to feeling whole again. For a short time, this may be successful. People who repeatedly injure themselves do so because the wound has a beneficial effect.

The problem is, of course, that the consequences of the wound creates a stigma that can lead to shame and secrecy. Here the stigma is a literal skin mark as well as a figurative cause of social scorn. Unfortunately, this can perpetuate or even extend (and strengthen) the internal boundaries that a person is trying to break down.

As so often in mental health, the symptoms that professionals try to remove are often the client's attempts at self-healing. Stopping someone cutting themselves may be legitimate if their wounds are likely to result in permanent injury or a threat to life. However, if this does not apply then stopping someone cutting may not be the most important focus of treatment. Our experience has shown us that it is important to be aware of the injuries that a person is making, but that the therapeutic focus should not be on the wounds, but on the person's attempts to change their identity or – as occurs in some cases – simply establishing a clear identity for the first time in their life.

BORDERLINE PERSONALITY DISORDER

Anzieu's metaphor of a psychic skin (as with our metaphor of internal boundaries) is also at the root of the diagnostic category that is most often called on to explain self-injury. Borderline personality disorder (BPD) was originally named, because it was thought to be a condition that lies on the border between neurotic and psychotic disorder. More recently, though, it has been taken to refer to the lack of boundaries that is thought to be typical of borderline personality disorder.

We too have suggested that people who injure themselves may lack a boundary where one is expected, but we think that this does not mean a lack of boundaries, or indeed a thinning of boundaries – something also associated with borderline personality disorder – is the problem. In fact, we would argue that people who injure themselves repeatedly often have too many boundaries.

There are many studies, using rating scales based on the internationally accepted criteria of BPD, that show that people who qualify for this diagnosis are more likely to harm themselves and, conversely, that people who injure themselves repeatedly have a raised incidence of borderline personality disorder. There are many overlaps, too, between our description of the difficulties facing people who repeatedly injure themselves and people diagnosed with BPD. Both have comparable problems with identity and self-image. Childhood abuse can play an important (but not an essential) role in the development of both. The emotional instability which is the most characteristic feature of BPD is also consistent with our idea of there being excess boundaries within the identity, since this might lead to a greater differentiation between emotional states, and sudden shifts from one state to another as boundaries are crossed.

One reason for thinking that people diagnosed with BPD have undeveloped boundaries is that those at risk of this diagnosis often form rapid and intense relationships with other people which can, as quickly, switch to being hostile or persecutory ones. Therapists, too, seem to have difficulty in maintaining a proper boundary and 'boundary violations' by therapists are more common with this group of people. We agree that this is likely to mean that the boundary between a person diagnosed as having BPD and other people may not be drawn in the expected place. The person with a BPD diagnosis may, for example, allow themselves to be controlled in ways that another person would normally repudiate. But we do not think that this means that the boundary is weak. Only that it has been drawn in a different place. Rather like the way that a person who self-injures treats their skin as not belonging to them, so they may also treat other people as owning aspects of their identity, of their life, that would normally be considered as inalienably belonging to themselves.

SELF-INJURY AS A TRAP

Every time that the skin is punctured or cut, blood flows, pain pours in, then eventually the skin heals, scars over, fibroses and thickens. So although cutting into the skin may seem like a way of cutting down some of the boundaries that separate a person from their emotions, the net effect is to thicken the boundaries even further. There is no possibility that one's identity can grow by creating more and more divisions, in the way that a slum landlord can create more rentable properties by sub-dividing more and more rooms. The immediate tension of over-crowding is relieved, as is the immediate tension of the spring, but in the long run the quality of life of the tenants, or the well-being of the person who self-injures, is not improved.

OTHER CONDITIONS ASSOCIATED WITH IDENTITY CHALLENGES

Psychology Today – on the same site from which we took the figures about cosmetic use – reported an even greater preoccupation with weight in the US, partly fuelled by a growing discrepancy between bodily characteristics of fashion models and of average US women. Models' height is increasing on average, and their weight is on average falling. The height of North American women is not increasing to the same extent. Their average weight is not falling, but is actually increasing. It is therefore no surprise that many Western women, and a growing number of Western men, consider that their body image deviates from their body ideal.

Body image is, as we have seen, a core component of identity. It is not therefore surprising that altering weight is one way of altering identity, nor that the eating disorders, which produce this effect, are more common in people who injure themselves and vice versa. Obesity is an eating disorder in which the short-term benefits of a relief habit – in this case comfort eating (Korte et al., 2005) – produce an alteration in identity in a direction which is socially undesirable and undervalued. It is in its own way an avoidance of a more effective or socially valued identity – one in which a person feels that their real identity is trapped inside their public identity.

Anorexia nervosa is more common in people who injure themselves. In this eating disorder, there is a paradoxical reaction to the impulse to comfort eat, so that the anorexic finds the experience of hunger rewarding and may, indeed, become addicted to it (Szmukler & Tantam, 1984). The effect of course is that the young woman, or rarely the young man, loses weight. Weight is one of the important triggers to sexual maturation and therefore to the identity change associated with the development of secondary sexual characteristics like sexual hair, increasing size of the genitalia, deepening voice in men and breast development in women. Losing weight reverses this process and some have argued that anorexia is motivated by a fear of sexuality. Whether or not this is so, anorexia is clearly an example of avoiding identity change.

Bulimia nervosa seems to have features both of anorexia and of the overeating that leads to obesity, but our experience is that this is misleading. People who are bulimic experience their desire to binge eat as bad and something to be suppressed. In order to do so they purge, over-exercise and, particularly, make themselves vomit. To do this people usually stick their fingers down their throats (usually only when alone) and there is in this something very reminiscent of the skin penetration that is involved in cutting. There is a strong association between self-injury and bulimia. A history of abuse seems to predispose to both, both are associated with dissociation, and both are a means of changing personal identity without changing one's public face.

People with bulimia may harm themselves by their uncontrolled eating, and it is true that the feeling of being full is what the bulimic tries to get rid of by vomiting. But contrary to what many people with bulimia believe, our clinical experience is that recovery comes not through stopping the over-eating, which is a physiological response to the hunger of being empty, but through tolerating the feeling of fullness and accepting the identity of being a greedy, hungry or angry person that is associated with it. Vomiting, like self-injury, is a way of getting rid of bad feelings in the hope that identity can be maintained. And so it can, since vomiting can be concealed from almost everyone other than the dentist, and self-injury can be concealed from anyone who does not see one unclothed. However, the effect is that the personal identity – who one feels oneself to be – becomes shrunken or divided.

CONCLUSIONS

If a person decides that a change in identity is unacceptable, they have several choices, all of which involve trying to express the emotion that would otherwise drive them to change. Cutting or burning oneself, like other kinds of self-harm, seems to be able to do this. But it results in an alteration in identity even so, albeit not one's public identity but one's private identity.

If one has the luck to be provided with a new, socially sanctioned identity – as Zelda was – then it is possible to find a shortcut. But this is unusual. Most often the only way of overcoming problems like self-injury is to find a way of making a new identity stick. This means pushing outwards to fill out the identity, which is there in potential, but also in finding a space in which that identity can be fully realized. We consider these two factors – the pressure to change identity and the space for a new identity – in the next chapter.

Chapter 5

Moulds and Matrices

INTRODUCTION

This chapter is all about the development of identity, and we begin it with quotations from two famous self-injurers (one an actor, the other a guitarist). Both are part of a celebrity culture in which the belief that a person is able to choose and develop their 'identity' is central.

> There is a website devoted to celebrities who cut (http://self-injury.net/doyousi/famous/). One of the male stars reported on there has a series of scars on his forearm where he has cut himself with a knife on different occasions to commemorate various moments or rights of passage in his life. In a 1993 *Details* magazine interview this star explained his self-injury:
>
> > 'My body is a journal in a way. It's like what sailors used to do, where every tattoo meant something, a specific time in your life when you make a mark on yourself, whether you do it yourself with a knife or with a professional tattoo artist.'
>
> In a 2001 *Movie Star Magazine* interview he talked about how he is currently the happiest he has ever been:
>
> > 'My upbringing made me as I am now. But I can become merry and happy at once. There were many years I was feeling at a loss about my life or how I grew up. I couldn't understand what is right or what is precious. At that time, I was so miserable and self-defeating. I was feeling angry with various things. My anger came up to the surface then. I don't say such tendency has disappeared. Even now there are anger and the dark side in myself. But it's the first time I've been so close to the light.'

> Richey James Edwards, a former guitarist and co-lyricist with the Manic Street Preachers until his mysterious disappearance in 1995, made no

secret about cutting his skin. In an interview on Villa 65, a Dutch radio programme, Richey talked openly about his self-injury:

> You know, maybe a few days later you get a certain amount of pain as the skin starts to heal, but when you're in that frame of mind it's really natural. It's the only logical thing to do. Otherwise you feel you could almost do something to another person, and that is something that I would – again, like I said, I would never ever take it out on somebody else. Maybe the things I do, it's more concerned with the fact that I don't like myself very much, and so I would not expect anyone else to judge me that highly; so if I discipline myself I can feel relatively content with my mental state and my physical state. If I can balance those two then I feel OK, and I'm not really worried what people think about me. Because I judge myself harsher, and on more strict terms, than they ever could probably. I – I think. Mm. (quoted at http://www.self-injury.net/doyousi/famous/).

Both Johnny Depp and Richey Edwards saw their self-injury as very much under their control. Johnny Depp saw it positively, as a commemoration. Richey Edwards more negatively, as discipline. Both also mention not liking themselves very much and Johnny Depp mentions his upbringing, but these are not given as explanations of the self-injury.

So far in this book we have considered cutting the skin as a means of changing feelings, and the habit of repeatedly cutting or wounding the skin as a means of establishing or reinforcing personal identity. Our treatment does therefore seem consistent with the accounts of these two celebrities. But celebrities get to where they are by taking control of their identities. The celebrity culture of which they are a part is underpinned by the presumption that each of us can have the identity we choose, so long as we work hard enough at it. In this chapter we will consider an alternative view, and how it might affect the choice of self-injury as a means of expressing or changing – 'crafting' – identity. We will start with a very simple analogy.

STORIES OF IDENTITY

A place in the world

Roger, who we met in a previous chapter, was told that his mother had tried to abort him and was left feeling that he didn't really have a place in the world any more. His idea is an important one because all of us need to feel that in some way we have been given a place and hence that we have a right to exist.

In the back of our mind, there is a sense of having a space to exist created for us. This might be a literal space – the word territory is often used – which we tend to become most aware of when that space is violated or taken away. Think of how it would be to reside in an invaded country and to have troops from another country billeted in one's home or, a more common experience, to be told at work that someone was moving in to share your office or work space. However, the notion of 'own' space at the back of our minds is more commonly a mental space. It is perhaps a status, a social identity or a feeling that we have a part to play in the local community. We may say of someone who inherits a title or achieves acclaim that 'from that moment, he or she took up their rightful place in the world' as if the place had been made ready for them and was just waiting for them to step into it. But we have a different way of thinking about plants. We see them struggling against competitors until one manages to grow higher and thrives, whilst the others die. Until then, all of the competing plants might be stunted or thin and spindly. It is only when one or two win out over their competitors that they are able to fill out into their typical forms.

Both of these are stories about identity. In the case of the person coming into a title, it is their new identity of Lord So and So that the expression 'their rightful place' indicates is their true or proper identity. In the case of the plant, it may only be when it has overcome the competition and grown into its proper shape that we might be able to identify it at all.

How does identity work?

By identity we mean the kind of answer that one gives to questions like 'What is it then?' Let us use an analogy to make this clearer. Imagine standing in a field at a large festival, watching people blowing up their hot air balloons in preparation for flight. In recent years, hot air ballooning has become something of a spectator sport and attracts large audiences. These balloons have always been both large and colourful, but many are now custom built to take on specific shapes when inflated (often for advertising purposes). To the spectator, however, there is no way of knowing what form any particular balloon will take until it gets inflated with hot air. Standing in a field and watching the various balloons as they slowly inflate we might ask, 'What's this one going to be?'. Only when it is inflated sufficiently can we can see the final shape, and can then say, 'Oh, That's a bottle of Guinness' or 'That one's a cow' or 'Look, a can of Heinz baked beans!' It is this final shape that defines the identity of each balloon. This shape is determined by the form into which each balloon's PVC skin has been cut, but there is something else to consider. Whether or not that final shape is attained depends on adequate filling with hot air from the propane burner, on whether the shape was cut right in the first place, and also on the medium in which the inflation is occurring. If there is not enough room for inflation to take place, then the balloon won't blow up into its planned shape and its identity will be altered. Now the bottle of Guinness is oddly curved like a banana, the cow seems to have no head and the can of baked beans is all wrinkly.

So, to summarize, the final form of the inflatable figure is a product of three things: the potential final form that is inherent in the PVC (that is, the way that it has been cut and glued together), the pressure that fills it out and the medium in which inflation occurs.

Similarly, most of us think that there is probably a finite potential to each of us, too. This is determined by our heredity, our biology, the society and the place in it into which we are born as well as our culture. Unlike the inflatable PVC balloon, we do recognize that this potential changes during our lifetime – one that occurs as a result of the impact of events and the way that those events 'shape' us. Even so, we can imagine what our children might develop into if given the chance. What we imagine is sufficiently vivid for us to mourn the lost possibility if we perceive that our potential, or that of people we love or honour, has been diminished by an accident or by the malicious action of someone else.

How are we able to imagine this so clearly? One explanation is that we infer our final form from our current shape, and the sense either that we are being stretched beyond our limit, or that we are being cramped into too small a space. The sensors that provide us with this information are the emotions. Emotions like excitement, anger or 'anomie' (a word coined by the sociologist Durkheim for the situation in which custom breaks down, so that no-one knows what is required or expected of them) make us feel that we are being over-extended or over-stretched or full to bursting with new ideas or hopes. Emotions like shame, humiliation or social anxiety make us want to hide. We feel as if we are shrinking into ourselves, and that our lives are being constricted.

THE IMPORTANCE OF 'VITAL ENERGY'

Heated air is what inflates an inflatable hot air balloon. Many of us suppose that there is something akin to this that inflates our identity. In fact, we some-times make use of this image. For example we might say of someone that they have an over-inflated sense of their own importance. The notion that there is an energy that drives psychological development is closely related to the notion of 'vital energy' or vitality. This is one of the oldest health beliefs, according to which we are alive because our bodies are animated by a vital energy whose correct flow is a pre-requisite of health.

What do we mean by 'vital energy'?

This vital energy is called Qi in Chinese medicine (ki in Japan), doshas in Ayurvedic medicine, and also, variously, chakra, shakti, prana, etheric energy, fohat, orgone, odic force, mana and homeopathic resonance (Hintz et al., 2003). Prana in Hindu belief is derived from the air we breathe, and this is one reason why correct breathing is thought to be so important in yoga. There are many names for this in the Western medical tradition, too (Sourkes, 2006): vital energy or élan vital in French, libido in psychoanalysis, narcissistic supplies in object relations theory, 'drive', strength of character, strength of mind, ego strength, psychic energy, life-force, buoyancy, bounce, resilience, pushiness, grit, staying power, self-efficacy, self-esteem and ... determination.

The reason that there are so many words for the same thing is that they are not quite the same thing. Most of the words derive from a particular theory of motivation. Libido is, according to Freud, derived from sexual excitement; narcissistic supply and self-esteem are supposedly derived from the love or respect that other people have, or have had, for us. Some of the words are based on the idea that we move forward in life not so much because we have a motive power, but because we can resist damage, either through material strength ('grit') or because we are resilient ('bounce' or 'buoyancy').

Vital energy and self-injury

It is possible that too much vital energy is what causes self-injury, since this would, on our model, press the mould of identity hard and create tension. However, this is where the hydraulic model seems to break down. The problem that people who injure themselves face is a lack of self-esteem, of vital energy. It is not that their energy crushes them as they try to expand against a rigid mould. Minimal pressure from outside can result in a failure for someone to fulfil their identity if they lack vital energy, and this seems to be the case for people who injure themselves. Their more vital brothers and sisters force their way into the social matrix and create their own impressions. It is the person who is already ready to fold, who fails to unfold fully. There is empirical evidence for this. Deiter and colleagues developed a scale to measure what they termed the self capacities of *'ability to tolerate strong affect, self-esteem, and the ability to remain connected to others'*, but which is recognizably a scale measuring what many would call vital energy (Deiter et al., 2000). They found that in their sample of 233 people receiving psychiatric help, self-capacity was significantly lower in the 135 people (58% of the sample) who injured themselves than it was in the remainder.

Vital energy and previous abuse

Deiter et al also found that there was a link between a lack of vital energy and previous sexual abuse. Both had independent effects on self-injury, but there was also a synergistic effect. Sexual abuse reduced vital capacity and contributed to self-harm in that way, too.

The preoccupation of Western culture with sexuality, an unwitting consequence of Freud's emphasis on it perhaps, has detracted from the other childhood experiences that drain vital energy. These include bullying, physical abuse and other less easily quantified experiences, such as those associated with lack of social status.

MOULD AND MATRIX

It seems to us that for Roger, who was told that his mother had tried to abort him, it was as if the space in which he had grown had suddenly collapsed. Christine, too, found herself unable to expand beyond the limited space that her family created for her. It is as if each of us has to find it in ourselves to grow, but we can only grow into the space that is provided for us by others and, unless we are particularly vigorous, this space forms us into our permanent shape – our identity. But at least we can tell ourselves that the space we are given is ours by right. To be told that this space was only created as second best, because an attempted abortion failed, is to take even that away.

Impact of the social environment

Christians argue that the eternal soul – our fullest or completed identity – is the form that we aspire to. Buddhists and Hindus would deny that there is a final form, since this would itself be yet another illusion born of desire, but they do consider, like Christians, that spiritual development is constrained by our preoccupations with the world and our emotional reactions to it. Unlike the inflatable figure where we can ignore the surrounding atmosphere in which it is being inflated, we cannot ignore the impact of our environment in which our identity is being created. This is what the ethnologist Jakob von Uexkull called 'die Umwelt'. We have already mentioned the notion of a mould for our growing identity and suggested that this is a potential constraint, but a mould may also be a facilitative environment during some stages of development. The group analyst and psychiatrist, S. H. Foulkes, coined the term 'matrix' for this. He played on the double meaning of this word, both 'womb' and 'network', and thought of a social group as structuring the development of a person by bathing them in a network of communication. The model only works if the womb is nutritive: if there is a relationship of care.

To return to our analogy, inflating a figure successfully – developing a robust identity – requires that the atmosphere that surrounds the figure is one that does not damage the boundary. The PVC of which inflatable balloons are made does not require much looking after, but our own psychological boundaries need maintenance. They need 'strokes', tactile or social reward to maintain their strength and therefore their integrity. So the social mould in which our identity grows must not only be non-constricting, it must also have the positive virtue of providing what our boundaries need to maintain their strength so that they do not break down as our identity inflates (Kashani et al., 1994).

Constriction

The permissive aspect of our social environment is care. But as we have seen, the social world can also be restrictive. Other people can deny us the space to enable our ideal form, our full identity, to manifest. If this occurs, we have to negotiate a greater space for ourselves, break out altogether or, to speak metaphorically again, change our form or our identity. We might think of this as lopping off the bits that we cannot fit in; or of puncturing our emotional container and deflating ourselves to fit in; or of our safety valves deflating us as a result of the increased signal from negative emotions. Whichever metaphor we choose, there needs to be an acknowledgement of violence being done to us as a result of the constriction of the social mould into which we have been cast. This is a violence that causes an answering violence in us which may be turned outwards to break the mould, or inwards to deflate our identity.

We will consider in a moment how well this analogy fits with what is really known about human psychology, but we do want to draw one last conclusion from it. Negative emotions like shame or fear of other people are, according to our analogy, signals of other people wanting to force us into a different shape to the one that is naturally ours. This is, of course, not always destructive. In fact, there is a tradition of Christian pedagogy that assumes that children are born with original sin, which must be combated by fear of punishment in the after-life. Control is, according to this view, the only route to social harmony and spiritual perfection, but is must be applied with loving care. An opposite view, originally attributed to Rousseau but also strong in the writings of Kierkegaard and Nietzsche, is that social control is society's means of reducing everyone to the same mediocrity, a procedure that is motivated by what Nietzsche called 'resentment' or envy, rather than any kind of concern for the individual.

Self-injury and over-control by others

While there can be no closure to this philosophical debate, self-injury is a reaction to over-control by others, as we shall see, and not under-control. The only way to overcome over-control is by bearing shame, anxiety, and rejection in the hope that the final shape of one's life will be an enhancement and not, as society supposes, a travesty of one's potential. But this is hard to do, requiring as the theologian Tillich famously wrote, the 'courage to be'. Failing this courage, or rather failing to have sufficient grounds for belief that one's potential is to be a lovable human being, a person may take refuge in a kind of alternative but secret identity. Alternatively, they take into themselves the hostility of other people by accepting their shame and allowing this emotion to drain their vitality so that they no longer expand and put pressure on the mould around them. Self-injury is a kind of temporizing strategy. It reduces the pressure for a while, but only for a while. One could imagine that it does this by reducing vitality, much as cupping or leeching were once thought to improve medical conditions that were associated with inflammation or excess energy.

The most effective way of dealing with negative emotions is – if our analogy is applicable – a matter of dealing with the social mould that constrains us. We might be able to do this by negotiation, but it is unlikely that this option is open to someone who has already had to resort to self-injury because of negative emotions, since these emotions are typically caused by the hostility or uncaring reactions of others.

Breaking the mould?

The way forward might be to break the mould. So another way to understand a person reducing their identity to fit into the constricted shape available to them is that they open their boundaries against the outside world to allow these negative emotions entry. They then let these negative emotions deflate the expansion of their identity so that it fits more comfortably with the mould into which others have cast it.

TRANSFORMATION

Types of 'world'

There are particular times in our life when our identity is brought into question. Pursuing our analogy further, this is particularly likely to occur when changes occur in the world in which our identity has been inflated. Van Deurzen (Deurzen, 1994) – following Heidegger and Binswanger – extends von Uexkull's Umwelt as it applies to animals, to human beings. This requires additional 'worlds'. As well as the physical environment ('Umwelt'), there is the social environment ('Mittwelt'); the inner world ('Eigenwelt'); and the heavens, our spiritual world ('Überwelt'). When we break the mould around us, we have to find a new world to inhabit, a new atmosphere in which our identity can be inflated with safety. To some extent we can choose to have our identity mainly in one or other of these worlds, but we still have to maintain a sufficient existence in each of them to survive.

Consequences of breaking the mould

This all sounds very abstract, so let's make it more specific. If we break out of our mould, then we lose out on any care that we received from it, and also the control that it provided for us. We will see that many people who repeatedly injure themselves tend to have experienced their parents as having provided them with little care, but lots of control. So breaking out of that mould is less likely to increase emotional isolation, or to lead to more loneliness or emotional emptiness. Those feelings are likely to have been common companions already. But breaking the mould *is* likely to result in a loss of external control that can be disorientating. We can find ourselves lost in the risk of inflating more and more, and even 'bursting'. To prevent this from happening we can look inside ourselves (into our Eigenwelt) for regulation; we can also look into the spiritual world (our Überwelt); or we can look to our social world (the Mittwelt). The social world is the world that has usually broken down already. Zelda was lucky that her social world was reconstituted by her pregnancy: her new baby changed her social world, and her personal world (her Eigenwelt) changed accordingly. This new world facilitated the expansion of Zelda's identity in a way that the old social world, with her coercive father and her cowed mother, could not.

Transformation involves the loss of both care and control. The loss of control creates a sense of possibility and freedom. The loss of care, conversely, is associated with isolation, loneliness and a lack of comfort. These adverse effects are what puts may people off taking the risk of transformation. They are, we suppose, what makes it seem preferable to limit oneself by puncturing one's self-esteem rather than maintaining one's personal integrity and breaking the mould.

SPIRITUAL ENDS

One of the reasons that Favazza's book *Bodies Under Siege'* (Favazza, 1996) has been so widely acclaimed is, we believe, because it recognizes that the motive of self-injury is often spiritual – and that transgressing the very basic boundary of the safety-catch against self-harm arouses an energy that involves the gods themselves. We must therefore note here that the 'soul' is conceived very differently in world religions. We have largely taken a Christian perspective. Christ's parable of the talents defines how Christianity views the ideal soul: it is the culmination of self-actualization, a realization of the God-given potential of each person. Each of us has an immortal soul (other traditions call this by a different name; for example, anthroposophy calls it the 'astral body') which is our ultimate potential. However, there are religious traditions that arrive at very different conclusions.

Confucianism prioritizes not the inherent shape of the soul as Christianity does, but the space that we each are given. It is the ultimate duty of the Confucian disciple to inhabit this shape to his, or her, fullest vigour and obedience. Contrariwise, the Hindu or Buddhist perspective is that there is no individual soul, since individuality is an artefact of the veil of ignorance. Our ultimate aspiration should be to expand our identity until it encompasses the whole of humanity, until our self is absorbed into the universal self-consciousness, or Atman.

WHAT DOES THIS MEAN FOR SELF-INJURY, AND FOR PEOPLE WHO INJURE THEMSELVES?

We have seen that self-injury is linked to a failure to establish a satisfactory identity. We can consider that in two ways, as we have seen: that society does not make a space for a new identity which is consistent with the potential that a person has, or that a person does not have the vital energy to expand against the jostling constrictions of other people's identities. We have considered that 'creating a space' is not just leaving a gap, but providing a matrix, or mould, in which identity can naturally develop. Whether or not the right space is being made available is, we have suggested, signalled by emotions: comfort or security for when the right space is being made; or humiliation, shame, despair, anger or fear for when it is not.

We have also suggested that there needs to be a fit between the space made available, and the potential final identity of the person filling it. We have also intimated that there is a kind of filling pressure, an energy, which needs to be available for the filling to take place. This is because, as in the world of plants, there is always competition. We have argued that the energy store is depleted by just those negative emotions that indicate the wrong kind of matrix: shame, anger, despair and anxiety. These are, it will be remembered, the very emotions that act as triggers for self-injury.

THE MATRIX, HOLDING, AND THE 'GOOD ENOUGH' ENVIRONMENT

One of the most resonant metaphors for the function of the social matrix was coined by Winnicott, who said that the infant (and we would argue any of us when we are needy or vulnerable, and not just the infant) requires a 'holding environment' (Winnicott, 1945) for the development of a stable identity. Winnicott called this a strong ego. Holding requires only a 'good enough' (another Winnicottian term) environment. However, to make the environment good enough there needs to be a degree of predictability, of nurturing, and of adaptation of the environment to the needs of the infant. This is usually achieved by giving the infant progressively more control over its environment. The control given is gradually increased in proportion to the infant's ability to accurately evaluate its own needs.

The following quotation is how one of the participants in a recent study (Sinclair & Green, 2005) of people who harmed themselves by poisoning described the situation that led to their overdose.

> My stepmother ... was a nutcase [had manic depression], when she was not high or low she was actually a very nice woman ... but then she had an episode ... I actually felt quite scared of her; she went really high and was just very scary ... I did feel very rejected which was really hard, and my father is very old school and just couldn't be doing with this teenager who was crying over this pathetic guy who was a complete loser anyway, and my mother didn't want to know, you know 'you went to live with your father, let him deal with it'.
>
> (Sinclair & Green, 2005, p. 1114)

Sinclair and Green's list of the factors that undermined the identity of their participants, and led to their self-harm, could equally apply to people who injure themselves. These were (a) 'unpredictability and powerlessness within family situation'; (b) 'a lack of validation of unique personal experiences'; and (c) 'a sense of not being heard or of being unimportant' (from Sinclair & Green, 2005, p. 1114).

As some of Sinclair and Green's other descriptions indicate, there may be many circumstances that can lead to a lack of a holding environment. But four mentioned in their quoted accounts are commonly involved. These are family breakdown through divorce or separation; emotional commitment to an unreliable partner; harsh or inappropriate discipline; and family mental illness or substance misuse. Quantitative studies support these findings. For example, in a retrospective study of 17,337 adult health maintenance organization members in California, 3.8% reported at least one episode of self-harm, but this rate was increased by a factor of between 2 and 5 times if the person concerned also reported emotional, physical or sexual abuse; household substance abuse, mental illness or imprisonment; or parental domestic violence, separation or divorce. Only 1.1% of this large adult sample reported ever harming themselves if they had never experienced any of these factors, but over a third (35.2%) of those who had experienced 7 of these factors reported doing so (Dube, 2001).

THICK OR THIN SKIN?

In our balloon analogy, we noted that for a hot air balloon to inflate to its full size it needed not only inflation pressure and the room to expand, but also a strong and impervious skin. Hot air balloons are made of PVC. Their plastic skins do not need much looking after, but can crack or tear if not given reasonable attention. The 'skin' or boundary defining an identity is not made of a substance that needs physical care, but it can be helpful to think of it as a something that needs looking after, even so. There is perhaps some direct link with the skin itself, too. Early maternal care involves caring a great deal for a baby's skin. Grooming in primates (including human beings) has an important place in restoring emotional harmony, re-establishing social relationships and reinforcing social identity.

The expressions 'thick skin' (meaning resilience with perhaps an overtone of insensitivity) and 'thin skin' (meaning sensitivity, but also a readiness to take offence or to experience humiliation) reflect commonsense psychology's recognition that the properties of what Anzieu calls the 'psychic skin' (Anzieu, 1989) influence identity. In relation to self-injury, though, it is not the permeability of the skin that is important, but its capacity to be expanded to its full potential. This is what we might call its suppleness.

Keeping the body's skin supple involves care. Mothers start early on their babies' skins using protective creams, soothing ointments, lotions and special soaps to prevent nappy rashes or sores. Unguents to be rubbed into the skin continue to be an important, and costly, element of self-care in later life. Their efficacy is enhanced if accompanied by attachment-securing vocalizations ('cooing'), by kind words, by expressions of admiration or love (one advertising campaign for Olay cosmetics cunningly linked the product with the catchphrase 'because you're worth it') and by loving gestures. Caring for the psychic skin may not involve physical grooming, but does involve all of these accompanying actions. As usual, commonsense psychology recognizes these links in terms like 'ego massage', 'scratching the itch' (an increasingly common term for sexual intercourse or other appetitive behaviour), 'soothing' (used for the reduction of both skin discomfort and psychological discomfort) and 'stroking'.

We could say – if we continue with our metaphor – that the psychic skin can be either too thick or too thin to stretch to allow a person unable to expand their identity to the full, and that both of these conditions can be produced by a lack of emotional care. The psychoanalyst Fairbairn imagined this in a different way. Carers, he thought, had to deal with their children's negative feelings effectively if the child was to grow up feeling positively about her or himself. Like the attachment theorists, he stressed the importance of dealing with the child's fears, which meant not going away from the child too far emotionally, and not punishing the child's fear to suppress it. He also thought, and this is his main original contribution, that the child had to be helped to tolerate the carer's disapproval. If disapproval meant not just gentle chiding but a loss of all love momentarily or if disapproval was associated with disgust, Fairbairn thought (Tantam, 1996), that the child would become over-preoccupied with forestalling these very painful responses by the carer, even at the cost of inhibiting exploratory or sociable behaviour.

Later on, as the child developed an inner narrative and a sense of identity, there would be a series of stories or simulations about what is disgusting to other people about the child. The child could then try to anticipate and forestall disgust reactions by running simulations of how others would react to aspects of the child's identity were they to be disclosed. The net effect of doing this, of having what Fairbairn called an 'anti-libidinal ego', is that a person would come across to others as emotionally distant, even calculating. Further social rejection might follow with an increase in self-monitoring and the addition of more elements of identity to those which the child had tried to suppress or, to use the term used by Fairbairn, to 'split off'. 'Splitting off' is an Anglo-Saxon version of the term 'dissociation' that we have already used quite frequently. There is evidence that children who have experiences about which they cannot tell anyone, such as being abused, are more likely to develop a readiness to dissociate about other experiences as well.

The disgust of a mother for a child is a sweeping experience. This is particularly so if it is associated with a sense, for that moment at least, that any vestige of positive feeling that a mother may have had, has been withdrawn. A child's response is likely to be equally all-or-nothing. One alternative is to accept mother's version and consider that it is true and that he or she really is a bad person, or has a 'spoilt identity' to use Goffman's resonant phrase. This is the way to developing a thin skin, because hints of disgust or emotional rejection are likely to be enough, in future, to produce this overwhelming sense of being bad. The other alternative is to be the sort of child who laughs when he (or more rarely, she) is being slapped. This is the sort of child who, when told not to touch the fire, immediately stretches out his hand and touches it. In later life, such children may grow up into thick-skinned adults who seem oblivious of other people's negative opinions.

Either of these reactions – being thick or thin-skinned – can be considered to be the effects of shame on emotional reactivity and therefore identity. People may become brazen and apparently insensitive to shame; or shame-prone and inhibited by shame, embarrassment or even the fear of these emotions (Tantam, 1998). We define shame as the combination of three elements: negative appraisal of the self by another person; an acceptance of that negative appraisal by the person themselves; and an intense wish to hide from the cause of the negative appraisal, and from the appraisal itself. In one small group of women who had cut themselves many times that we studied intensively, the readiness to experience shame was strongly associated with a perceived lack of maternal care. Shame was also one of the three commonest triggers of self-injury, after feeling uncared for and feeling powerless. The women who cut themselves the most were the women who most often dissociated, and who 'switched' into injuring themselves. These women also reported their mothers as being least caring, and shame also seemed to be a more important trigger for their self-injury.

Having a low care upbringing, like having an avoidant carer, results in making close relationships in adolescence and early adulthood that are also low in care (McCarthy & Taylor, 1999). This may be because someone who is brought up without care may as a result have failed to develop their own ability to care for others, or it may be that an uncaring parent is less likely to provide appropriate advice and support when choosing a potential partner or friend. Uncared-for children are also less likely to be popular and more likely to be socially isolated. So when uncared-for adolescents turn to peers to get the nurturance and support in developing their identity, they are not likely to find it. Instead, they will be offered not affection but other kinds of bonds with peers, through sexual excitement, shared intoxication, or crime and antisocial behaviour. These bonds are no respecter of individuality and tend to disrupt, and not assist, the development of identity. Not surprisingly these behaviours are associated with self-injury and also with the development of eating disorders – in themselves possibly a means of asserting an identity.

ABRADING THE PSYCHIC SKIN

We have so far dealt with why a person might grow an inability to expand to their full identity. But the psychic skin can also be weakened at the critical moment, during the later years of childhood and into early adolescence when identity is beginning to expand – leading to a constriction of identity development similar to that which occurs as a result of life-long developmental problems. These abrasions of the psychic skin can result from family breakdown or from family stigma.

Family breakdown does not always cause psychological harm to children and, when it appears to, it may be that the conflict that preceded it are what causes the real harm (Kelly, 2000). There is no doubt though that family breakdown reduces the security and increases the anxiety of all family members. Other common, although avoidable consequences, are depression in one or both of the separating partners and loss of income.

To grow up in a family where there is a constant worry about money, or where there is a constant lack of care, may have less impact than to be suddenly faced with a parent becoming depressed – and therefore unable to care – or with new acute financial hardship. Both of these may be experienced as being excluded from a previous world of relative safety and ease. Exclusion means being thrust out of the caring matrix prematurely, and this may have more of an effect, especially if it comes at a time – in early adolescence – when social ties with peers are the crucible for the development of a desirable adult identity.

STIGMA

Having a depressed parent, like having a parent with other kinds of mental illness, may increase social exclusion through the stigma that extends from social judgement of the parent to every family member. Stigma threatens identity (Balsam et al., 2005) and self-injury may be a response – perhaps as a means of regaining control over their identity. A sexual orientation that is different from that of the mass of society may be a significant cause of stigma in adolescence (Radkowsky & Siegel, 1997). In one large study, the mental health of over 1200 women and men who identified themselves as lesbian, gay or bisexual was compared with their siblings (79% of whom were heterosexual). Being lesbian, gay or bisexual was associated with an increased use of psychotherapy and mental health services, and also with thoughts of self-harm and with self-injury (Balsam et al., 2005). Substance abuse by a family member or the imprisonment of a family member may also be sources of stigma that can result in a challenge to the developing identity, and to self-injury.

CONTROL AND OVER-CONTROL

Studies find that there are limited ranges of emotional themes that are likely to trigger self-injury. In our own research, the two that were far and away the most frequent were feeling powerless and feeling uncared for. In our analogy between identity and hot air balloons, we have considered being cared for as being analogous to looking after the skin of the balloon, and making sure that it can take the pressure and not burst before it expands fully and we see its final, realized shape or identity. We have considered the important role of mothers in looking after the baby's skin, and caring for and strengthening the psychic skin of the child.

The function of the father in many families is rather different. His conventional role (we accept that this is conventional, and that there is no necessity for caring roles to be divided up in this way) is to protect the family in transactions with the outside world. In our analogy, the father must create a space for the family to live in, and thrive – if we were using our balloon analogy, we would say to keep any other balloons far enough away that they do not prevent full inflation – and this means also giving individual family members the freedom to develop in their own way, without constraint.

In our research, we found that the fathers of people who injured themselves tended to be perceived as over-protective. Whilst they may have defended the family by controlling external threats, they also extended this control over family members and inhibiting them, too – or at least this is how they were perceived. Feeling powerless was associated with this perceived control, and fathers of the women we studied who injured themselves were perceived as much more over-protective (controlling) that the average.

We noted in an earlier paragraph that self-injury is a harsh way of treating oneself. Religious self-injury is explicitly advocated as a means of taming or chastening the flesh with a view to controlling 'fleshly desires'. Private self-injury too has an element of self-punishment or, to use the term used by Richey Edwards in the extract from the interview quoted at the beginning of this chapter, of 'discipline'. Where does this harshness come from? Just as a lack of care for oneself is a consequence of being uncared for, as we saw in the previous section, so treating oneself harshly is probably a consequence of being harshly treated.

Care and control are both important parental functions, and it is the mother in human families throughout the world that seems particularly concerned with care, and the father with control (Bales, 1955). Parents – and this may apply more often to fathers – can sometimes think of control as a kind of care. It is easy to see the folly of this in extreme cases, as in this recent news story.

> Police today raided a house in Texas where three children were being kept in conditions that were, in the words of one law officer, not even suitable for keeping hens. The oldest of the three had been confined to an outhouse resembling a kennel for the previous 11 years. She had not been spoken to by another human being during that time. Food had been pushed into her kennel and she, and it, had been hosed down when it became necessary. Otherwise her parents did no more for her than ensure that she remained confined.

The measures were instituted by the father and were, he said, to protect his children from the evils in the world around them. The mother was over-awed by her husband and dared not protest. She was discouraged from going out herself, although she had the run of their house. The house was described as a normal, everyday home by neighbours who said that the family kept themselves to themselves, but were not suspected of any misdemeanour. In fact, the neighbours were unaware that they had children. The father worked regularly at a local factory where he was described as 'quiet' and 'a bit antisocial'. Psychiatrists later concluded that the father had a paranoid disorder and was mentally ill.

Repugnant as this seems, the father seems genuinely to have believed that his children benefited from being confined as they were. He had taken control to its furthest limit, mistakenly or deludedly thinking that this was a kind of care. Of course, the children lacked love, comfort, companionship and all of the other components which would be recognized by right-thinking people as care. They were the victims of extreme emotional neglect, a kind of child abuse. But some of the elements of this story can be detected in a much less severe form in the backgrounds of people who self-injure repeatedly. There is an increasing replacement of positive regard, negotiation, cajoling and coaxing by negative regard, prohibition and control by punishment or physical restraint. There is the belief that gentle handling of the child has failed, or will fail, and the further belief that this is either because the child is bad, or the world is too full of temptation, or both. Finally, there is the gradual isolation of the child and the parents in a closed world where the family's values and beliefs go untested or unchallenged by others. Isolation of this kind is more likely to happen if there is no-one who has the power or the inclination to reflect on the behaviour of one or both parents if the parent him or herself lacks self-reflectiveness, or if the family is threatened or embattled by the wider community.

Over-control, or emotional abuse as it is sometimes called, may also contribute to the lack of trust in other people, or male aggression towards others, that can be associated with self-injury (Bierer et al., 2003). But not everyone who experiences over-control ends up injuring themselves. We have already noted that there are some remarkable people who have the courage to endure other people's negativity (although this may be less a quality of these individuals and more a reflection of at least one formative experience of being valued somewhere along the line). There are others who can make use of their imagination to go beyond the self-loathing induced by an over-controlling parent; Franz Kafka, for example, who felt bullied by his father all of his life and imagined being sliced up by a butcher's knife. Kafka could never bring himself to marry, was considered unfit for military service and was throughout his life a considerable disappointment to his father. His fiction was, Hayman argues (Hayman, 1983), an elaboration of the discussions that he and his loving sister Elli would have in the bathroom as children, discussions in which they pleaded against their father's dissatisfaction with them. 'The Trial' and 'The Castle' – Kafka's best known novels – both describe a man about whom little is known except that he is either on trial for his life for an unknown crime, or a prisoner who has never been convicted and does not know what offence he has committed. Neither the crime nor the offence is ever divulged.

ABUSE

We have already observed that there is a particular association between childhood sexual abuse and self-injury. It's worth noting here that, irrespective of the effects of abuse on a child's self-perception, abuse (and particularly sexual abuse) is likely to be associated with the two factors – powerlessness in the face of paternal control and lack of care particularly from the mother – that we have considered in this chapter as the most important triggers of self-injury.

THE RED BADGE OF COURAGE, OR THE MARK OF SHAME?

Injuring oneself is, we have argued, an act of rebellion and an impulse towards self-healing. It may enable the creation of a new identity when an earlier one has been crushed. Why then should it be considered also to be a kind of psychopathology?

One reason is that the experience before, during and after self-injury becomes an addictive one. The emotional flavour of self-injury becomes so effective in absorbing and altering negative feelings that a person feels drawn to it more and more frequently, and less able to handle negative feelings in other ways. Another reason that self-injury is a problem is that it is just too successful in enabling a person to create a new identity for themselves. But the new identity is a secret one. So self-injury fosters the development of a secret life. The secret life may be shared with a few others, who may themselves be anonymous and therefore willing participants in a covert life. The Internet offers many opportunities for such relationships.

Covert identities are, by definition, 'deviant' (we use this term not in a scornful way but simply to emphasize the deviation from a public, transparent identity that is taken to be the norm). 'Deviancy theory' or 'labelling theory' introduced the notion of secondary deviance as a way of accounting for why a person who has put a foot wrong seems to be increasingly likely to step out of line, rather than to learn from his or her mistake and keep to the straight path. Sociologists have not found evidence to support the original assertion of deviancy theory, which was that calling or 'labelling' someone a thief or a murderer would actually increase the likelihood that a person would become a thief or a murderer. But labelling oneself does have consequences for locking in an identity. Telling oneself that one is a thief does increase the chances of future theft because it opens up values and feelings pertaining to being a thief which make future theft easier to contemplate and carry out. Identities can act as traps because of our own labels for those identities, and the assumptions that go with the labels. So it is with labelling oneself as a 'cutter', for example (Adams et al., 2005).

It is intoxicating to have the power to disturb others just by revealing what one does to one's skin. But investment in the power to shock may mean giving up on other ways of influencing people, and an increased commitment to other affirmations of 'deviance'. This is probably the reason for the association of self-injury with other badges of counter-cultural identities like Satanism (Noshpitz, 1994) or being a 'Goth' (Young et al., 2006).

The trap of a counter-cultural identity can be, in the language of covert intelligence, a 'honey trap'. It can provide gratification as well as confinement, so much so that even if a person gets free of the trap, he or she may re-enter it again. The honey in the self-injury trap is the relief of negative feelings that we have considered previously. In fact, the combination of a secret life and the seemingly magical suffusion of that life with relief can create a kind of glamour, which can be intoxicating and transforming. The shabbiness of scarring, razor blades stained with old blood, dressings and a wardrobe full of long-sleeved clothes can all seem all right, even attractive and welcoming, under the influence of this glamour. No wonder fairy tales and myths are so often preoccupied with enchantments in which young women are carried off, lose all sense of time and see monsters or hideous animals as charming young men. These stories are accurate reflections of a psychological truth about covert identity.

Chapter 6

Challenges for the Carer

INTRODUCTION

Self-injury is carried out in private, but sooner or later other people come to know about it. Knowing that someone you are close to has been secretly harming themselves can have a profoundly upsetting effect. If this chapter we will consider the burden on others of self-injury and how their reactions can help (or hinder) the person who self-injures to cope, and to change if they want to. We also consider its effects on health care professionals and how self-injury can present different challenges to the professional and the non-professional carer, even though the underlying principles are the same.

There are advantages to drawing attention to these differences. Doing so increases one's awareness of other peoples' concerns, obligations and roles. It allows a wider perspective on self-injury and people who self-injure, which can be helpful for someone who (professionally or non-professionally) is beginning to feel isolated. It also helps to avoid misunderstandings that can occur when a member of staff is constrained to act in a particular way as a result of some legal or professional requirement.

DIFFERENCES BETWEEN PROFESSIONAL AND NON-PROFESSIONAL CARERS

We view a non-professional carer as someone who has some personal relationship with the person who self-injures. This might be a family member, a close friend, a partner, a spouse or simply someone who cares about the person and wants to support them. In contrast, professional carers are people who care for other people as part of their job or occupation. They include doctors, nurses, psychologists, psychotherapists and counsellors, as well as volunteer health care workers.

The basic principles of caring for someone who repeatedly self-injures are similar for both groups, but there are important differences as well. Some of the challenges faced by the friend, partner or family member are made easier for the professional by virtue of his or her training, working environment and, to some degree, emotional distance. Of course, professional carers also have their own unique sets of challenges to face.

Professionals

Some things are easier for professional staff. Because the care they offer is part of their working day, they are required to take breaks from time to time. Their training often allows them to model the care they give on a series of underlying principles, which means they are (in theory) less likely to find themselves not knowing how to proceed. The role of the professional gives some licence for detachment when the atmosphere gets too emotionally charged, and the nature of their work means that they are required to detach themselves and go home at the end of the working day. Access to support and supervision is increasing regarded as essential to most professional health care roles, and many of those who work in residential settings work in teams, which makes it easier to share problems with colleagues and feel supported when making difficult decisions.

Having said that, some aspects are more difficult for the professional carer. They are at all times accountable for their actions, and are at risk of losing their livelihood if they behave in a way considered to be unprofessional. They have a responsibility of care to their patients, and so need to come to terms with who takes what responsibility for the patient's safety. Health care professionals also need to be able to justify any treatment they provide or action they take, and need to be cautious about 'experimenting' with unorthodox interventions. They are often bound by confidentiality restrictions, which can leave them unable to pass on information to a partner or family member without their client's express permission. This can make it appear as though they are 'taking the side' of the client and refusing to allow significant others to get involved in the care or treatment. Finally they may, in some circumstances, have legal obligations under mental health legislation.

Non-professionals

Many of the things listed above as being 'easier' for professional carers are unavailable to their informal counterparts, and so become significant challenges. For example, it is often difficult to take a break from caring for someone who self-injures without feeling at least some anxiety and guilt. With no training to fall back on, a friend, family member or partner can feel very out of their depth. The difficulty of not knowing what to do 'for the best' (something that is difficult to know without an understanding of self-injury and considerable experience of dealing with it) is further compounded by the intensity of feelings it raises. When these feelings surface, there may be no one to share them with, and no one close by to turn to for support. This can feel even worse when there is someone nearby who offers support and a listening ear, but that person is someone with whom the carer would be embarrassed about sharing his or her 'true' emotions. These might include considerable anger at the person who self-injures, or strong feelings of guilt about aspects of their upbringing.

The non-professional cannot easily take the option of 'assuming a professional distance' without making him or herself open to being criticized as being cold, uncaring or even heartless. If an attempt is made to share difficult feelings with other family members or involve them in difficult decision making, the person who self-injures can feel their privacy betrayed. Finally, there is the challenge of having a 'history' with the person who self-injures, which can provide much material on which (probably quite unreasonably) to base guilt and blame.

Some things are, however, easier for non-professionals. They can sometimes be more flexible in their approach and more innovative in their interactions with the person they are caring for. If the person agrees, they can accompany them in less formal activities (going to the cinema, swimming, cooking or shopping). Furthermore, non-professionals can usually call for professional help if things get serious.

IMPACT ON EMOTIONS

Emotions and the safety-catch

In Chapter 3 we discussed what we took to be universal aversion to witnessing the skin being deliberately cut as something which could be of evolutionary value, since its effect is to protect the integrity of the skin barrier to infection. We called this a 'safety-catch' because it has to be released or overcome to enable a person to injure themselves. We have also discussed the fears that people who injure themselves experience, particularly the fear of loss of control and of negative appraisal. We have observed that the wound itself can have a calming effect, but that when the safety-catch fails, those who witness another person self-injuring (or simply the wounds that result) can experience the disgust and horror vicariously.

It is not difficult to see what a volatile mix of emotions these various reactions are likely to produce in people who deal both with the wounds and with the person who has self-injured. Carers will be threatened by the evidence of the failure of the safety-catch and will not be reassured if the person who has self-injured seems calm. A carer meeting the situation for the first time might ask, 'How could you do such a thing?', but their bafflement is likely to be tinged with anger or hostility.

Managing emotions

A number of studies have explored the range of feelings that surface in professionals who work with people who self-injure (see, for example, Allen, 1995; Arnold, 1995) and in family members who provide less formal care. In each circumstance the range of feelings generated is considerable and includes horror, disgust, anxiety, sadness, coldness, detachment, incomprehension and confusion. Sometimes a strong desire to over-protect also emerges. It is important to be able to monitor one's feelings and to be able to understand that many are normal reactions to difficult circumstances. It is not unusual, for example, for a parent to experience guilt with worries that they may have contributed in some way to the behaviour or the disturbance that gives rise to it.

Professionals may also find that working with a self-injuring client powerfully challenges their views about their own competence, role and autonomy (Breeze & Repper, 1998); this can be a particular difficulty if the client is knowledgeable about wound care and wishes to be actively involved in decisions about his or her treatment. On the other hand, non-professional carers, particularly if they are in a close relationship with the person who is self-injuring, may feel driven to find something that will stop the cutting or burning happening again because they themselves feel unable to bear it. A mother might typically say 'my daughter may not worry about her cutting ... the pain ... the scars, but I do. I can't bear the thought of her doing it again. It's like I worry for both of us. It gets me so anxious that I'll try anything to stop her doing it.'

One of the best solutions for managing difficult emotions such as these is to talk them through with another, trusted, person. For the professional, this is most reliably achieved through formal supervision. As we have already noted, provision of appropriate confidential support is increasing regarded as essential to most professional health care roles. In addition, staff who work together in teams can often make use of each other to talk through what they are feeling. Identifying the various emotions and being able to express them verbally to another person in a safe, supportive environment can be invaluable; it is also an effective way of 'handing over' one's concerns and thus effectively sharing the burden. There are, however, two caveats to this apparently straightforward solution to managing difficult feelings for professional workers. The first arises when boundaries are not properly set between the type of supervision that is offered to front-line staff (often termed 'clinical supervision') and the type of supervision used by managers as a way of reviewing performance. It is clearly quite difficult to be honest about one's feelings if one feels one's pay or promotion could depend on what is said. The second difficulty arises when a member of staff finds that the team in which he or she is working has become split into discrete sub-groups of workers who have very different views about how a self-injuring client should be managed. This is discussed in more detail in a later section.

The same principles apply for the non-professional carer, only here it will be even more important to find a source of support and a safe place to express one's feelings since he or she is often trying to cope in relative isolation. Other family members can be helpful in this respect, but are not always the best source of impartial support. A trusted friend from outside the family may be less emotionally entangled and more able to listen in a non-judgemental way. The services of a professional counsellor may also be sought, although there will be a cost involved in most cases. Family doctors (GPs) may be able to suggest other suitable sources of support, and there is a section at the end of this book listing resources, including resources for carers.

Being able to say how one is feeling can also be valuable in interacting with the person who self-injures as long as this does not come across as apportioning blame. As Arnold and Magill point out, there is a big difference between saying '*I feel really upset and worried about your self-harm*' and saying something like '*How can you do this to me?*' (Arnold & Magill, 2000, p. 20).

ATTITUDES TO SELF-INJURY

The 'attention-seeking' argument

One argument for the badness of self-injury is that it makes demands on others which are illegitimate, and therefore any response to those demands is undeserved. This is the 'attention-seeking' argument, and one that weighs particularly strongly with some carers. A clinical variant of this argument is the 'displacement of the deserving patient' argument that states that more deserving patients are forced to go without care because of time spent on less deserving self-harmers.

Most nurses and doctors feel compassion for injured people, and a wish to help them. Indeed, for many this will be one reason for their choice of profession. But this feeling is generally based on a conception that the injury is a consequence of ill fortune. Attitudes to people who are injured doing dangerous sports, especially if they have not taken proper precautions, are slightly different (examples might include racing drivers, rugby players and enthusiastic skiers). Medical and nursing staff sometimes think these people have courted injury, almost as if they are happy to be injured. Sometimes this kind of activity is even termed 'slow suicide'. Attitudes to people who have injured themselves are even more negative. Self-injury is often called 'deliberate self-injury' to bring out this aspect of calculation. The term implies that a person who injures themselves knows what they are doing and its consequences, including the consequences for the trouble that other people will be put to. Furthermore, so the argument goes, the time taken to stitch up someone who has cut themselves might be time that could otherwise be given to a 'genuine' emergency.

Whether or not patients are more or less deserving is currently a contentious area of medical ethics. For example, should someone who is overweight be given the same priority for a hip replacement, if they had previously been warned that their obesity would cause osteoarthritis in their hip, but they had failed to heed the warning and go on a diet? Doctors are increasingly reluctant to replace arthritic hips in obese individuals, but their argument is not that the patient is undeserving. It is that the prosthesis breaks down too quickly when the recipient is obese. Similar arguments have been applied to cosmetic surgery to remove the scarring of previous self-cutting. If the person is still injuring themselves, there is a significant chance that they will cut into the newly grafted skin, thus obviating the benefits of the operation.

However, few ethicists would recommend denying urgent medical treatment on the grounds that it is undeserved. So this argument cannot be applied to the urgent treatment of self-inflicted injures. In ordinary life, outside the clinic or the emergency room, we might become exasperated by someone who gets harmed or injured over and over again despite our advice about how to avoid this. But we would not normally argue that they are deliberately harming themselves in order to gain our attention. We might need to consider why the person is not paying us enough attention, or why they cannot change their dangerous habits, but the discomfort of being harmed and also of bearing the brunt of our exasperation means that we cannot really think that that is the explanation of why they are doing whatever it is they are doing.

Even if self-injury is an illegitimate means of getting attention or care (and we would not take that view ourselves), it does not follow that getting attention is why people injure themselves. In fact, we find the opposite tends to be true. As we have seen, one of the characteristics of the kind of self-injury that we are considering in this book is that it is private. People who injure themselves do not flaunt it, or seek attention as a result of it, but usually hide it. In one unpublished study of one month of attendances at the accident and emergency department of a large district general hospital, or requests for an ambulance to be taken there, there were 172 attendances or ambulance calls identified as being for self-harm. Of these, 40 were for self-injury and an additional 14 for self-injury in combination with an overdose of drugs (Brian Hockley, personal communication). Of the 118 people for whom an ambulance was called to take them to hospital for treatment of self-harm, 54 (45%) refused to go in it. It is not known what proportion of these had injured themselves, but since most people who take an overdose are stuporose by the time an ambulance is called – and so are unlikely to resist being put into it – it is likely that a substantial proportion had self-injured. So even if a self-inflicted injury is serious enough for other people to want the injured person to go to hospital to have it treated, many will refuse. This does not seem like attention seeking – far from it – but one might forgive the carer who called the ambulance for thinking that the person that they were trying to help was causing unnecessary trouble.

The 'attention-seeking' argument also seems to fail when we consider the majority of those who repeatedly injure themselves. Our experience of working with nurses who regularly offer a wound care service in day hospitals and other non-emergency community settings is that most regular self-injurers prefer to hide their injuries, seeking professional help only when something has 'gone wrong' with a wound, which usually means it has become infected. For those who repeatedly self-injure, it is probable that the vast majority of their wounds go unseen by another person until they are healed and a scar is the only evidence.

Other components of attitude

We might say that someone who views self-injury as 'attention-seeking' has a particular attitude to the behaviour, although in practice this normally means that their attitude is to the person who does the behaving. Attitudes can be extremely powerful for they can operate unconsciously and may have a considerable impact on the relationship between the person who self-injures and the person who tries to provide help, support or professional care.

Relatively little work has been done to explore professional attitudes specifically towards people who self-injure, although there is a considerable literature relating to attitude to self-poisoning, attempted suicide and self-harm in general (NICE, 2004). According to the NICE report, these studies have demonstrated that attitudes to self-harm are generally more negative than attitudes to other medical conditions; that depressive motives tend to be viewed as more acceptable than 'manipulative' ones; and that people who harm themselves repeatedly are viewed particularly negatively. Consequences of such attitudes included the avoidance of self-harm patients and diminished attention to any pain they may experience, although there are also reports of some staff responding with 'compensatory attentiveness and attention' (Antonowicz et al., 1997).

One recent study (Friedman et al., 2006) explored the attitudes of casualty staff towards patients who self-harm through laceration. Respondents were unsure of the relationship between self-laceration and both mental illness and risk of suicide, and the majority had previously received little training in managing this condition. For staff who had not received previous training, a longer period working in an accident and emergency setting was correlated with higher levels of anger towards patients and an inclination not to view patients as mentally ill.

Our own study, which aimed to identify factors governing professional attitude towards self-injury in a large group of mental health staff, used a postal survey to discern reactions to a case vignette (Huband & Tantam, 2000). The hypothetical case vignette was based on two frequently cited descriptions of a typical self-injuring patient and provided limited information about a 24-year old woman who had cut herself on several occasions, but exhibited no symptoms of psychosis or major depression. Five key factors were identified, the most dominant being *'ability to be in control of her actions'* which reflected perception of her capacity for consciously determining and moderating her behaviour. Other factors were *'tendency to be undemanding vs. difficult'* (reflecting a perception of how troublesome she was likely to be in her interactions with staff), *'eligibility for tolerance and empathy'*, *'difficulty in understanding her actions'* and *'therapeutic confidence'*. While it can be difficult to generalize from a single exploratory survey, these findings do focus attention on staff perception about the locus of control in people who self-injure. Furthermore, the first and third factors from this list ('control' and 'eligibility') seem to sum up the 'attention seeking/displacing the deserving patient' viewpoint described above.

Managing one's own attitudes
Although it may initially seem strange to be reading about managing one's own attitude to someone who self-injures, it is often a valuable exercise. Awareness of one's own attitudes helps to avoid extreme reactions and reduce defensive manoeuvres that were previously automatic (Rayner et al., 2005). Here the focus is on how to be, rather than what to do or what to say.

Being positive and upbeat is generally helpful, although it can come across as not genuine if excessive or if it appears to discount sadness, grief or loss. Clinicians often report that drawing attention to those positive aspects of a client's life that are unconnected with self-injury helps to increase self-worth. It is also worth concentrating on being comfortable with the client taking control whenever this is appropriate, as is being willing to listen to what the client wants to express verbally, and being keen to avoid misunderstanding what is said.

It is also important to strike a balance between, on the one hand, not being critical or judgemental and, on the other hand, not colluding with or overtly supporting self-injury as the preferred coping strategy. Noticing how often one uses words and phrases that imply a negative view of self-injury as a coping behaviour rather implying a negative view of the person who self-injures is also valuable.

PREFERRED MANAGEMENT STYLE

'Firm' and 'soft' styles of management

Attitudes are important for many reasons, but particularly because they can determine the style of management which people prefer to use when dealing with individuals who self-harm. As we have often said, self-injury is emotive, and any behaviour that raises strong feelings is likely also to raise strong opinion about how best to deal with it. This has consequences not only for the lone carer, but also for carers who try to work together as a team: either formally in the case of the hospital ward or the outpatient clinic, or informally in the case of the family.

The classic study by Tom Main in the 1950s exemplifies the difficulties that people can face when trying to work together to care for 'difficult' or 'special' patients, and the strong differences that can emerge within a group (Main, 1957). Main's study focussed on a group of professional staff caring for a group of hospitalized patients described as exhibiting recalcitrant distress. Many of these patients self-injured, and most did not 'get better' despite the enthusiastic efforts of those who offered them care and treatment. Staff anxiety tended to increase over time, and once it had grown beyond a certain point, there was a blurring of roles and therapy became mixed with management. By then the staff had effectively divided themselves into two groups. The first of these Main termed the 'Out-group', who were not closely involved in treatment and whom the patients had not honoured. This 'Out-group' felt unworthy, resentful and envious of their counterparts. The second he termed the 'In-group', who were close to the patients and who tended to offer them ever greater amounts of care and attention as time went on. These two sub-groups eventually polarized leading to the near disintegration of the staff team. They differed strongly in their attitudes. The 'In-group' tended to see the patients as overwhelmed with psychotic anxieties and, as their condition worsened, considered them to be finally revealing the true and serious illness that they had previously kept hidden. In contrast, the 'Out-group' tended to see the (same) patients as hysterically demanding, and felt that they were playing up the staff and were 'getting away with it'.

The type of subdivision described in Main's study is often termed 'splitting', and it is certainly true that when a group of carers subdivide into two (sometimes more) sub-groups, they are effectively 'split'. This can, of course, occur in any group of carers and is not unknown in families. When it does occur, it is generally to the patient's detriment and is almost always upsetting for the carers. There is, however, an unfortunate confusion around the word 'splitting', which has come to have three rather different meanings (Gabbard, 1989). The first relates to disagreement and sub-division within a group of carers, as we have illustrated. We agree with Burnham (1966) and others that when this type of division occurs, it does so along lines of cleavage that are already present in the group (although the cleavage lines may be well hidden). The second meaning relates to a perception of manipulation by the patient. For example, borderline patients are widely regarded as having potential to actively split professional carers into groups by somehow making them disagree with each other. The implication here is that the splitting is a conscious and wilful process, and one in which the person doing the 'splitting' is seen as blameworthy. The third meaning derives from psychoanalytic theory. Here splitting is viewed as a normal stage in every person's mental development, occurring where intrapsychic experience becomes separated, usually into 'good' and 'bad' parts. In the latter, splitting is seen as a defence mechanism and so is unconscious (and thus not a wilful process).

One way of exploring preferred styles of management and potential for subdivision is to examine attitudes. In our study of mental health staff described above which focused a self-injuring woman described in a case vignette (Huband & Tantam, 2000), we examined the innate potential for our sample to self-polarize using a statistical technique called cluster analysis. A line of cleavage emerged between (a) less tolerant staff who perceived her to have more control over her actions and to be more difficult to understand (who we interpreted as favouring 'firm' management), and (b) those with opposing views (who we interpreted as favouring 'soft' management). Interestingly, opinion about the patient's ability to be demanding (or undemanding) was not significant in this division. These two sub-groups seemed very different in the way they prioritized empathic comforting and, we suggest, are not too dissimilar from those in the study by Main (1957) described above.

We called these management styles 'firm' and 'soft' because these are the terms that are often used in the debates, which can sometimes be highly conflicting – between mothers and fathers, parents and partners or staff and staff – about how to respond to self-injury. 'You're just too soft with her (or him)' is a common, exasperated comment. 'Spare the rod and spoil the child', 'give her an inch and she'll take a mile' or 'the absence of boundaries in the borderline means that it's essential for staff to set firm limits' – all of these adages seem to support the firm management position. Soft managers come across as, well, soft. It's difficult to seem to have a pro-active policy as a soft manager, or to come across as being in charge of a situation. But the reality of repeated self-injury is that it is not possible to be 'in charge' of it. So soft management styles are, at least, realistic.

Finding the middle ground
We believe that one of the key challenges when working with, or indeed being with, someone who repeatedly self-injures, is to be able to find a reasonable middle ground. This could be the half-way position between over-reacting to injured flesh and being completely unmoved by a wound, or between making heroic attempts to talk someone out of attempting another cut and rejecting the task as a futile waste of time. However, homing in on the middle ground is only possible once one has awareness of the extremes, and it is for this reason we have focused again on attitudes.

An intrigued reader may already have given some thought to where their own style lies on the spectrum between Main's 'In-group' and 'Out-group'; between our 'firm' and 'soft' management positions; and will probably have decided that they do not lie close to any of these extremes. This will be encouraging since it implies that the 'middle ground' is already in sight. However, the real difficulty is that one tends to be drawn a little nearer to one or the other pole when the emotional going gets tough. All others who are closely involved (for example, other family members and nursing colleagues) will find themselves similarly affected. The situation can then polarize quite quickly, and one suddenly finds oneself 'adopted' by one side or the other. Once adopted in this way, enduring loyalty is expected and it feels impossible to pull back to some less extreme position without appearing to have changed sides. This is a powerful group process that can lead to considerable discomfort, and its impact should not be underestimated. Fortunately, awareness of the extremes is of great help in monitoring such a situation and steering a middle course for oneself though it.

We can find no clear advantage to either extreme. Soft management can degenerate into laissez-faire, but rarely does so since few carers, or even bystanders, can escape the anxiety of discovering that someone has injured themselves, and with that anxiety, almost inevitably, comes the desire to try to prevent future injury. The one exception is when carers who have been emotionally involved – often very involved (or over-involved as some clinicians sometimes say) – begin to hate the person for troubling them so much. They may themselves feel rejected and also angry that all the time and effort they have expended has come to naught. Although nothing may be said, carers can become uncaringly laissez-faire as a result and, in our experience, this increases the frequency and severity of self-injury significantly.

Firm management can degenerate into punishment. Like uncaring laissez-faire, it is a reaction to being alarmed or troubled that often provokes this. For this reason, it is often staff who are experienced but who do not consider it their job to care for people who self-injure that are most at risk. Punishment may involve deliberately keeping people waiting before treatment, sewing wounds up without using local anaesthetic, or 'aversive treatment' in which something unpleasant is done to the person who has injured themselves as soon as possible after the injury on the premise that the noxious stimulation will reduce the frequency of self-injury through operant conditioning. It is not unusual for carers who advocate such aversive treatments to justify their actions by saying they are administering 'behaviour therapy' or 'doing a bit of CBT'. This is unfortunate, since an experienced behaviour therapist would first want to be sure about what was and what was not reinforcing for a particular person, and second would normally seek to involve the client in the process rather than making him or her an unwitting recipient.

Since being uncared for and being the recipient of negative feelings are, as we have seen, the two most common themes leading to self-injury, there can be no benefit to the self-injurer in being punished, only some relief for the carer if they can externalize their tension by blaming it on badness. Badness is, of course, a moral judgement, and it might be difficult at first sight to see what is morally bad about injuring oneself. There may be explicit prohibitions against doing so – many societies have prohibitions against suicide which may be extended to people who harm themselves. Mostly, these prohibitions arise from the writings of the great monotheistic religions, where the power to give or take life is thought to be an expression of the divine will that should not be usurped by mankind. In secular societies, suicide is usually decriminalized (this occurred in the UK in the 1950s). So self-injury is not illegal and, in some circumstances and cultures, may even be positively valued.

TROUBLE WITH SHIFTING IDENTITIES

We have concentrated so far on how self-injury is troubling to other people. For the layman, and sometimes for professionals too, the trouble due to the injury can often generalize to trouble being due to the person. This is not entirely without justification. As we saw in the previous paragraph, people who injure themselves can be a lot of trouble even in such an apparently straightforward situation as getting the appropriate treatment.

Some professionals feel comfortable categorizing this kind of trouble-someness as a personality disorder. This can be unhelpful because it treats difficulties in relationships as if they are a kind of illness and, perhaps more damagingly in the long run, is often taken to mean that the troublesomeness can never be overcome because, as most people assume, our personalities do not change much. We do not wholly agree with this assumption, either, but that is another story and, in any case, there is evidence emerging that attitudes to a diagnosis of personality disorder are becoming less negative, at least in the UK. Finally, focussing on the trouble that someone causes other people may distract carers and professionals from thinking about the trouble that the person him or herself is experiencing.

What trouble do people who injure themselves cause to other people?
In this section, we will argue that much of the 'trouble' that self-injurers cause for other people are fundamentally related to problems with unstable iden-tity. We begin by observing that by far the most common personality disorder diagnosis applied to people who injure themselves is 'borderline personality disorder' (BPD). In fact, over the last 20 or so years, this has become far and away the most common personality disorder diagnosis, tout court. However, its characteristics do seem to apply particularly to many people who injure themselves. The characteristics of BPD described by the American Psychiatric Association in the 4th edition of the Diagnostic and Statistical Manual are summarized in Text Box 6.1.

Text Box 6.1 DSM-IV criteria for Borderline Personality Disorder

- Frantic efforts to avoid real or imagined abandonment
- A pattern of unstable and intense interpersonal relationships characterized by alternating between extremes of idealization and devaluation
- Identity disturbance: markedly and persistent unstable self-image or sense of self
- Impulsivity in at least two areas that are potentially self-damaging (e.g. spending, sex, substance abuse, reckless driving and binge eating)

- Recurrent suicidal behaviour; gestures or threats; or self-mutilating behaviour
- Affective instability due to a marked reactivity of mood (e.g. intense episodic dysphoria, irritability or anxiety usually lasting a few hours and only rarely more than a few days)
- Chronic feelings of emptiness
- Inappropriate, intense anger or difficulty controlling anger (e.g. frequent displays of temper, constant anger and recurrent physical fights)
- Transient, stress related paranoia or severe dissociative symptoms

There has been considerable professional criticism of borderline personality disorder as a construct. Like histrionic personality before it – a diagnosis which it has largely superseded – it is applied overwhelmingly to women, raising the possibility that there is a strong gender bias in diagnosis. It seems also to be used as much as a measure of how disturbed or disturbing a person is, as to indicate a particular pattern of characteristics. Unfortunately, the scientific study of self-injury is often badged as the study of borderline personality disorder and we cannot therefore dispense with the term. What we will do, though, is not to refer to people with BPD but to people who have been diagnosed as having BPD.

What makes clinicians diagnose borderline personality? In one study (Wilkinson-Ryan & Westen, 2000) of clinicians in Boston, Massachusetts – where standards can be expected to be high – clinicians were asked to complete an 'identity disturbance questionnaire' about patients currently in psychotherapy. This questionnaire was based on the same literature we drew on in Chapter 5 to consider identity and self-injury. Fifty clinicians contributed ratings about 95 of their patients: 34 of these had been diagnosed with borderline personality; 20 with another personality disorder; and 41 had no personality disorder diagnosis. Identity disturbance questionnaires were scored and the scores factor analysed (a statistical procedure to try to reduce the number of essential items in a questionnaire to a minimum). It turned out that only four items (factors) were needed to explain half of the variance. Importantly, all four factors distinguished patients with borderline personality disorder. This means that only four questions about identity are enough to explain the majority of the differences between the group diagnosed as having borderline personality and the rest. We can conclude that there is a considerable overlap between the concept of an identity problem that we considered in Chapter 5, and that of borderline personality disorder. We shall see that dissociation, which we have already described as being linked to repeated self-injury, accounts for a large part of the remaining difference.

So what were the characteristics of identity that led to a diagnosis of borderline personality disorder? The weakest one – a lack of commitment – turned out to be linked to a diagnosis of any personality disorder, and the researchers concluded that the lack of commitment was not specific to borderline personality but was an indication of degree of personality disturbance or, to use less technical language, was an indication of a person's lack of control over their emotions.

The researchers described the three identity descriptions that were most associated with a diagnosis of borderline personality as follows '*The first factor was role absorption, in which patients appeared to absorb themselves in, or define themselves in terms of, a specific role, cause, or unusual group. The second factor, painful incoherence, reflected patients' subjective experience and concern about a lack of coherence. The third factor, inconsistency, was characterized less by subjective than objective incoherence (i.e., did not imply distress). ... The factors all showed high internal consistency, with the following reliabilities (coefficient alpha): factor 1=0.85, factor 2=0.90, factor 3=0.88*' (ibid., p. 534).

We have quoted what the authors themselves said because we do not want to twist their findings to fit our own clinical impressions. We hope that the reader will conclude, as we do, that what we described in the last two chapters as troubling people who self-injure – not being able to develop a primary identity fully, and coping with this by developing one or more covert identities based on the particular practice of self-injury and the hidden community of people who self-injure – is pretty much the same thing as Wilkinson-Ryan and Westen are describing, but in different words. Since Wilkinson-Ryan and Westen found that identity disturbance is the greatest single reason for a diagnosis of BPD, it seems to us that we lose nothing by sticking to a description of the identity problems that people who self-injure have (and their tendency to dissociate) and we gain the advantage of avoiding a term that many people who are diagnosed with BPD find pejorative and pessimistic.

Identity trouble: troubling to me, troublesome for others

We have discussed identity at length because we think that it provides some clues about why people who self-injure can be so puzzling and often challenging to their carers – and indeed, themselves.

Getting close to someone presupposes that we have a reliable sense of who that 'someone' is. We expect from our friends and colleagues that they will react predictably, particularly in their loyalty and positive feelings towards us. If they do not, we automatically think of them as being upset and look for reasons: in a recent loss or an alcohol problem, for example. In other words, we can tolerate a degree of unpredictability if we can find an external reason. If we cannot find one, we feel betrayed.

The following example illustrates how people may react to someone whose identity is not fixed but which shifts around. In his novel, 'London Fields', Martin Amis introduces his main female protagonist, Nicola Six as having the delusion that she could predict the future. The delusion was supported by the inevitability of Nicola not being able to sustain close relationships: '*Considered more generally – when you looked at the human wreckage she left in her slipstream, the nervous collapses, the shattered careers, the suicide bids, the blighted marriages (and rottener divorces) – Nicola's knack of reading the future left her with one or two firm assurances: that no one would ever love her enough, and those that did were not worth being loved enough by*' (Amis, 1989, p. 17).

Nicola has many jobs, and many identities. When she is alone, she seems unsure of who she is though. She uses drink, watching herself in the mirror and long baths to cover this up. Most of her identities are created for a man, and when she is able to influence men sexually she feels in control, even though men disgust her. In her relationship with the book's male protagonist, Keith, she hits upon the idea of videoing herself in sexually provocative poses and then inviting Keith to her flat to masturbate watching these videos in her bedroom whilst she goes and has a bath, or does her hair in another room.

Nicola is introduced as a 'murderee' and although she does not injure herself at any time in the book, there is the underlying theme that she is looking for, and to, violence as a solution to her emptiness. '*I'm so cold*', she kept saying. '*I'm so cold.*' And: '*Please. It's all right to do it … It's all right.*' *And after the first blow she gave a moan of visceral assent, as if at last she was beginning to get warm*' (ibid. p. 467). Nicola's murder, of which the previous extract was a description, is not carried out by Keith, even though Keith is introduced at the beginning of the book as her murderer. It is carried out by the book's narrator, because she burns the manuscript of the novel that he is writing, the novel that is based on a description of what is presented as the real-life relationship of the novelist and the inspiration for the Nicola's character.

It is a disturbing male fantasy that a woman would 'give a moan of visceral assent' to an act of domestic violence. Injuring oneself is not at all the same as being injured by someone else, even if the victim planned it to happen. Self-injury is, as we have already noted, an assertion of control over one's own skin and therefore over one's own identity. Being injured by someone else is the opposite.

Our reason for quoting these extracts from London Fields is not to illuminate Nicola's character, but to illustrate what we have been saying about other people's reactions to someone whose identity is not fixed. Sam, the narrator/author, cannot in the end complete his book because Nicola destroys it.

She supposedly burns the manuscript, even though the reader is obviously reading the manuscript, but the character really does destroy the book in that the author, Sam or perhaps Martin Amis himself, cannot manage the plot any more. Nicola's shifting identities defeat him and, as a result, he turns on her and murders her.

Amis correctly gauges how (murderously) strong other peoples' reactions to an unstable identity can be. Carers beware. The shifting identities of people who injure themselves can provoke strong, possibly violent reactions.

Unhelpful ways of coping with shifting identities

In real life, there are plenty of ways of insulating oneself from someone who causes this kind of troublesome frustration and anger. Experience has shown that some of these ways tend ultimately to be unhelpful to all parties. One way is to blame people who self-injure, and sometimes we wonder whether diagnoses of personality disorder are invitations to professionals to do this. Another way is simply to exclude people. We know of a woman who worked in a sandwich shop and one particularly hot day, she rolled up her sleeves (like most people who cut their arms repeatedly, she habitually wore long sleeved tops). The manager caught a glimpse of her scars and sacked her on the spot, 'because it would put off the customers'.

In families, self-injury and identity can often be tied together and become a justification for exclusion. One typical scenario might be that the first wound, and perhaps the second or third if they are repeated, are attributed to a 'suicide attempt' and considered to be prima facie evidence of depression or of a personal crisis with an external cause. Since self-injury often begins in the early teens, between 11 and 16, the causes are often those that commonly occur at this age: a change of school, bullying, burgeoning sexual feelings, examination stress, splitting up with boy or girlfriends and so on. This is by no means an irrational response. There may indeed be an external cause. What the family, and sometimes the professional carer, are reluctant to admit is that the cause has disclosed how trapped the young person feels. They are trapped in the sense that they feel their public identity is not who they really are, but they either will not or do not know how to renegotiate a new and better identity.

Family members know about each other without being able to formulate their knowledge explicitly. Unfortunately this knowledge can sometimes lead them to precisely the wrong thing with as much uncanny precision as sometimes they do precisely the right thing. The wrong thing in these circumstances – but a common reaction nevertheless – is for a parent or another carer to say something along the lines of, '*You don't know how upsetting it is for me to think of you hurting yourself like that. Even if you don't care enough about yourself to stop it happening again, I care. I want you to promise me that you won't do it again and even if you can't promise that for yourself, I want you to promise it for me. If you really love me, spare me going through that again.'*

What this kind of statement amounts to is a bid by the parents to own the child's actions, creating even more tension between the acceptable identity of the child, and the wished for identity. However, the really bad consequence of this move is that when the child does injure themselves again – and this is made more likely by the gap between public and private identity – the parent concludes that it was done because the child did not love them enough. The parent may then feel justified in turning their face away from the child because the child does not reciprocate their affection (as the parent views it). This, in turn, can be a pretext for marginalizing the child because the child has failed to fulfil their obligations as a family member – they are 'unnatural' or 'ungrateful' perhaps – or, much more simply, because the child does not realize 'how lucky they are'. We can imagine a parent saying in this situation, *'Perhaps it would be better for you to live on your own for a bit. Then you might realize how much your father and I (or your mother and I, or the medical and nursing staff) do for you, and it would make you a bit more inclined to do your bit for us.'*

A version of this exclusionary process sometimes takes place in hospitals and therapeutic communities. This is the so-called 'No Self-Harm Contract'. The notion of such a contract is based on several correct premises. The first is that if self-injury increases during the course of treatment, then the supposed benefits of the treatment should be called into question. The second is that self-injury can be contagious and if one member of a therapeutic community injures themselves this will demoralize other community members (and also the staff) and may trigger off emulation. The contract is designed to prevent the repetition of self-injury, and if it were a contract by the institution to provide the client with a therapeutic service, this would be fine.

For example, such a contract might say, 'We regret that we are unable to provide our therapeutic service to people who are continuing to injure themselves' or 'Past experience has shown that once a person injures themselves whilst in our treatment programme, they are more likely to injure themselves more seriously if they remain in the programme than if they are discharged. Our policy is therefore to ask people to leave the programme if they should injure themselves.' However, contracts usually place the duty on the person who self-injures. He or she has to sign a statement to the effect that they promise not to hurt themselves (and not to do other things that the institution disapproves of), and that they are aware that any breach of the contract will result in discharge.

Contracts assume that when the person signs, they are signing for all time, or until the contract is revoked. But when a person's identity can change substantially, he or she is not in a position to be able to commit themselves for every circumstance. This, as we have seen, can be particularly exasperating. To impose a contractual approach on someone with an identity problem is to deny this truth. It is either an indication of inexperience or (and we have come across this often) a disingenuous means of ensuring that the people most in trouble, and most troublesome (that is, those with the greatest identity problems) are most likely to be excluded from treatment. Not surprisingly, such contracts are at best ineffective at reducing repeat self-harm, and may even increase the likelihood if they are seen as uncaring (Drew, 2001). Contracts are one of the management strategies that are particularly associated with 'firm' management. This is because the presumption of 'firm' managers is that self-injury, unless it is associated with psychosis or intoxication, is an action for which a person can be held responsible. If someone cuts themselves while in treatment, they should therefore be held responsible for their actions, even if that includes discharge.

Helpful ways of coping with shifting identities

More helpful ways of coping with this difficulty do exist, however. One mechanism is to provide a supportive, nurturing environment into which a stable identity can develop. This is most easily achieved within the relationship between the carer and the person who self-injures, but it requires considerable effort on the part of the former to remain stable, supportive, non-judgemental and, most importantly, not over-defensive. This is difficult to achieve consistently, even for professionally trained staff.

Some people are lucky enough to have a kind of natural stability that comes from being very comfortable with themselves, and as such are able to exert a calming influence over the type of person whose identity seems to shift from hour to hour. They have a natural constancy and rarely seem to go on the defensive. However, most of us do not fall into this category and so need to take steps to recognize (and so reduce) our defensive reactions, and contain ourselves so that we present with a reasonably consistent identity.

Again, the focus is more on how to be, rather than what to do (or what to say) in a given situation. Someone who is able to create the type of nurturing environment defined above is likely to display many of the characteristics summarized in Text Box 6.2.

Text Box 6.2   Creating a nurturing environment

- Taking care to treat the person like an adult (but also remaining sensitive to the vulnerability inherent in any child-like presentation)
- Behaving in a way that minimizes shame (such as suggesting that even though his/her behaviour is difficult, this does not mean that he/she is bad)
- Focusing on positive aspects of the person (rather than on negative aspects of the behaviour)
- Helping to encourage realistic target setting (rather than setting goals that are clearly unattainable)
- Having clarity about their own limits (but not stating these aggressively or in a defensive way)
- Talking and acting as consistently as possible (thereby modelling a stable presentation)
- Avoiding being over-protective (such as taking away blades)
- Avoiding over-reaction (such as seeing every injury as a potential suicide attempt)
- Avoiding being over-controlling (such as insisting they stop self-injury)

It can sometimes also be helpful to demonstrate that one does not always take things too seriously (unless appropriate to do so), to use humour and to avoid saying or doing things that come across as 'clever' or 'devious' and so get interpreted as attempts to trick or coerce.

Another way of helping someone cope with identity disturbance is to establish whether there is a particular way of being that the person prefers, and then work with them to strengthen that aspect of their psyche. This type of work tends to fall more within the domain of the professional therapist since it requires the existence of a strong therapeutic alliance between client and carer. The therapist needs to maintain a neutral yet supportive position, and such neutrality can be difficult to achieve if one is closely related to the person who self-injures. This type of therapeutic contact tends to be more long-term than short-term, and so we leave further description of it till Chapter 8 where we consider the process of recovery.

TROUBLE WITH UNPREDICTABILITY, DISTRUST, AND DISSOCIATION

People who get diagnosed as having borderline personality disorder can also cause trouble to other people because they have a tendency to dissociate and, when dissociated, can do or think things that are unexpected, sudden and out of character. Even more disconcertingly, they may forget having done these things afterwards, and even deny that they did them.

Dissociation often means danger. There are many stories of it consuming people. Dissociation was once upon a time attributed to divine or diabolical possession. Maenads were women, who were possessed by the god of wine and on the night of the festival dedicated to the Bacchic rites, would reputedly hunt down, and kill men. Berserkers were men whose dissociation in battle led to wanton violence and sometimes to grotesque cruelty. Amok, as in 'running amok', is another example of dissociative violence.

Dissociation has its ordinary side, too, though. 'Being on automatic pilot' is something that many of us experience during tedious and repetitive activity. People 'switch off' in boring situations, and 'blank out' unpleasant memories. Sometimes they can also do this with unpleasant sensations, like pain.

The difference between the alarming and the prosaic dissociation is partly one of degree. The person who is wool gathering can come to if recalled, but the Maenad or the berserker cannot so easily come back to themselves. They are too far gone, as people say. There is also a difference in the extent to which identity is affected. The person who has managed to dissociate from the pain of the dentist drill is not likely to seem like a different person while that is happening. But the person who appears to be in the grip of divine possession is alarming because they are possessed of another character. They do not seem like the same person that they used to be (and might be again). They have, as we would now say, multiple identities. Once we know this about a person – that they can change into someone else – it is difficult for us to fully trust them, particularly if they do something shocking or reprehensible when they are the someone else.

Many people who injure themselves have multiple identities, if only their everyday identity and their hidden identity as a self-injurer. A number of studies, including our own, have found that the more a person dissociates, the more likely their injury is to be severe (e.g. Matsumoto et al., 2005). So a carer of a person who self-injures whilst dissociated may not only have to confront a very different side of their husband or wife, but the evidence that they are capable of extreme and emotionally disturbing violence to themselves. 'How could you do such a thing?' or 'What took over you?' are natural reactions in such circumstances. These questions herald a reassessment of what the carer really knows about the person who injures themselves, and this reassessment may lead to an increased emotional distance and coolness. This may in turn increase the risk of further self-injury if it is experienced as the carer being shamed, angered or disgusted.

Dissociation is one of the consequences of repeated self-injury that weakens other people's trust and can lead to relationship breakdown. But it also places possible obligations on carers if they believe that the self-injurer needs protection from themselves (see below).

In the next chapter we look at ways of dealing with crises and helping someone to cope in the short-term with their distress. It is there that we consider the various methods that mental health professionals may use to help someone reduce their tendency to dissociate and the frequency of their dissociative episodes. These include psycho-educational sessions; exploratory work to discern what triggers dissociative episodes for that particular person; and methods by which client and carer can reach an agreement of the best way to manage flashbacks and other disturbing symptoms.

PROTECTION AND RESPONSIBILITY

Responsibility, safety and sharp objects

Leaving a sharp object in a baby's clothing is irresponsible behaviour by a carer. No responsibility attaches to the baby if the baby is injured by it. The baby does not have the capacity to detect the danger or to deal with the sharp object. But what if a carer discovers that an adult is carrying round a sharp object in their clothing? Perhaps a husband discovers this about his wife, or a staff nurse about one of the patients on the hospital ward. The carer would want to know if the adult knew the sharp was there and if they had the capacity to know how dangerous it was. The carer would probably want to know why the person was carrying a sharp object: perhaps it was going to be used as a weapon, which would be a particular concern of the nurse on the ward.

The adult – let's call her Joan – says that she is feeling increasing tension and she knows that it may soon get to the point that she will only be able to deal with it by cutting herself. She wants to have the reassurance that she has the remedy to hand if it does get to that point. Joan is aware of the anxiety that carrying a razor blade (the sharp object that she has chosen) causes and she tries to be reassuring. *'I'll make sure that I just cut myself the minimum necessary amount'*, she says, *'on a non-vital part. My arm probably. I've wrapped the blade up. So it's nice and clean. I'll do it without you even being aware of it, and I'll be much easier to live with afterwards.'*

Many carers would fail to be reassured completely by Joan's words. One reason is that, for many people, it just doesn't seem right to cut oneself. It seems immoral, or if not immoral then not really decent. We have argued already that this reaction is a consequence of the disgust or horror that is produced when someone overrides the safety-catch by cutting or burning their skin. Perhaps something of this instinctual reaction was evoked in a recent case in which a group of men were found to have inflicted injuries on each other's genitals. They were all adults, had all consented and all said that they had enjoyed this practice, as they were, each of them, turned on sexually by giving and receiving pain. The injury was carried out in private and no record was made for later public consumption. The charge was not assault but an offence against public decency, of which the men were found guilty. The defence argued that the public decency could not have been offended by an act committed completely in private. The judge argued that the public's decency could only be upheld by prohibiting such acts and enforcing that prohibition whenever possible.

A close carer, a spouse or counsellor for example, might also be offended that Joan was keeping the feelings that led to her cutting herself, private. Joan might say that she could see no point in discussing them, but from the carer's point of view it would be as if Joan was keeping herself at a distance, or implying that the carer could not be trusted with her feelings, or both. Self-injury injures the relationship as well as someone's skin.

Joan's intentions might upset the carer even more because of the dilemma that they pose. Should the carer try to stop Joan hurting herself? Obviously in the baby scenario that we considered first, there is no doubt that the carer should take responsibility. But can one adult take responsibility for another? Presumably any carer would try to dissuade Joan, but should the carer take responsibility away from Joan if persuasion fails? For example, would there be a case for forcibly removing the razor blade from Joan, or at least keeping all other sharp objects locked away in future? In practice, it might not be so easy to physically coerce Joan and, in the process, someone may get even more hurt than would have been the case if Joan had injured herself. In a hospital setting some kind of physical confrontation might be easier to manage, however.

We have been considering Joan's intentions assuming she is behaving autonomously. There are, however, certain situations where the person in question is not fully autonomous and in which other people have to take some responsibility for them. This occurs with children and with people who have profound learning difficulties, brain damage or dementia. It may also occur in certain presentations of intoxication, such as a drunken person with a blade in their hand. People who are in prison or who are confined against their will in other forensic settings live in circumstances where they are only partly autonomous. Their full autonomy is denied them and so they are generally expected to take responsibility for their actions while at the same time being under the control of others who ultimately are expected to take responsibility for them.

You'd have to be mad to think that
One argument in favour of control would be that anyone who wanted to injure themselves cannot be in their right mind; that a person not in their right

mind cannot be held to be responsible for their actions; and so, like the baby we already discussed, it becomes someone else's responsibility to protect them. According to this argument, Joan's intention to cut herself with a razor blade if she gets too upset is, in itself, an indication that there is something adrift in her thinking. Since her brain is apparently working normally (she is not intoxicated, does not have brain injury, or a mental handicap and so on), then it must be some kind of mental disorder that is affecting her.

Professional carers like doctors and nurses share the idea that mental disorder can be associated with an increased risk of self-injury or other self-harm. But they have a much more restricted view of what mental disorder is and how it affects people's responsibility for their actions. Mental health professionals are also much less optimistic about the ability of one adult, or even a group of adults, to make another do something for their own good.

Different perspectives and the potential for tragedy

It will have become clear to the reader that the issue of where responsibility for a person's safety lies is often far from straightforward. As we shall see in the next section, the law is not always as helpful as it might be in clarifying the situation. Professionals who care about people who self-injure may – because of their position or because of the position taken by the agency for which they work – be constrained to a different perspective on responsibility and safety than another professional group. Non-professional carers may have yet another viewpoint. Unfortunately, the difference in perspective about responsibility can lead to a breakdown of relations between carers, and sometimes to tragedy. An example that concerns a different type of self-harm (substance inhalation; 'paint sniffing') illustrates such a tragedy. Here is what an Australian mother told a Drug and Crime Prevention Committee inquiry into the inhalation of volatile substances in May 2001 (Drug and Crime Prevention Committee, 2002).

> 'My 16 year old daughter is slowly dying, her memory is fading, her sight, hearing, lungs, kidneys, bone marrow and liver are being damaged. Her blood oxygen is being depleted and this can directly induce heart failure. This can also cause death from suffocation by displacing oxygen in the lungs and then the central nervous system, causing breathing to cease. Her personality has changed. Her system is slowly being poisoned. She buys a can of paint legally from a store, sprays it into a plastic bag and breathes the fumes deeply into her lungs. She doesn't notice the paint stains on her mouth and hands. I do. My beautiful daughter is a 'chromer'.

'The girl I gave birth to 16 years ago is killing herself. And I cannot stop her, help is too far away, hands are tied, this practice is not illegal. I can no longer sit back and allow this practice of our youth to continue.'

'I would like to have it made hard for these children to destroy their lives or kill themselves. As the law stands at the moment it is not illegal for cans of paint to be sold to minors. According to authorities, it is not a drug, BUT she has all the hallmarks of a drug addict, no longer at school, roams the streets day and night, is in trouble with the law, is destroying our family. Everything is locked up so it doesn't 'vanish'. She has no respect for herself, others or their property … I have been on an endless merry-go-round for 18 months trying to find assistance for my daughter …'

MENTAL DISORDER AND RESPONSIBILITY

The legal framework in the UK for dealing with these issues is given by the 1983 Mental Health Act, by legislation about crime and punishment, and by legal judgements based on this legislation which establishes precedents for the particular interpretation and application of the legislation. The Act applies only to people who are suffering from a 'mental disorder'.

How does the UK Mental Health Act define 'mental disorder'?

The legal framework governing both mental disorder and responsibility is surprisingly vague and elastic. The 1983 Mental Health Act defines mental disorder as: (1) mental illness; (2) arrested or incomplete development of mind; (3) psychopathic disorder; and (4) any other disorder or disability of mind. Mental illness is not further defined. Arrested or incomplete development of mind is defined in a Code of Practice published in 1999 to be learning disability (otherwise known as mental handicap) and a necessary criterion is that a person's intelligence is substantially lower than the average. Psychopathic disorder is not otherwise defined, either, except that it must be associated with abnormally aggressive or seriously irresponsible conduct. It is usually taken to mean that a person has a personality disorder.

Psychiatrists, managers and social workers using the Act as well as the Mental Health Act Commissioners who supervise them, expect that patients who are compulsorily detained under the Act will have, or will be reasonably expected to have, evidence that their minds are disordered other than their intention to do something that would upset other people. To ensure this, the Act specifically excludes promiscuity, other immoral conduct, sexual deviancy, or dependence on alcohol or drugs being sufficient evidence of mental disorder on their own. Other evidence of a mental disorder is also required. Most psychiatrists would consider that an intention to injure oneself would be, like other immoral conduct or sexual deviancy, the kind of upsetting and self-damaging action that does not, in itself, constitute sufficient evidence for diagnosis as a mental disorder. So, for example, if Joan had no symptoms of mental illness, mental handicap or personality disorder, but did say that she intended to cut herself with the razor blade in her pocket, she could not compulsorily be detained in hospital to stop her from carrying out her threat.

In fact many psychiatrists would go further than this and consider that even if Joan had a personality disorder or a mild mental illness, they might be reluctant to consider compulsory admission to hospital. This is because, they would argue, Joan can only become more uncontrolled in her self-injury if someone else tries to take responsibility away from her.

Detainment and compulsory treatment
The importance of the Mental Health Act is that it is the only legal procedure to ensure that a person has treatment for a mental disorder without their consent. Suppose Joan is in hospital and telling the staff that she has the razor blade in her pocket, and the staff decide that it must be taken away but Joan refuses. The staff cannot force Joan to give up the blade, as it is not an immediately life-threatening situation, unless Joan is detained under the Mental Health Act, since removing the razor blade is a kind of treatment. So unless Joan meets the criteria for detention and is then detained, she cannot be forcibly prevented from carrying out her threat.

Under what circumstances can the Mental Health Act be applied?
The tests of the Mental Health Act that doctors apply are to determine whether or not someone has a mental disorder and whether they are a danger to themselves or others, or whether their condition is treatable. Arguably a person could fail one or more of these tests and still be responsible for their actions. A person could also not be responsible for their actions, and yet not be suffering from a mental disorder. An example is an 'automatism': an action which is carried out by a person who is unaware of what they are doing.

'Automatisms' include post-hypnotic suggestions, acts during sleep, actions influenced by epilepsy (perictal automatisms) or physical conditions like low blood sugar, actions carried out when people are so drunk that they 'don't know what they are doing' to use the commonsense expression for such situations, as well as dissociative acts. Legally, a person whom a jury accepts to have committed an offence 'automatically' has no intention to commit the crime and so has to be innocent of any of the more serious offences for which a person needs to have the intent to commit a crime ('mens rea'). In practice, automatisms due to a remediable cause 'extrinsic' to the person (like hypoglycaemia in association with a glucagon-secreting tumour) may lead to a complete acquittal. However, automatisms due to something which is considered to be an affection of the mind, including epilepsy, are considered to be 'insane automatisms'. Here, although the person may be innocent of the offence, they are 'not guilty by reason of insanity' and so must be detained in hospital under the Mental Health powers that are granted to judges.

UK law deals with automatisms, including dissociation, as if they render a person unable to be held responsible for their actions. The UK Homicide Act of 1957 introduced a further category of 'diminished responsibility' in homicide cases, and once again the legal definition of responsibility is wider than the scope of the psychiatrist's interpretation of the Mental Health Act: in fact, juries are advised specifically to be guided by, but to be independent of, medical opinion. The jury needs to consider only that the person concerned has an abnormality of mind which substantially impairs the mental responsibility for his or her actions. This might include someone who flies into a rage when told by a spouse of their infidelity, or someone who panics when they think that they are being attacked, and attacks first.

The law would appear to be on the side of the parent who considers responsibility to be fairly easily diminished by emotional turmoil, but psychiatrists typically are much more conservative. No wonder that there can be such confusion!

Should mental health workers take more responsibility for people who self-injure?

The law (ultimately the intuition of the 'man on the Clapham omnibus') and parents agree that people who injure themselves have a kind of compulsion to do so that reduces their responsibility for their actions. Dissociation leads to automatic behaviour, which must be considered as reducing responsibility further.

So should carers – whether parents or professionals or others – take over responsibility? As we have seen, the UK Mental Health Act is quite permissive, and a legal framework exists for people who are at risk of self-injury to be detained. Other countries' legislation is equally permissive. But in practice, professionals restrict their use of the Mental Health Act to people who are suffering from clear-cut mental illness, such as depression (although just to confuse matters, some psychiatrists argue that many people currently diagnosed as having borderline personality disorder do, in fact, have a depressive disorder).

Psychiatrists justify compulsory detention to themselves because in almost all cases they believe that it will benefit the patient (Alexius et al., 2002). They often use, as a test of this, whether or not the patient will recover with treatment and, when recovered, whether they will be glad that they have received treatment. Experience suggests that few people who injure themselves benefit from compulsory admission or are grateful for receiving treatment. In fact, self-injury may increase following detention, and can increase again at the point of discharge from hospital, especially after a lengthy admission. Discharge from a psychiatric inpatient facility is also associated with an increased risk of suicide, and so hospital admission cannot be assumed to be without adverse health consequences.

Those who provide residential care for people who self-injure may need to take account of such issues. We are aware of two examples in the UK where self-injury is tolerated (but not promoted) in an attempt to minimize some of these difficulties. The Crisis Recovery Unit at the Bethlem Royal Hospital, London (to our knowledge the only NHS specialist inpatient facility specializing in treating people who self-injure), does not insist that inpatients stop injuring themselves; and St George's Hospital, Stafford, where adult inpatients are being allowed to keep their blades as part of an investigation into the care of people who self-harm.

There is no useful guideline about compulsory detention, or coercion of any kind, in the treatment people who injure themselves. It is clear, at one end of the spectrum, that a young person who has scratched their arm superficially on a few occasions, and announces that they intend to do so again should not be placed under any kind of external restraint. It is equally clear that, at the other end of the spectrum, a middle-aged woman who has repeatedly been injuring herself over years, whose marriage is breaking down, who is drinking heavily, whose injuries have been becoming increasingly frequent and life-threatening and who says that she intends next time to cut her throat, should be supervised in a place of safety, even if this means compulsory admission to hospital. Restraint can be justified in this situation by the duty to protect another person from imminent harm. In the UK this is covered by 'common law', but there may be specific legislation in other parts of the world. For example, in New South Wales, the Crimes Act of 1900 stipulates in section 574B that '*It shall be lawful for a person to use such force as may reasonably be necessary to prevent the suicide of another person or any act which the person believes on reasonable grounds would, if committed, result in that suicide.*'

But where should the line be drawn between these two extremes? The guidelines on deliberate self-harm produced by psychiatrists in Australia and New Zealand could not reach a conclusion because of a lack of evidence, and it is this lack of evidence that makes the decision so difficult. We think that most mental health professionals with experience in this area would probably agree that the threat of further self-harm is not enough to justify restraint in itself, but that the following are also needed:

- An inability to exercise responsibility through a lack of capacity caused, for example, by mental illness or mental handicap, OR
- A definitely increased risk of suicide, OR
- A definite risk of permanent disfigurement or mutilation

We will consider how to assess these risks in detail in the next chapter.

The car without a driver

It will be clear from what we have written that there will be situations in which a person who self-injures is apparently heedless of the consequences of continuing to do this, and the carers (who are only too aware of the consequences) are not morally or legally justified in taking responsibility. The results can sometimes be fatal. When such a fatality occurs, it seems that someone, somewhere should have done something to prevent it, but this cannot happen because there is a 'responsibility gap'.

The trajectory to tragedy can be very short, sometimes only a few years. Self-injury is a particular problem of young people, and adverse outcomes may develop rapidly. It is a tragedy when a young person loses their life, and almost as much when their life chances seem blighted. But the 'responsibility gap' we have described occurs in many other conditions that are not so emotional. Smoking shortens life, but many people continue to smoke even with that knowledge. The same is true of drinking heavily over a sufficiently long period, over-eating and becoming obese, or driving unsafe vehicles too fast. When pressed, people who do these things first off deny that the consequences apply to them, and, if pressed further, then say that they cannot help themselves, sometimes adding that they are addicted. Neither of these explanations, though, explains other unhealthy behaviour, like eating lots of animal fat, not exercising or taking prescribed medication fitfully. One possible explanation for all of these behaviours is that they make sense when immediate satisfaction takes priority over long-term benefit.

Many factors influence the health choices that young people make. What their parents do and what their peers think are important. But a limiting factor is the young person's sense of their own agency: their potential for acting responsibly. Many people who injure themselves lack, as we have seen, faith in their own agency. They believe that they are the victims of circumstance.

It is not therefore surprising that acting responsibly, which implies a belief in one's capacity as an effective agent to bring out a desired future, is not a goal. Dealing with the responsibility gap means – for many people who injure themselves – dealing with their experience of others as agents or perpetrators, and themselves as passive targets or victims.

AN IMAGINARY ENACTMENT

We conclude with an imaginary dialogue between a mother and her daughter in the hope that it might illustrate some of the issues we have raised in this chapter so far.

'Er … Anna, I found a razor blade in your bag today. What was it there for?'

'Mum, what were you doing looking through my bag? That's private you know.'

'Surely it's OK for a mother to look into her own daughter's bag? After all, it's only right that …'

'You don't seem to realize you can't just run my life any more. If I want to have a razor blade in my bag, that's my business.'

'Anna, I'm sorry. I know I shouldn't have looked into your bag. … But you've been looking so tense, and I was so worried that you might have begun to cut yourself again. … And I was right, wasn't I? You have started again?'

'What if I have? It's no business of anyone except me.'

'That's assuming that when you cut yourself it has no effect on anyone else, Anna.'

'Well, why should it? It's my skin, my blood, my injury. Not yours.'

'That's true, but it's a bit disingenuous to think that when you do it, it has no effect on anyone else. You know I'm a bit squeamish. I could never watch you have injections when you were a kid. When I think of you cutting yourself with a razor blade, well, uurgh, it makes me feel a bit sick.'

'I think that's your problem, Mum, and not mine. Perhaps you need to toughen up a bit.'

'I agree it's my reaction, and not yours, but I don't think it's a problem. I don't like looking at skin with holes and cuts in it. I don't want my skin to be off-putting to other people, and I don't want your skin to look like that, either.'

'That's typical of you, to bring it back to what someone else thinks of me. What about what I think of me? Anyway, who's going to look at my skin … ?'

'Er. … '

'Don't start that whole boy-friend thing again. You've got sex on the brain. I never want to have someone else looking at my body, *let alone* having them touch it. Never.'

'Anna, never is a long time. Perhaps you'll change your mind. Anyway, even though it makes me squirm just thinking about you cutting yourself, that's not really why I get bothered that you do it. What really worries me is that I'm afraid that you'll get dependent on it, and won't be able to stop yourself.'

'Please give me some credit, mother. I'm not stupid. Anyway, what's this 'dependent', anyway? Your generation were so hypocritical. Always against drugs, but doing them anyway. Against sex, but for free love. You used to smoke, what did you call it, 'pot', didn't you? Did you get dependent on it?'

'I didn't, Anna, no. But some did. And free love – that was a big mistake. Love isn't after all like a free sample at the cosmetic counter. But I somehow knew that, even then. I felt that all this liberation could be a trap: more freedom, less liberty, you know.'

'Not really, Mum, I don't. You talk in riddles. Well, that's not fair. I do know a bit what you mean; you're talking about experimentation. Everyone has to do that when they're young. I'm experimenting with my skin, come to that.'

'Let's come back to that, young lady. Do you know what you are doing? What happens to you when you cut yourself? What's the result of the experiment? Why are you messing with your head, I think that's what you call it? Why can't we talk about what's bothering you?'

'God, you're such a nag. So many questions when what you want to do is give me orders. Well, you can't.'

'Anna, I'm not trying to order you to do anything. I know I can't. I know that if I did order you, or try to force you to stop cutting yourself, it would give you a golden excuse to do it more, because you had a controlling mother.'

'Well, that sounded bitter!'

'I'm sorry, Anna. It came out more mean than I wanted. I was trying to express something that's not too easy for me. I know that you are an adult. I know that you are no more and no less a responsible person than I am. I know that however much I want to protect you against yourself, I can't. …'

'Er. … '

'Yes, I know that it's not a question of protecting you against yourself, but of protecting you against what I fear might happen. … And that, of course, ignores you and your own control over your life.

But I can't help thinking that you are stirring something up in yourself that may be very difficult to control. ... '

'Mum. ... '

'I'm sorry, Anna. I keep allowing my own distress to get control of me. What I want to say. ... The most important thing that I want to say ... is that you are not an island. When you choose to deal with your feelings by cutting yourself, you are closing down any possibility of talking them through with someone else. That might, or might not be me. That's not the point. The point for me is that you are becoming more alone, and more out of contact emotionally. And that frightens me, for you and for me. Each time you cut yourself, I wonder why I should make the effort to reach you and each time it's a little harder to do so. What frightens me most is that sooner or later I will give up trying to reach you, and you will no longer know how to reach out to anyone else, because all your feelings will have become closed up by the scars of your old injures.'

Anna starts to cry.

Chapter 7

First Professional Responses to Self-Injury

INTRODUCTION

Self-injury usually comes to professional attention because the person who has injured themselves discloses this, and asks for help. It will therefore be professionals on the front line – counsellors, school nurses or general practitioners – who will be the first to know. It is actually quite rare for someone to seek medical treatment for a recently inflicted wound and so casualty officers are less likely to be the first to know. This is in contrast with self-poisoning which often first comes to attention when a person is taken to hospital for emergency treatment. When a person does need urgent treatment, it is usually because the wound is deep, gaping, infected or otherwise requiring surgical intervention.

This chapter focuses on a range of factors that will need to be considered by a professional on first contact with someone who has self-injured. We consider the importance (and also the limitations) of assessing risk of suicide or serious further self-harm; what can be done to reduce the risk of repetition; when coercion or compulsory detainment may be appropriate; and strategies that can be used to help a self-injuring person who asks for help in averting an imminent crisis. The focus here is on the psychological rather than the physical. The issue of how best to care for the wound itself is dealt with separately at www.reconciliation.org.uk.

A LIMITED EVIDENCE BASE

There have been several recent reviews of how to manage people who harm themselves (National Institute of Clinical Excellence, 2004; Skegg, 2005; Royal College of Psychiatrists, 2004; Kapur, 2005), but they are all disappointingly

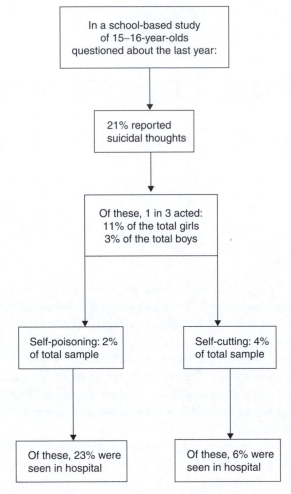

Figure 7.1 Epidemiology of self-harm (from Spender, 2005)

inconclusive. As the authors of one have written: '*The overriding conclusion from this review is that the evidence base for the treatments of self-harm is extremely limited. Most studies are small and tend to recruit fairly specific groups, making generalisation problematic. This is true for most of the studies upon which recommendations are made. Moreover, as a group, people who self-harm are highly heterogeneous, and what works for one subgroup may be useless for another*' (NICE, 2004; p, 177).

The implications of published research which focuses specifically on self-injury are even more meagre, mainly because people rarely seek professional help for their wounds and partly because even if professional help is sought, many people do not get in the ambulance when it comes, or else discharge themselves before they can be assessed in the Casualty department. The published literature is therefore relevant only to the minority of people who stay to be assessed, and sometimes the even smaller minority who are willing to follow advice after assessment. Those that stay to be assessed will mostly be people who have poisoned themselves (see Figure 7.1), and we have had to rely on studies of self-harm in this chapter particularly. In practice this means studies of people who poison themselves with a very small admixture of people who self-injure. We will try wherever we can to extract the lessons for self-injury from this evidence, but this can be difficult.

THE IMPORTANCE OF ASSESSING RISK

Young people who harm themselves are more likely to cut themselves than to take overdoses of medication (see Figure 7.1, taken from Spender, 2005). In comparison with other adolescents, they are more likely to suffer anxiety and depression, to have lower self-esteem, to have friends who self-harm, to have difficulty in coping with problems, to get angry and to have fewer people in whom they can confide. When faced with problems, young people who harm themselves are also more likely – compared to other adolescents – to blame themselves, to shut themselves in their bedroom or to drink. They are also more likely to have concerns about sexuality (if they are girls) or to have experienced physical abuse (if they are boys).[1] Self-injury is likely to be provoked by a recent stress, for example a problem with schoolwork. However, family conflict or a breakdown in the parental relationship often sets the scene by reducing parental well-being and increasing maternal health problems (Sourander et al., 2006).

As we have seen, many young people injure themselves at least once, probably in the context of some degree of social or emotional turmoil. Usually, the actual harm caused is slight and the limited evidence that is available suggests that only a minority of young people will repeat the injury more than a few times. However, there are a small number of first injurers who will go on to serious self-harm which might even be fatal, and another small proportion who will fall into a pattern of repeated self-injury. Some researchers have described this as being a suicidal process in which people get more and more caught up as they repeat their self-injury (Neeleman et al., 2004). This presumes that self-injury is always 'suicidal', which we doubt. But even if there are two or more processes that people get caught up in, caught up they certainly get. Those at risk of getting caught up will need more intervention, and assessing risk will therefore be an important second step in responding to the disclosure or discovery of self-injury.

The balance of risks changes as injury is repeated and as it becomes a regular part of a person's life. Suicide risk increases, and so does the risk of permanent damage as does the likelihood of continuing self-harm. Risk assessment therefore becomes even more important.

STAGES OF RISK ASSESSMENT

We believe there are three discrete components in the process of assessing risk, and that it is important that these are carried out in the order indicated in Text Box 7.1 below.

Text Box 7.1   Risk assessment stages

Step 1 – Creating a relationship
Step 2 – Assessing the risk of future suicide
Step 3 – Assessing the risk of repetition

CREATING A RELATIONSHIP

Conducting a formal risk assessment should not be the first step in a dialogue with a person who has self-injured. Nor indeed should there be focusing on the wound at the expense of focusing on the person. This is because people who injure themselves are highly ambivalent about the impact that their wounds make on others – on the one hand, it is the emotional significance of breaching the safety-catch that makes self-injury emotionally effective; on the other hand, a person who injures themselves feels affronted if their injury is 'seen' but they are not.

It is more important to develop a rapport. This will involve relating to the person like a regular person – without showing inappropriate emotional responses to the wound or to the idea of self-injury – and forms an essential beginning for developing the working relationship. Deciding what is and what is not an appropriate emotional response is not always straightforward, however. It is difficult to generalize since individual circumstances need to be taken into account, but it is worth noting two extremes. Over-reacting is almost always unhelpful; for example, expressing outright disgust at the sight of a self-inflicted wound is easily misinterpreted as expressing disgust for the person who has self-injured, and does little to help develop a rapport. Extreme under-reacting can also be inappropriate as this can easily be interpreted as a cold and rejecting response. A sensible balance will need to be struck between acknowledging the person, acknowledging the wound(s) and acknowledging one's own reactions to both.

Developing a sound working relationship is important because many people who injure themselves expect to be shamed or shunned if their self-injury comes to light, and will already be predisposed to withdraw from contact. This can occur when self-injury is not openly disclosed but is accidentally revealed as, for example, when a sleeve rides up to uncover a scarred forearm. In such situations, a calm non-judgemental approach that invites further discussion is more likely to lead to development of a sound working alliance than is direct questioning about the origins of the scars, or about how often the person self-injures. It is also important not to over-react to other aspects of appearance, and carers should not be put off by piercings, studs or tattoos which many people who injure themselves will have. These are the marks of violence, but it is often helpful to see them as violence at the expense of the person themselves with, perhaps, a corresponding reduction in violence to others. Many people who injure themselves will also be particularly sensitive to any kind of pressure or coercion. So a gentle approach will be important, too.

ASSESSING RISK OF FUTURE SUICIDE

Once a rapport is established, certain specific pieces of information need to be gathered if an attempt is to be made to assess the risk of future suicide. Some of this information may already be known, and the missing details can be obtained by sensitive questioning of the person who has self-injured or, in some cases, from a carer who accompanies them.

Whether or not someone kills themselves depends on their openness to death as a solution to problems in life; on psychological and social risk factors; and on transient factors that may push someone over the edge or pull them back. Not surprisingly, the assessment of risk requires a high degree of clinical judgement. Even when such risk assessment is carried out diligently by experienced staff, the relationship with outcome can be poor. Having said this, there is a fair consensus about the factors that contribute to risk. We show a recent summary of these in the Text Box 7.2 below, and awareness of these will help to formulate some of the questions that may need to be asked.

Text Box 7.2   Risk factors for suicide after self-harm
(adapted from Skegg, 2005)

Male sex, older age, previous psychiatric care, psychiatric disorder, socially isolated, repetition of self-harm, hopelessness, attempt made to avoid discovery at the time of self-harm, medically severe self-harm, strong suicidal intent, substance misuse, poor physical health.

We shall consider some of these factors in more detail, including a history of self-harm, the nature of the injury itself, previous patterns of self-injury, the reactions of others, suicidal intent, hopelessness and social factors.

PREDICTORS OF FUTURE SUICIDE

Previous self-harm

It is important to remain aware that there is a substantially increased risk of suicide when a person has harmed themselves at least once. Following one recent systematic review, approximately 15% of men or women who had attended hospital at least once for treatment of self-harm attended again for a similar reason within the year, and somewhere between 0.5% and 2% had completed suicide within the year. With increasing years of follow-up, up to a quarter repeat and it is estimated that up to 5% actually kill themselves (Owens et al., 2002). The longer the follow-up, the greater the cumulative risk of suicide with an increased risk being evident even 37 years after the original episode of self-harm in one study (Suominen et al., 2004b). The risk estimates given here are based on self-harm and so may be an unreliable guide to the risk of suicide following one or a few episodes of self-injury. They may however be a better guide to the risk in that minority of self-injurers who present for treatment to a hospital, or in those who both injure and poison themselves; both these groups are likely to contain significant numbers of people who self-injure repeatedly.

The injury itself

The perceived lethality of a suicide attempt is an indication of how much a person was aiming for death. In one 2-year follow-up, the intent to kill oneself in a suicide attempt was a predictor of completed suicide in the future (Brown et al., 2000). However, only a proportion of people who injure themselves have an accurate expectation of the consequences of a particular injury, and so gauging intent by the objective dangerousness of the injury may be unreliable.

For example, a client may present with superficial cuts to a vulnerable area having made such wounds in the belief that the outcome would be fatal once blood had started to flow. Trained medical staff do not automatically assume that bleeding from a cut to the wrist is imminently fatal without first inspecting to see if a major vessel has been severed, whereas it is not unusual for untrained person to assume this is the case – especially the younger person.

Culture may influence the choice of method. For example, in Lithuania almost two-thirds of adolescents think that a person should be free to choose whether to live or to die (Zemaitiene & Zaborskis, 2005), and the most common method of self-injury is by hanging. In India and Sri Lanka, self-immolation (committing suicide by setting fire to oneself) is more common than anywhere else in the world (Laloe, 2004) possibly reflecting the significance of fire to Hindus and the now outlawed former practice of suttee (an old funeral custom in which the dead man's widow burns herself to death on her husband's funeral pyre). Burns account for 20% of UK suicides in Indian women (Raleigh, 1996), and are particularly dangerous because of the use of accelerants such as petrol (gasoline). Indeed, 44% of people who had set fire to themselves and were admitted to a burns unit in the UK Midlands eventually died (Rashid & Gowar, 2004). In some parts of India as well as in China and other rural areas where agrichemicals are more widely available, swallowing herbicides or pesticides can be the most common means of self-harm (Yang et al., 2005). This is frequently fatal, even though the precipitants of the self-harm (breakdown of a relationship or family difficulties) are no different from those that lead to an overdose of drugs in the UK, which is rarely fatal.

The surgical risk of a self-inflicted injury should not be used on its own as an indication of suicide intent, and therefore of the risk of a future suicide attempt. However, a potentially fatal wound should always raise the possibility that the aim was not to injure, but to die. Sites that are used for suicide are the throat, the chest, the inside of the wrist and the abdomen. Penetrating injures to the chest or the abdomen are also an indication of a wish to die. The depth of the wound may also be important, particular in someone who has never or only rarely injured themselves previously. However, depth can be an unreliable indicator and, as we have already observed, relatively superficial wounds may have been made in the mistaken belief that they were potentially fatal and as a genuine suicide attempt.

Self-injury patterns and others' reactions

When self-harm comes to attention, it influences significant others. Self-poisoning, as we have seen, usually comes to attention, but self-injury is usually concealed. Research on self-harm has often concentrated on the kind that comes to attention, and that is usually self-poisoning. This research has suggested that self-harm is motivated by trying to change relationships with other people, and that a person becomes hopeless only when this seems impossible (Williams, 1986). Hopelessness, and therefore suicide risk, increases when a person feels that the people who they are close to (or who they seek to be close to) finally reject or abandon them. Although this may also be a factor in self-injury, the motive of concealed self-injury – the commonest kind – cannot be to influence others, since others often do not know about it. Rather, it is aimed at altering how the person who self-injures feels.

In our experience a pattern of repeated self-injury in which the time between injuries shortens progressively – and sometimes in which successive wounds are deeper or more dangerous – is a particular indication of hopelessness, since it indicates that each wound has not had the intended effect of putting right the distress that led to it. Sometimes this crescendo of distress is accompanied by a kind of emotional numbing on the part of carers. The phrase 'burned out' is sometimes used in this context to imply that they have come to feel drained of compassion and weary of attempting to respond empathically to the person who repeatedly self-injures in this way. Perhaps they, too, become hopeless. This numbing may mean that the person who self-injures feels that even if they did seek help from a carer, it would not be forthcoming.

Many people who repeatedly injure themselves also poison themselves. Death more commonly results from the latter because the immediate motive for death is, in our experience, more often reckless and angry unconcern for oneself rather than the deliberated, designedly fatal act. Very few professionals now repeat the adage that was common, say, thirty years ago that 'people who talk about suicide don't do it'. It remains true that there are a great many people who talk about suicide who do not go on to kill themselves, but whether or not someone talks about it is not a predictor of later completion. However, it is equally untrue that adolescents who cut themselves superficially do not kill themselves. Many adolescents who injure themselves do so, as we have seen, once or only a few times, and their wounds are rarely life threatening. But a small proportion of these adolescents continue to injure themselves, often in association with other acts of self-harm, and as the injuries become repeated the wounds tend to become deeper and to have more lasting surgical consequences. This group is at high risk of suicide.

Hopelessness

The determination to kill oneself has been found to be the single most powerful predictor of eventual suicide in some studies but not in all (Suominen et al., 2004a, b). One reason for the variation is that intent is not always easy to judge.

A person's intentions may change, or they may conceal them. Other, indirect measures may therefore be more useful. One of these is hopelessness. Hopelessness is a predictor of suicide mortality both in the short and the long term. The Beck Hopelessness Scale (Harcourt Assessment, 2006) has been found to be a reliable measure still predictive of suicide even after 20 years (Brown et al., 2000). The 4 items from the scale listed in Text Box 7.3 below seem to be almost as good as the total scale (Yip & Cheung, 2006), with the single item 'My future seems dark to me' being the most predictive single item.

Text Box 7.3   Predictors of hopelessness from Beck Hopelessness Scale (adapted from Yip & Cheung, 2006)

- Item 6: In the future I expect to succeed in what concerns me most (negatively correlated)
- Item 7: My future seems dark to me
- Item 9: I just don't get the breaks and there is no reason to believe I will in the future
- Item 15: I have great faith in the future (negatively correlated)

Psychological disorder

There is a substantially increased risk of suicide in anyone with a mental illness; addictions (including dependence on alcohol or drugs, eating disorders and even repeated self-injury); or a physical illness associated with chronic pain or discomfort. The risk is not confined to people suffering from a depressive disorder although depressed mood may be the final common pathway leading to suicide (De Leo et al., 1999) since it is characteristically associated with hopelessness. Depression and some other mental illnesses are also associated with thoughts about death – and with sleep disturbance – each of which independently adds to the risk.

Mitchell and Dennis (Mitchell & Dennis, 2006) – in a very practical and useful brief review for the casualty officer or general practitioner – note that the current UK national guidelines indicate that every person seen urgently after an act of self-harm should be assessed by a psychiatrist or trained mental health worker (NICE, 2004), but that that the Royal College of Psychiatrists and others have argued that this is not practicable, at least not in the UK (Royal College of Psychiatrists, 2004). Michell and Dennis recommend that every patient be questioned about 5 areas (see Text Box 7.4), including questions about mental illness. They also suggest that at the end of the interview, the assessor should plan what action is to be taken collaboratively with the patient, and in our experience this may reveal previously undisclosed psychosocial information relevant to suicide assessment. According to Mitchell and Dennis, risk assessment tools are unreliable and do not add to this clinical assessment.

Text box 7.4   Screening for suicide risk
(adapted from Mitchell & Dennis, 2006)

- A careful history of the events surrounding the self harm attempt, concentrating on factors that indicate significant intent
- Symptoms indicating previous mental health problems (including previous self-harm)
- Harmful use of alcohol or illicit drugs
- Social circumstances and problems (Are family sympathetic and can they be recruited to help? Are difficulties likely to improve or worsen after self-harm?)
- A forensic history and a mental state examination, paying particular attention to symptoms of depression, current suicidal thoughts and plans or intent to self-harm again

---

One perceived benefit of suicide for many people (unless they have a conviction of eternal torment or punishment in an after-life) is the relief of suffering and escape from emotional pain. However, escape always results in loss and very often the transfer of one's own suffering to others.

The balance between escape and loss

An influential view of suicide, which can be traced back to the French sociologist Durkheim whose book was first published in 1896 (Durkheim, 1970), is that the risk of suicide increases when a condition of anomie or 'lawlessness' supervenes. Anomie occurs at times of personal or social change or transition, when the chances of loss increase. This loss is not just of material goods, nor just of family and friends, but also loss of certainty and security, loss of mastery, loss of expectations, loss of faith, as well as pre-eminently loss of the connection between personal effort and social reward. This is a concept similar to what Janoff-Bulman calls the loss of a sense of a 'just world' (Durkheim, 1970; Janoff-Bulman, 1992). Suicide increases because the balance between escape and loss changes. When there is less and less to lose, only a small impulse to escape may be enough to make suicide seem preferable to drifting on in life. This kind of suicide – which we will call 'anomic suicide' – is often associated with social isolation, which we discuss below. It is the paradigm that most often fits the elderly or the exhausted, and also the socially excluded younger person. It does not fit so well with suicide as a complication or alternative of self-injury.

Suicide in self-injury is often described as impulsive. Impulsivity is often cited as being increased in both borderline personality disorder and in substance misuse, but it promises more as an explanation than it delivers. Although some would like to consider it a biologically determined trait, the evidence is that it is strongly influenced by life experience (it is strongly linked to feeling uncared for and uncaring) and is not just one trait but several (Bornovalova et al., 2005). Another way of looking at this kind of suicide – which we will call 'escape suicide' – is that, although the person has a lot to lose, the desire to escape is so great that the threat of loss is not enough to offset it.

Emotional states

What would be so intense that a person would want to kill themselves to escape from it, if there was no other way? There is no word that sums all of them up, but we will use the word 'anguish' as the best descriptor because, we think, anguish is a 'hot' kind of pain. It is a kind of mental suffering which will not let us rest because it has such a strong admixture of anxiety, worry and rumination. If we can compare it with pain, anguish is like the kind of pain that makes use squirm or contort (renal colic for example). It is different from the kind of pain, such as that of peritonitis or migraine, which makes us want to lie as still and as quietly as possible.

Emotional states that lead to anguish include extreme fear (the tortured prisoner might be an example); the admixture of anxiety and depression that used to be called agitated depression; post-traumatic stress; anger or hate which is stifled because there is no action which can assuage it; and shame.

The reader will recognize these from Chapter 3 as being very similar emotions to those associated with self-injury. This reinforces the point that we have already made in this chapter, that self-injury which becomes repetitious because it does not succeed in reducing dysphoria can lead on to suicide in a significant minority. Shame might be particularly important here since it is a link between abuse and bullying, both of which may be associated with suicide in young people.

It is important to note that our discussion of the prediction of suicide has been influenced by our experience of working within the UK and its culture. The UK has an increasingly multi-cultural and multi-ethnic society, but our remarks, and the evidence we cite, is strongly influenced by the European culture that continues to dominate in the UK. There is some evidence that the relative importance of the factors that we have been considering might differ between ethnic groups and this should be taken into account (Gutierrez et al., 2001).

Social factors

'Anomic suicide' (which Durkheim saw as linked to a loss of standards and values in society) is associated with social isolation which may follow from social exclusion, migration, institutionalization, or the death of family and friends. Anomic suicide is a lonely event, but the kind of 'escape suicide' that is most associated with a history of self-injury often, in contrast, occurs when a person has a high level of social contact. Suicide in people who were admitted to hospital most often occurs in people who are away from the hospital, on leave or who have been recently discharged – and who therefore find themselves alone and socially isolated. People who kill themselves on the hospital ward, in the midst of other people, are more likely to have a history of self-harm (Dong et al., 2005) and to fall into the 'escape suicide' group.

Social contact in itself does not therefore protect against suicide in the 'escape suicide' group, which includes people who have previously injured themselves. What matters for them is the quality of social contact. Our own experience parallels that of colleagues working as family therapists with young people who have repeatedly self-injured. Like them we have the experience that even when the contact and emotional involvement of the family increased, the young person actually began to cut even more and, in some cases, went on to kill themselves. In retrospect, the family therapy had sometimes led to disclosures that changed the family irreversibly and led to an increase in shame, or to blaming the patient for forcing this situation into the open. On other occasions, the parents had explicitly rejected the young person, either saying that they were fed up with them and no longer willing be involved, or going further and saying that they had never really liked them. One patient to whom this happened was on a shopping trip with friends to buy Christmas presents (it was Christmas Eve) and without warning ran into the road in front of a car which could not stop in time.

Social rejection in young people may also increase the risk of suicide and also self-injury. Young offenders remanded in custody are at particularly high risk, since in them anguish may occur alongside being placed in close social contact with unsympathetic or even abusive fellow-inmates or staff (Morgan & Hawton, 2004).

PREDICTORS OF REPETITION

Factors predicting repeated self-harm and suicide

The single best predictor of repetition is the number of previous acts of self-harm (Gilbody et al., 1997), whether by self-injury, self-poisoning or other self-harm. However, predictors of repeated self-harm and predictors of suicide are sometimes differentiated, as if what causes suicide is different from what causes a person to harm themselves. This is true if the contrast is made with anomic suicide, but not with escape suicide. The factors that lead to a person escaping into death are qualitatively no different from the factors that may lead a person to self-injure.

Text Box 7.5   Commonly listed predictors of repeated self harm
(adapted from Colman et al., 2004)

unemployment, previous sexual abuse, alcohol or drug abuse, hopelessness, antisocial personality, previous psychiatric treatment (especially if depression or schizophrenia)

The predictors shown in Text Box 7.5 are non-specific and although each is cited in more than one study, there is no study in which all are cited. One reason for this is, as the NICE guidelines that we quoted indicate, that the motives for repeating self-harm differ so much from person to person.

A more useful approach is to remind ourselves that a person self-harms for a purpose (as we have seen, this is especially true of self-injury) and the self-harm is likely to be repeated until that purpose is either served or replaced. Often, the purpose is to relieve feelings, improve a bad social situation or relationship, or both. Cedereke and Ojehagen (2005) have provided a set of risk factors that capture this underlying dimension that we find more clinically relevant (see Text Box 7.6).

Text Box 7.6   Psychological risk factors for the repetition[2] of self-harm (adapted from Cedereke & Ojehagen, 2005)

- Lower level of psychosocial functioning and less improvement over follow-up period
- Higher suicidal intention which is more sustained over follow-up period
- Greater need which fails to be met over follow-up period

Younger age

Our clinical experience is that age is also a factor. Self-injury is principally something that young people do. We are aware that children under 12 rarely injure themselves deliberately (although they may headbang and intentionally harm themselves in other ways), and that people who repeatedly injure themselves often give up doing so when in their twenties and thirties.

One way of understanding this is that repeated self-injury is a kind of self-healing, but one that only works during a particular phase of adolescence and adulthood. Perhaps, one could speculate, it is the phase when appearance and skin care are at their most important and, if so, it will be interesting to see if the growing market in skin preparations for the middle-aged will lead to an extension of self-injury into that age group.

Another way of looking at this same phenomenon is that self-injury is a symptom of a time-limited psychiatric disorder, one that often begins in early adolescence and remits spontaneously in middle age. Borderline personality disorder, although originally thought to be a life-long condition, actually behaves more like an episode of disorder which does occur most commonly in this developmental phase. Some have even argued that borderline personality disorder is not a disorder at all, but an episode of depression, albeit one that lasts for an unusually long time and one that is unusually refractive of the customary treatments for depression.

A third way of looking at the situation is that self-injury is a means of establishing an identity against resistance from other people. The risk period for self-injury is explained by that being the period when a person has to do most to claim an identity. As a child, it is almost inescapable that one accepts the identities associated with being a child that are conferred by society. Later in life, there are usually welcome identities that carry status, like being a father or an expert at something or a skilled worker, which can be accepted without personal diminishment.

We think that each of these perspectives is valid, but the one that dominates the published literature is the perspective of the health professional – that is, that of self-injury as a symptom of a disorder. The following section may therefore put off some of our readers who will consider us to have pathologized people who injure themselves, as if we are assuming that every self-inflicted injury is an expression of a disease, almost as though it was caused by some kind of parasite that broke through the skin on a regular basis. We apologize for this. We have concentrated on a medical perspective because, as we have written above, there is little information available otherwise. We are also influenced by the concerns of the likely readers of this chapter. A person who injures themselves might think, 'will I have to do that again because of the things that other people make me feel?' and not 'will I find myself having to do that again because I cannot help myself?' The notion of repetition that needs predicting does not apply to the first question, since it is what other people do that determines whether or not one has to injure oneself. So the people who read this section of the chapter with attention are likely to be those who are already thinking of repetition as the symptom of some persisting disorder.

Despite this, we think that there is something for everyone in this section. We believe that few people who injure themselves repeatedly and in secret regard it as an affirmation of themselves. It is more likely to be considered to be the only defence against what other people do, and it is the only defence because nothing else seems to work. Having only one choice of action – and that a destructive one – is a trap; this trap is set, however inadvertently, by other people. Even though the repetition literature is written from the disorder perspective, it does give lots of useful information about how a person gets trapped into having to injure again.

Addiction to self-injury

An additional factor comes into to play when injury is repeated for a sufficient length of time that it becomes an end in itself. The more a person injures themselves, the more likely they are to reach this point and to have become addicted to self-injury. By that we mean that self-injury becomes more than a means of dealing with the tension of perceived rejection, hostility or abandonment by other people; it becomes a craving which generates a new, inner tension. Once this craving develops, the chance of repetition increases considerably. Craving can be enquired about directly, but it may be hard for someone to distinguish craving from the kind of inner tension associated with their 'spring' getting wound-up.

A more useful indirect measure might be how often a person experiences 'switching' into self-injury. A direct question about this might be, 'Do you ever become suddenly aware that you have cut yourself (or whatever kind of injury is relevant) without having planned to do so?' or, alternatively, 'Have you ever had the experience of trying to do one shallow cut (or maybe a few shallow ones) and then suddenly finding you've done a big one that was much deeper than you intended?'

Craving is often associated with the development of other dissociative symptoms and it may therefore be worth asking a person specifically about these. One way of doing this is to make use of a questionnaire such as the Dissociative Experiences Scale (Bernstein & Putnam, 1986). This is normally completed by the person in their own time as a pencil-and-paper exercise, but it can sometimes be more valuable to use the scale as the basis for a semi-structured interview with the clinician reading out each question in turn.

The capacity for dissociation may be linked to the likelihood of developing a craving for self-injury. 'Dissociability' may run in families and so it is worth asking about a family history of dissociation, and a family history of repeated self-harm. Both are associated with an increased risk of repetition. Dissociability is also increased by a childhood history of abuse or neglect (Brodsky et al., 1995; Chu et al., 1999; Draijer & Langeland, 1999) and an assessment of both childhood family experience and current close relationships should be undertaken as part of an assessment of repetition.

WHAT CAN PROFESSIONALS DO TO REDUCE RISK?

We will spend the rest of this chapter considering what health professionals might do in an attempt to reduce the risk of self-injury being repeated, and to reduce the risk of suicide after an episode of self-injury. We begin by examining the predictive factors that emerged in one large study of self-harm in young people. Sourander and others followed up a random sample of all the children born following an antenatal clinic attendance in one region of Finland sometime during 1986 (Sourander et al., 2006). There were 1287 children who were potentially includable, all of whom were assessed at the age of three, 907 at age twelve, and 839 at age fifteen. At age twelve, 10 boys and 5 girls reported that they had harmed themselves, although this was not known to their parents. At age fifteen, 44 girls reported harming themselves, and 10 boys. Ten parents knew about their children having harmed themselves, which implies that three quarters of the fifteen year olds who had self-harmed had parents who did NOT know that their children had done so.

As we have noted from other studies, Sourander et al. found that the small number of children who had harmed themselves (or had thought of doing so) by age twelve were more likely than the other children to harm themselves again by age fifteen. The strongest single predictor was a mother's report of her own poor health at age twelve. Other predictive factors at age twelve of self-harm by age fifteen were being a girl, living in a broken family, having somatic problems, having worries, (on parents' report) being aggressive and having problems getting on with other people. Young people aged fifteen who had thoughts of suicide were more likely to have learning difficulties, and to be or have been bullied at school (see Text Box 7.7). Another important risk factor for self-harm in youngsters is awareness of peers who have self-harmed – as identified in a school-based study of fifteen-to sixteen-year-olds in England (Hawton et al., 2002).

Could these factors be used to predict children at risk, and would an intervention at age twelve prevent self-harm at age fifteen? One problem of prediction is that so many people would have to be screened to detect the children at risk. If we consider one of the most strongest predictors – mothers' self-reported health – and want to be sure of helping a child who would go on to harm themselves, four children would have to receive the intervention, and 97 mothers would have to be screened.

A combination of all of the relevant factors might be sufficiently specific to alert a counsellor or primary care practitioners to a future difficulty if a young person attends to see them, but it does not seem practicable to undertake a screening programme.

Text Box 7.7   Learning point – bullying
Children who are bullied, who have learning problems, who live with a mother who has had health problems – especially when these have followed a family breakdown – and in whom these have led to aggressiveness, worries about health as well as problems getting on with people are at particular risk. If a child goes to a counsellor with this combination of problems, it would be appropriate for the counsellor to consider this possibility.

There is a further problem. What intervention would reduce the risk? There has been no specific study of this, but many reviews of interventions to prevent repetition. If there is an intervention that reduces the risk after an episode, this might give some clue about an effective intervention for primary prevention. So we will consider this evidence first.

Two recent systematic reviews conducted by the British Psychological Society with the UK Royal College of Psychiatrists and the Royal Australian and New Zealand College of Psychiatrists have been unable to find any conclusive evidence of the effectiveness of any psychological, psychosocial or pharmacological intervention. There is some suggestive evidence of the effectiveness of dialectical behaviour therapy in people who harm themselves and dissociate a lot; of group therapy in young adolescents; and a single and unreplicated finding of the value of the antipsychotic, flupenthixol. The UK group came to the conclusions that '... *at the present time, there was insufficient evidence to support any recommendation for interventions specifically designed for people who self-harm*' and '... *that referral for further treatment after an act of self-harm should be determined by the overall needs of the service user, rather than by the fact that they have self-harmed per se*' (Anon, 2004).

CLINICAL IMPLICATIONS WHERE HELP IS NOT DIRECTLY SOUGHT

Not everyone who has injured themselves needs professional attention, but some will. There are two ways to ensure that a person who needs attention does, in fact, receive it. They can be pressurized by third parties, or the person concerned can make their own judgement about whether or not they should seek help or advice.

Private self-injury is often experienced by carers as a hostile or disruptive act, and there may be some justification for this. But it is unfortunate that care often ends up being foisted on people who injure themselves, rather than being available when it is needed. Wherever possible this adversarial relationship should be avoided – although too often this does not happen, and professional carers particularly may be angry or frightened by self-injury, and at times even welcome conflict with the self-injurer. It is important to remember that many people who poison themselves become stuporose or comatose. They are, effectively, throwing themselves at the mercy of others because they are too intoxicated to be competent to make decisions of their own. This is not true of a person who self-injures. Such a person may need surgical treatment, but is nonetheless competent to choose the kind of treatment that he or she wishes to receive. In fact, a person who repeatedly self-injures is often very knowledgeable about the most effective way to manage his or her injuries, and will sometimes have a greater experience of caring for complex or infected wounds than the professional who is charged with providing it.

Most societies agree that it is right to restrain someone from doing something that will bring about their death. Indeed many societies would recognize a common law duty to do so. Most societies would probably agree that it is right to restrain someone who intends to kill themselves and is very likely to do so within some finite time, so long that is believed that their mind is in some way impaired or in disarray. It is less clear, however, what constitutes disarray. It is also unclear whether the duty to prevent suicide would extend to a duty to prevent deformity or illness brought about by self-injury.

Coercive treatment has several side effects that are rarely discussed. One, which the Italian democratic psychiatrist Bassaglia thought made all compulsory treatment unethical, is that some treatments may be considered by their recipients to be a kind of violence, and that this in itself might increase the risk of them becoming violent in reaction. Bassaglia thought that compulsory detention, electro-convulsive therapy, long lasting or depot medication that is injected as well as psychosurgery were all violent treatments. Coercive treatment may also put people off seeking treatment in the future, and thus reduce their uptake of care or assistance in the long run. Finally, coercion may be experienced as a kind of abuse, and may itself perpetuate the need to injure oneself to reduce feelings of shame, impotent anger or abandonment.

Forceful management of people who injure themselves can be in the opposite direction, too. Doctors and nurses may sometimes argue against people receiving services, including hospital admission, which are requested by the person who has self-injured. The reason may be that the person is assumed to be seeking the service for a non-therapeutic reason, or the person may be mistaken in thinking that the treatment will help them.

Someone asking for help which seems inappropriate, like someone refusing help that seems essential, should, we think, be the starting point for a negotiation in which the professional should respect the genuineness and thoughtfulness of the other party or parties. Professionals engaged in working with people with self-injury need to develop these negotiating skills. They also need to develop skills at conflict management so as to reduce the hostility that may sometimes block negotiated solutions.

When is coercion justified?
Sometimes coercive treatment is justified to save the life of someone who would irrationally destroy it and arguably to prevent deformity in someone who is irrationally willing to create it. However, we think that it is necessary to show that a person is irrational. Just assuming that they are is not enough. Independent evidence of severe depression or other mental illness is sufficient for this. But we do not think that the presence of personality disorder is of itself.

A clear expression of a determined suicidal intent, in the absence of mental illness, presents one of the most difficult challenges. We think that if a person is thought to be at serious risk (which will not be true of everyone who says that they intend to kill themselves) then an independent assessment by two experienced clinicians should be carried out. If a period of detention is required to enable that assessment to take place, then a very strong argument can be made that there is adequate justification. Hopelessness and social isolation should be considered to be particularly important contributors to the overall risk of suicide in this situation.

Responding to high risk
Suicide in the short-term is only one of the risks, and probably not the most important one, that should be considered in assessing someone after an episode of self-injury. In principle, it is possible to separate out the risk of developing other psychiatric problems, the risk of repetition and the risk of suicide. However, in reality the risks of all of these – with the exception of anomic suicide associated with depression and hopelessness outlined in the previous section – are all linked to the same high risk factors that we have already considered. As we noted in that section, no scale or statistical combination of these factors can replace a clinical assessment, but the absence of any of the risk factors can usually be considered to indicate low risk.

'High risk' is a clinical concept, with the implication that people at high risk need treatment to reduce that risk. From the point of view of the person who self-injures, reserving the option of injuring themselves again in the future may not be something that they wish to give up. 'Treatment' of this may not be something that they want to consider.

There are two circumstances in which a person may be much more ready to see themselves in need of help: when repeated self-injury has become an end in itself, and when self-injury has started to seem like an unattractive or ineffective way of dealing with dysphoria and the person is seeking some other means of dealing with the problem.

Unfortunately, those at highest risk of repeating self-injury often tell themselves that they are not. The last episode, they prefer to think, was the last one. Perhaps social circumstances have changed, perhaps a close friend or family member has become less hostile and more kind, or perhaps the feeling of relief coupled with the embarrassment of medical care has been enough to set the person thinking that not only should they turn over a new leaf, but they have done so.

Keeping a life-line open

Many of the people, usually young people, who have harmed themselves are likely to find that enough has changed in their world that there will be no immediate wish to harm again (although, as we have seen, the disposition to cope by turning towards death or harm may reassert itself many years later). A significant minority will, however, find that there has been no deep change, and that the same problems and the same feelings reassert themselves days, weeks or months later.

Many of the interventions that have been developed to help people who self-harm have been developed to provide a lifeline back to treatment when the thoughts of self-harm resurface. They range from an appointment at a routine clinic (which is rarely attended), a referral back to the general practitioner or to primary care, a follow-up letter or phone call asking people how they are getting on, or a card that a person can carry (in the UK often called a 'green card') which gives the phone number of who to call if this happens. The green card scheme has, of course, to be linked with the provision of a suitable professional on the other end of the phone who can respond, and so has often been linked to the development of a specialized 'suicide prevention' service. A professional can give their contact details more informally to be used in an emergency even without a specialized service, but the turnover of the junior medical staff who usually deal with people who harm themselves and who are often in a training post, is so swift that the contact details become quickly out of date, and therefore unusable. The turnover of nursing staff working in some mental health services can also be significant, which leads to a similar difficulty.

None of these measures has been shown to be more effective than standard care (which often amounts to no after-care at all for this group) in an unselected group of people who self-harm. This should not put off professionals or other carers from negotiating an after-care plan with elements that match the needs of an individual patient. The best plans will often be those that use a wide range of potential carers across several disciplines: examples include practice, school or college counsellors; general practitioners and paediatricians; members of child and adolescent mental health services or of community mental health teams; befrienders or support workers; and where appropriate family members with whom contact can be maintained in family support sessions. None of these interventions should be prescribed, only offered. However, their appropriateness, and the confidence in them that the professional has, will influence whether or not they are taken up.

WHAT IS THE APPROPRIATE PROFESSIONAL RESPONSE WHEN SOMEONE WHO SELF-INJURES ASKS FOR HELP?

This is an important question that we will address by considering three contrasting presentations. We find it useful to consider each separately, although it will be clear that people do not always fit neatly into one of these three categories.

The first type of presentation arises when someone feels overwhelmed by emotion and has an intense urge to cut or burn their skin, but wants to avoid doing so. The sufferer seeks an immediate alternative solution, but usually acknowledges that this will not be a permanent one. This situation, where help is sought in the hope of circumventing a crisis, is addressed in the following paragraphs. We believe that the most relevant response is to explore a range of pragmatic coping strategies, and then to work collaboratively to identify those which the person is comfortable using and which seem effective in the short-term. The key aim is for the sufferer to assemble their selected strategies into a repertoire that will then be available whenever the urge to self-injure recurs.

The second type of presentation is one where a person has decided that he or she wants to break away from self-injury as a preferred means of coping. Someone who feels this way may be able to take a longer-term view of their circumstances. There is some acknowledgment that there will continue to be times when difficult emotions must be tolerated, but that it may be possible to manage them without resorting to self-harm. Arranging for a series of sessions with a counsellor, psychologist or psychotherapist, either individually or in a group setting, might be an appropriate response under these circumstances.

The third type of presentation occurs where someone asks for help with his or her underlying problems, but does not see relinquishment of self-injury as the first priority. There may be a strong need to hold onto the behaviour as a means of coping, even to the point at which this is a firmly held conviction. Someone who feels this way often seems to have a clear view of the order in which the elements of their progress should occur. He or she may say they would like to sort out other more important problems first, and then give up self-injury later. Here again there are advantages in engaging with a trained therapist, although the focus of the therapeutic work is likely to be different from the previous presentation.

SHORT-TERM INTERVENTIONS AIMED AT AVERTING A CRISIS

The value of a portfolio of coping strategies

Although people who self-injure are usually secretive about what they do to themselves, some are able to ask others directly for help when they sense the urge to self-harm growing inside them. In short, they anticipate a crisis and seek assistance in avoiding it. Deciding how best to react to such a request is a real difficulty for many carers – including those who have professional training – partly because there is little hard evidence about what works for whom in the short term, and partly because most people who self-injure will say they have already tried everything and found that nothing works.

In fact, our clinical experience suggests that many of those who repeatedly self-injure have come to the conclusion that once emotions start building and the thought of self-harm seeds itself, a self-inflicted wound as the end result is a foregone conclusion. Some would even say that the most that can be achieved is a delay of the inevitable. They may think: '*OK, so I try hard and maybe I cut my arm tomorrow rather than today – but I'll still end up cutting my arm. Is it really worth putting in the effort?*'.

Many therapists would be keen to point out that such thinking is evidence of a type of cognitive distortion commonly seen in those who self-injure, and one that is certain to help maintain a cycle of self-harm in response to bad feelings. We agree with this notion, but are also aware that such comments are not often experienced as helpful by a person who is finding it hard to focus on anything besides their current distress and the anticipation of a self-inflicted injury. The client desires something more pragmatic and down-to-earth at such times, and the carer (professional or otherwise) can feel under pressure to conjure up a coping strategy without delay. It is not surprising that many carers feel stressed and negative when placed in such a position, since it is easy to feel as though one has been somehow forced into a no-win situation. To make matters worse, there is added irony if time has been spent trying to persuade someone to seek out help when they feel dysphoric rather than immediately resorting to self-harm – the irony arises because, now that person is actually taking responsibility and asking for assistance, the carer is not at all certain what to offer.

We believe that it is preferable under such circumstances to be aware of as wide a range of short-term coping strategies as possible, and to work with each client individually to explore which of these appeal and how effective each is. Professional staff who spend a considerable amount of time with self-injuring clients tend to gather for themselves a portfolio of simple techniques and interventions that they have found to be helpful to people who are becoming distressed and are anticipating self-harm. They then draw from that portfolio when asked specifically for help and, consciously or unconsciously, will try to select a technique that they feel is most likely to suit the person before them.

Choice and collaboration as essential components

It is important to allow someone who self-injures the choice in selecting which strategies they try and which they eventually take on as part of a personalized repertoire of coping techniques. There are three reasons for this. The first is that the person needs to take an active role in experimenting to discover what is effective and when. Being actively involved tends to encourage a more positive outlook so that the client becomes less likely to say or think: '*nothing ever works for me*' and more likely to think: '*doing [A] didn't work brilliantly, but it helped a bit and it was definitely better than [B]*'. The second is that many self-injurers have difficulty asserting themselves. Insisting that choice is an essential part of the process minimizes the chance that the client will just go along with a suggestion because it feels difficult to refuse. The experience of having to make choices in this way can be particularly helpful for someone who tends to use their self-harm in attempt to control or influence others. The third reason concerns the risk of dependency. Feeling overwhelmed can be a common experience for people who repeatedly self-injure, and though not all will seek assistance when they feel a crisis looming, those that do may make many such requests. It is surprisingly easy for a health care worker to become drawn into repeatedly responding with suggestions for new methods of coping. This can lead to an unhelpful dependency in which the client starts to believe that coping with distress is only possible when there is a resourceful member of staff close by (or at the end of a phone) to provide suggestions about what to try next.

Exercising choice in this way helps to develop a collaborative relationship between client and professional which is essential when evaluating progress in this type of short-term work and also when moving to the more formalized interventions described in the following chapter. Exercising choice also helps focus the work on what the client is motivated to control, rather than what staff and carers would most like them to control. In saying this, we realize that the degree of choice available to the individual will vary with the type of setting in which they find themselves, and is likely to be less for prisoners and people detained in forensic mental-health settings for example.

Coping strategies that distract

Many coping strategies work in the short-term because they distract the sufferer, temporarily diverting attention away from the perceived need to self-harm and onto some new path. Activities that seem particularly absorbing or engaging are not always the best choice, however, and it is unwise to assume that the activity requiring the most concentration is the one most likely to focus the attention away from self-injury.

In practice, a distraction strategy needs to be simple. It must be easy to understand and easily executed, since someone already struggling with a downward spiral of dysphoric feelings is unlikely to be able to concentrate on anything too complex. Choice is again important, since what can help one person may actually increase the distress of another; a common example is when the activity that is suggested takes the client back to an unhappy school experience or triggers memories of past abuse. Fortunately, most clients are very aware of the type of situation that can trigger such memories for them and are usually able to avoid making an inappropriate choice.

Lists of potentially suitable strategies are available from many sources. These include published books, pamphlets from voluntary organizations or charities, and many websites that focus on self-harm (see Appendix). Some of these publications take the form of a self-help manual, such as the 'Hurt yourself less workbook' (National Self-Harm Network, 1998). Others target a specific sub-group, such as 'The Rainbow Journal' (produced in the UK by the Bristol Crisis Service for Women), which is written specifically for young people who self-injure. Many of these sources summarize ideas which have been contributed by people who self-injure. Most recommend taking some basic steps to keep oneself safe (e.g. avoiding situations known to trigger self-injury, avoiding intoxication, deciding to dispose of blades safely rather than hiding them for later use and destroying stockpiles of medication which have been stored 'just in case'). Many suggest identifying a safe place in the house which is kept as somewhere where skin cutting or burning never occurs and to which one can retreat when feeling vulnerable. The value of having company around when urges to self-injure are strong is also advocated.

Some suggestions involve distracting oneself though physical activity (such as walking, jogging or gardening), mental activity (such as card games, paper-and-pencil puzzles, planning tasks for the day or writing one's own life story) or expressive activity (such as painting, drawing, doodling, writing poems, ripping paper or moulding clay). Others focus on improving mood (for example by listening to music, watching a video or cartoons, reading old Christmas cards or writing a self-addressed letter forgiving some of one's recent mistakes) or on delaying tactics (such as deciding not to self-injure for the next ten minutes). Further ideas may be found in Arnold & Magill (1996, 2000) and in Schmidt & Davidson (2004) who provide a chapter of what to do in a crisis that includes useful suggestions for developing distraction skills and self-soothing techniques.

Many of these ideas, though simple in concept, have potential to be executed in a myriad of different ways. This offers much scope for customization to suit the individual client, and involving the client in personalizing his or her own repertoire of distraction techniques has obvious benefits. Another advantage is that most of these activities can be approached in a relatively light-hearted frame of mind. This contrasts with other more 'serious' therapeutic interventions that are often seen by clients as rather cold and humourless. Although its role in the therapeutic process is often underappreciated, humour can be powerful in its ability to defuse stressful situations (Garrick, 2006).

Strategies to help manage flashbacks and dissociative episodes
Some of the activities listed above can also be beneficial for an individual who is prone to dissociating prior to self-injury and who wants to try to prevent this occurring, but they are less relevant for someone who is currently experiencing a dissociative state. In such situations a member of staff may seek guidance on how best to assist a client who appears unresponsive and disconnected from the present.

Kennerley (1996) and Benham (1995) describe a variety of cognitive (or cognitive-behavioural) methods that clinicians have found useful in helping clients terminate flashbacks, depersonalization symptoms and transient trance-like states. These include grounding and refocusing techniques that aim to keep the client in touch with what is happening in the present. Examples include encouraging changes of posture rather than remaining 'frozen': asking the person to pay attention to the sensation of the chair beneath their arms if sitting; or the ground beneath the feet if standing; and asking the person to name out loud what he or she sees. Encouraging the counting of objects (such as the number of chairs in the room) can also be effective, as can focussing on a benign object (such as a soft toy) and describing out loud its colour and texture. It is also helpful to ensure that the room is well-lit (with few shadows), well-ventilated and that the environment is not over-stimulating (not too busy or noisy). The overall approach should be calm and confident, and frequent reminders of the present should be given in a voice that is steady and clear. Attempts to shock the person out of a dissociative state are ill-advised (as would be trying to suddenly 'wake-up' a person who is sleep-walking).

A client experiencing a flashback presents a particular challenge. Here it is useful to provide clear verbal reminders that he or she is, in fact, able to exert some control over the experience rather than giving in to it. The client can also be reminded that he or she is living in the present and that any flashback only relates to the past. Sometimes a person will experience flashbacks frequently and will regularly ask for help in controlling them. Here it can be useful to have a pre-arranged object so that when the situation recurs he or she can be encouraged to focus on it as a comforting reminder of the present. Some clients are able to discern the start of a flashback or else find that the involuntary recall commences with memories that are less disturbing but which carry with them a great dread of what will follow. People in this situation often ask for help to avert the horror they see ahead of them; they can be encouraged to write down some of what they are experiencing (focusing on where they are now rather than where they anticipate their flashback is taking them), and to then write boldly underneath that 'this is in my past'. The piece of paper can then be crumpled and destroyed, or else handed to the member of staff for safekeeping or destruction. Our own clinical experience is that this procedure can sometimes be remarkably effective.

Various other schema-focused approaches and cognitive techniques have been developed to help manage the dissociative process. These include psycho-education; cognitive restructuring; goal setting; problem solving; procedures that help to self-soothe, control impulses and contain anger for those who regularly dissociate; and also to manage flashbacks by image modification. Specialized therapeutic procedures such as eye movement desensitization and reprocessing (EMDR) and dialectical behaviour therapy (DBT) have also been found helpful for dissociative symptoms. We discuss some of these procedures in the following chapter when we consider how dissociative processes can be managed in the longer term.

Strategies that substitute for some of the effects of self-injury

Behavioural alternatives to self-injury can sometimes be useful as short-term interventions. Some people find that marking their skin with an indelible red pen can act as a temporary substitute for skin cutting. This strategy requires the sufferer to carefully draw a red line exactly where the injury is anticipated and, though not infallible, can exert its effect long enough for the intense desire to self-injure to pass. A similar outcome can sometimes be achieved by applying a dummy bandage at the site where the sufferer anticipates making the next cut, and some people report finding it helpful to combine both methods.

Two other behavioural alternatives to self-injury appear popular. The first involves holding an ice cube, either gripping it firmly in the hand, or else pressing it hard against the skin at the site where a cut or burn is anticipated. Loss of body heat to the melting ice produces localized cooling and discomfort but without tissue damage. Some people find that the discomfort so produced can temporarily substitute for the effects of self-injury, and a similar outcome can sometimes be achieved by holding the hands in ice cold water, or even taking a cold bath or shower. The second strategy involves placing an elastic band over the wrist so that it is always in place when the urge to self-injure presents (the elastic band should be a loose rather than a tight fit). When the sufferer suddenly experiences the desire to self-injure, he or she 'flips' the rubber band so that it snaps back sharply against the wrist. This again is uncomfortable and the sensation may temporarily distract from or substitute for self-injury, usually without any damage to the skin.

Strategies like these are simple to execute and can sometimes be very effective. We have already noted in Chapter 4 that some people who self-injure can feel that their skin has disappeared from their body image, and it is possible that the sight of the red ink, the sensation of the bandage and the sting from the rubber band all help to reaffirm that boundary. The main disadvantage is that these particular behavioural alternatives can be viewed by others as 'playing at' self-harm, and so the sufferer may be ridiculed if he or she does not keep secret that there is no actual wound under the bandage. This can be a real difficulty if there are many people around, such as in an acute ward or in the family home. As we have already noted, someone who is trying to reduce their self-injury is unlikely to benefit from further experience of shame. There will also be some observers who will have ethical concerns and view these techniques as actively encouraging the client to focus on self-harm rather than distracting from it. Another disadvantage is that repeated use of this type of behavioural strategy can inadvertently reinforce the idea that difficult feelings are best managed by physical action (Conterio et al., 1998).

Expressing emotion

Being able to express pent up feelings is generally regarded as more positive than trying to pretend that they do not exist, and many people who self-injure say they find it occasionally useful to spend time expressing feelings like anger through physical activity. Almost any vigorous activity can serve this purpose

such as speed walking, jogging, cycling, pillow thumping and energetic dancing. There can, however, be disadvantages. Using intense physical activity in
attempt to dissipate intense anger is often counter-productive for someone who
feels that they spend much of their life in a struggle to control their inner rage,
and it may even be dangerous at times. If the angry feelings are very strong,
the sufferer may feel as though he or she has little influence over the intensity
or duration of the physical expression. The rageful eruption continues to build
over time instead of dissipating as a result of catharsis, and only wanes when
exhaustion takes over or the person is restrained for their own safety or the
safety of those close by.

Developing the ability to identify feelings and learning to express these
verbally (rather than physically) is often regarded as a valuable skill for people
who are trying to reduce their reliance on self-harm (Dallam, 1997). The difficulty here is that someone who has a life-long difficulty naming and differentiating their feelings is likely to take some time to learn 'emotional literacy'.
Verbal expression of feelings may not be a realistic strategy for avoiding crises
in the short-term for such a person. However, clients who are aware of their
feelings can gain considerable relief though expressing them verbally – the
term 'ventilation' is often used – to someone who has agreed to take the role
of listener and who is able to hear what is expressed without over-reacting or
taking what is said as a personal affront. Short-term management of feelings
can also be achieved by writing them down (White et al., 2002), and this can
also set the scene for further diary work to help identify triggers and precipitants as described in the following chapter.

LOOKING FOR UNDERLYING PROBLEMS

Self-injury may be a means of trying to come to terms with an underlying
problem which the person cannot bring into focus, or cannot address. People,
especially young people, do not always recognize when they are being placed
in an impossible situation by someone else; too often they blame themselves in
these circumstances.

One important part of the assessment of a person who has self-injured and is
at high risk is to respectfully and caringly search out any underlying problems of
this kind. The most severe, and the one most often linked to self-injury, is abuse.
This might be sexual abuse, but might also be physical or emotional abuse.

Abuse is one of the rarer causes of people injuring themselves, and should
not be the exclusive focus of enquiry. Other 'impossible' problems from
which a young person may feel they cannot flee and cannot solve are bullying
at school or at work; marginalization because of social phobia; an autistic

spectrum disorder or other condition affecting socialization; and a struggle with gender identity or sexual orientation. Other problems that cannot be shared include struggling against substance misuse, a broken relationship which has had to be concealed and being caught up in the legal system as an offender. Twenty years ago, we would have included unemployment on this list, but that has stopped being the source of shame, financial worry and social isolation that it was then.

PROVIDING SOLUTIONS

If an underlying problem does emerge, then counselling or psychotherapy directed towards alleviating the problem is indicated. Text Box 7.8 lists some of the more common existential difficulties experienced by young people.

Text Box 7.8   Common existential problems in young people

Bullying; emotional, physical or sexual abuse; coming to terms with sexual orientation; autism spectrum disorder; social phobia; family conflict; substance abuse; bereavement or broken relationship; being caught up in the legal system; racial harassment.

If there is no particular problem, or rather if there is the usual accumulation of small problems that we all face, then it is worth considering whether a person lacks coping skills. In our experience, it is rare for someone to have a primary lack of such skills – usually an apparent lack comes about because a person feels increasingly ground down and unconfident in their own abilities, but a primary lack may occur. This may happen if there has been little family encouragement to develop independence. There is one study that suggests that teaching young people how to cope, using a cognitive behavioural approach, can reduce the risk of repetition of self-harm, but this has not been replicated in other studies.

This chapter has focussed on professionals' initial responses following contact with someone who has self-injured. In the following chapter, which is entitled 'Recovery', we explore ways in which a sufferer can be helped, over time, to disengage from the 'trap' of self-injury.

Chapter 8

Recovery

INTRODUCTION

We focus in this chapter on how to get out of self-injury when it has become a trap. This might happen because a person has become addicted to it, because it has become so central to personal identity that a person could not imagine giving it up, or because it is the only way that a person knows to relieve themselves of intolerable feelings.

ADDICTION TO SELF-INJURY

The following fictionalized account provides an insight into how a person can come to feel as if they are controlled by their self-injury, and how self-injury eventually becomes addictive.

'I really don't think it's possible for anyone to understand fully what a person who self-harms goes through unless they've experienced it themselves. For me, it was something I came to rely on. In fact, when things got tough it was really the only thing that I was able to rely upon. My life was out of control. I felt as worthless as anyone could possibly feel. I really didn't want to feel this anymore. I think that was what made me start harming myself.

I started self harming when I was twelve years old. It started by chance really. We had a bit of a nasty cat at the time, and she would scratch people, and particularly me. But it made me feel alive when she did it, and I used to want her to do it. In fact, I used to wind her up so that she would do it, and I ended up scratches all over my arm.

I was on my own such a lot then. My Mum was drinking, and my Dad just seemed to shout all the time, so I kept out of their way. I did have friends in school, but they never wanted to come to my house. School was good, but there were always the holidays and the weekends to get through. I thought of killing myself all the time, I think as a way of getting out of all the horrible feelings.

I did make one friend, but then my parents separated and we moved house. My Mum just became useless, and I was lumbered with looking after my two kid brothers. There was never any chance of going out in the evenings, and no chance of making new friends. There really was no escape. The cat had died, but I tried scratching myself to see if that would make me feel better. I quickly moved on to cutting my arms with a blade, because that really seemed to help. Cutting for me was a way of keeping my emotions in control. In the beginning I didn't really know what self harm was. I knew other people would disapprove, but I thought "Sod them. Why should they control my life?" and I kept it all to myself.

It has always seemed as though I've been in quite a focused state of mind whenever I've cut myself. It was as though self-harm was the only thing I had. My only goal was to do it. I didn't feel any pain at the time – only afterwards. In the early days, I got a huge feeling of relief from doing it. It seemed to work like magic to change my emotional pain into something physical. This somehow took my attention away from my thoughts and what I was feeling inside. I did feel ashamed and a bit sick at the mess I'd made of my arm after the feeling of relief wore off, but I mainly worried about how other people would react. I wanted to keep the cuts private, almost like a kind of intimate thing.

When I started cutting, it was simply a case of one cut at a time. Later I started doing several shallow cuts, perhaps as many as 15 or 20, but none were deep. Gradually, I did more and more each time. One time I did over 200 on my arms, and a few on the rest of my body. That's when I knew it was getting out of control. I tried to stop, but it had become an addiction and I began to resent it each time I did it. I now began to hate my body more and more.

I did manage to give up in the end, but then I started to burn myself. This worked even better than cutting because the pain lasted longer, but people couldn't help noticing the scars. Lots of things have got better in my life lately, but I still get this urge, and sometimes I still cut or burn myself. I guess it will always be there. Someone said I had to be positive and see my scars not as signs of weakness, but as symbols and signs of the hardships which I have been through. I'm really trying, but it's hard.'

Terri describes precursors of her self-injury that will be recognizable to those who have read this far in the book. But she also describes herself as 'addicted', feeling controlled by her self-injury and having a life-long urge to injure herself.

When thinking about when she got out of control, Terri refers to going from 20 cuts at a time to 200 and it then becoming impossible to stop. But at the same time she is seeking out ways of drawing out the pain and discovers burning as a way of doing so. Her shame about her scars is something that Terri implies maintains her self-harm rather than reducing it, and part of her recovery from addiction is 'trying to learn to love my body as it is – with all its scars'. If, she implies, she could accept her scars as signs of success and not as failings, then she would reduce the risk of harming again.

Terri considers two kinds of factor that have led to addiction: the power of her self-injury; and her own weakened resistance, undermined by shame and her imperfections manifested in her scars. She also considers two factors in recovery. The first is a change in her perception of self-injury from it being a helpful part of herself to being an outside influence that is making her an unwelcome dependent. The other factor is the possibility of seeing her body as something to love 'as it is', and not something to control or alter.

To fully understand the power of self-injury, or indeed any other addiction, we need to disentangle some of the emotional elements that contribute to it. To do so, we will use an illustration drawn not from self-injury but from driving, since that is something that we expect almost all of our readers can relate to.

A former client was referred because his marriage was breaking up. The immediate cause of this was his habit of getting up in the night and driving off in his car, leaving his wife asleep in bed. Sometimes she would only know he had done this when he rang her hours later, and hundreds of miles from home, and would talk to her in a rambling, almost intoxicated manner. This is not exactly how this problem developed: we have changed some of the details to conceal his identity.

John had never been good at standing up to his wife Jill. So when their relationship began to go through a really bad patch, he started to dread the rows. He did not know how to defend himself, and when a row started he got into the habit of not fighting back, but of thinking only about the row finishing. 'If only I could just get into my car and drive away' came into his mind one day, and this thought would recur with ever greater intensity every time that they had a row. One day it was so intense that he told his wife that he had to go to the bathroom, but actually went out to the garage and, before she could stop him, he drove away.

As he drove, his anger with his wife began to dissipate (tension relief) and he started to think of how upset she would be and how unkind it was just to drive away. After half an hour, he rang her on his mobile and told her that he felt he had to escape, and that he was sorry. When he came home, the row had been forgotten. The next time that they had a row, John felt an even stronger urge to escape and this time just walked out of the room, went to the garage and took the car out. He was away for longer this time before his own temper cooled and when he got back the row flared up again, making him want to leave again.

There were several further repetitions of John driving away, and each time he had to drive away a little further before he felt calm (habituation). There came a point when he still felt angry, but the thought came to him that he had shown her she could not push him around. He felt that he was not escaping at all, but becoming the master of his fate. He could go anywhere he wanted, he was bound to no one. An intoxicating feeling of power and calm stole over him, a feeling that he wanted to perpetuate. He stayed out longer than ever before, driving aimlessly but with the feeling that he was really going places emotionally (strong emotor).

His wife had gone to bed by the time he got back, and he slept in the spare room, which he thereafter continued to do. His wife, Jill, had become careful not to slip into rows in case John took off. John rarely felt the urge to escape. But he did now feel a yearning for that feeling of calm mastery that he had experienced on that one occasion in the car: a feeling that he did not normally feel when he had to drive somewhere for work or for the family. The yearning (or craving) became more and more intense and one evening he waited until his wife was in bed, and surreptitiously left the house, took the car, and set off. He did not know where he was going, and just let the car drive itself as a feeling washed over him that could have not been more intense had John been called into a meeting of the directors at work and told that he was being appointed as chief executive – except on that occasion, John would have been intensely nervous, whereas he felt calm and in total control. John only 'came to' (dissociation) when he realized that the car was running out of petrol: he had driven over 200 miles.

John began to live for those drives. They usually took place at night, and his work began to suffer as a result of his distractedness and his sleepiness during the day. His wife was sure that he was meeting someone and told John to leave. This was the situation when he was first referred. He almost did not come, he said, as he could not imagine giving up his nocturnal outings. They were what gave his life meaning, and made him different from other men (addiction).

> John initially used driving as an escape and as a means of tension relief. At this point, if there had been some other way that he could deal with his mounting tension during rows with Jill, it is likely that he would have taken it. But he gradually became addicted to driving. Driving was what gave his life meaning, gave him an identity ('made him different from other men') and was worth sacrificing his marriage and his job for. He had given the driving an enormous power over him.
>
> Self-injury, if repeated sufficiently, can develop a similar addictive power. In this section of the chapter we shall consider some of the steps from tension relief to addiction in John's story and see how they apply to self-injury.

DEVELOPMENT OF ADDICTIVE BEHAVIOUR

Strong emotors and mastery

We have already considered how sometimes two 'emotional flavours' can combine to produce something unexpectedly, and addictively, pleasing. John's relief at feeling his anger dissipating, his feeling of inadequacy at having to run away from his wife, his fatigue and his sense of mastery in his driving – all of these combined to give him an intoxicating flavour blend of calm, effortless mastery over others. Self-injury also produces a concoction of emotional flavours.

With self-injury there is mastery, as there was for John. However, in self-injury it is not the mastery that comes from exercising a skill, but the mastery over one's own body, which is the only inalienable property that we all have. John's tension relief came from escaping the row, and his wife's anger towards him. Self-injury has intrinsic tension relieving properties, perhaps due to a built-in effect of skin stimulation or grooming (see Chapter 3). The unpleasant flavours of self-injury include shame and pain, as instanced by Toni in the quoted extract. John experienced these to some degree – he was only too aware when he was discussing his 'escapades' as he called them that he was behaving badly towards his wife, and that he would be ashamed if his friends found out what he was doing. There was also a slight element of pain, in that it would often be when he was feeling most fatigued that he would have the urge for a drive, and sometimes there were brief moments when he was actually driving when an exhausted feeling would sweep over him and he would feel that it was all too much. Pain however was not a major contribution to the emotional flavour of driving for John, as it was to the emotional flavour of self-injury to Toni, and is to others who injure themselves.

Craving

Strong emotors are addictive because they become the basis of craving. One reason for this is that they are antidotes to the negative flavours which are contained within them. An analogy may make this clearer, and here we will use the analogy of a 'cocktail' drink. A cocktail is a type of alcoholic drink that always involves a mixture. There can be many components in the mix, but one is always alcoholic-based. So, for example, a dash of 'bitters' (a liquid infusion of bitter tasting herbs) makes a vermouth what it is, and a vermouth can consequently take away the bitterness of an olive – one reason for so often serving a cocktail with an olive in it. Similarly a strong emotor can absorb further amounts of the negative flavours that constitute it. Injuring oneself can therefore act as an antidote to shameful feelings or shameful memories, as well as painful feelings or even physical pain. Not only that, but just as an olive can pleasantly intensify the flavour of a martini, so these additional negative flavours may actually increase the comfort experienced as a result of self-injury.

TREATING CRAVING

Craving is, as we have already seen, mediated by neuronal networks in which the main transmitter is dopamine. Once a network has been created which readily leads to dopamine-induced craving, a small reduction in external reward (with a consequent small reduction in dopaminergic transmission and therefore synthesis) will result in craving being induced. The induction is more rapid if there is already a craving established. Unsurprisingly, it is difficult to find an effective treatment for cravings that have become firmly established.

Limitations of medication and psychotherapy

If this neurobiological theory is correct, then drugs that are dopamine agonists (that is, drugs which act to enhance the actions of dopamine) should reduce craving. The same should be true for drugs that reduce other pathways that are linked to the dopamine one, including ones mediated by gamma-butyric acid (GABA) and by endorphins. Dopamine agonists like pramipexole or buproprion; synthetic opioids like buprenorphine; and drugs active on GABA-ergic transmissions like acamprosate or the anticonvulsant vigabatrin have all been used as treatments for craving. Many have found a place in the treatment of addictions like alcohol dependence or smoking addiction, but they have received little investigation in self-injury. In fact, there is no drug treatment which has been shown to have a consistent effect in repeated self-injury. There is some limited evidence that drug treatment may relieve the rising emotional tension associated with the spring pathway, and we will discuss this later.

Psychotherapy is not consistently effective either, since it relies on a person having made the prior decision to change, and this is something a person with a craving is rarely prepared for. Craving does, however, diminish with time, perhaps because the less often it is acted on, the weaker it becomes. Having said that, craving may recur with fresh intensity after a long period, and for no very obvious reason.

Treatment using reward with, perhaps, attachment

The best method for dealing with craving seems to be to oppose it with some other equally strong, but opposed, reward. Craving involves the same pathways that mediate attachment and so an opposed reward that also involves the attachment system is probably the most effective. This might be a close relationship to another person, such as a partner or a therapist, but is most often a close relationship with a group of other people. Group participation in religiously oriented groups, such as Alcoholics Anonymous, or participation in web-based discussion forums may be effective if continued group membership is craved more than the self-injury. These methods only work if a person can commit themselves to this alternative.

TREATING DISSOCIATION AND SWITCHING

The important role played by dissociation suggests that one avenue of treatment lies in helping the individual to manage their tendency to dissociate. If a reduction in the number and intensity of dissociative episodes can be achieved, subversion of the safety-catch becomes less likely and a tendency for further dissociation should be reduced. Treatment for self-injury could therefore benefit through having more of a focus on dealing effectively with dissociation. The aim may be to speed the termination of a dissociative episode, or alternatively to find other ways of coping with intense affect without completely dis-associating from it. In our experience, people who dissociate do better when taught the skills to manage their own use of dissociation, either directly through using specific cognitive techniques or indirectly through learning to be more mindful of their current environment.

Techniques include the need to match treatment to individual presentation. This involves learning what factors govern the onset and duration of dissociative episodes for that particular client (assists in identifying precipitants which can then be avoided), educating the client about the nature of dissociation (helps to minimize feelings of powerlessness), exploring the strength and limitations of self-help as opposed to professional help and selecting and using appropriate cognitive techniques.

Switching and dissociation are closely linked and, since the types of treatment and management techniques suggested are similar to both, we consider them together in the following paragraphs.

Avoiding cues and precipitants

Cue avoidance is a useful technique, and one way to minimize switching is to teach greater awareness of switch situations (and the same applies to dissociation). A person who injures themselves repeatedly may be able to think of cues that can cause them to switch or dissociate. Some are common to many people who self-injure, so much so that people who post messages on discussion forums will, as we have seen in Chapter 3, place a warning or 'spoiler' in the subject line of the message to warn that there is something potentially 'triggery' contained in the text that follows. Keeping a diary and analysing its contents week by week with a therapist or key worker is a useful way for the client to build up knowledge about their own particular sensitivities and, ultimately, a reasonably comprehensive list of cues that might best be avoided. Individuals who regularly self-injure are usually able to describe some of their personal experiences peripheral to their cutting or burning and, with guidance, are often able to discern the degree to which they dissociate and the way in which dissociation fits into their regular cycle of self-harm. There is a further (and important) advantage to maintaining this type of diary. The perception of unpredictability gradually lessens for the diary keeper over time, which further increases the notion of being more in control of the situation.

A number of factors capable of promoting dissociative experience have been identified and examination of these can be a useful starting point when attempting to pinpoint specific individual cues and sensitivities. This list includes alcohol and a variety of illicit drugs including cannabis, 'Ecstasy' and ketamine. Dissociation may also occur as a side effect of indomethacin and certain other non-steroidal anti-inflammatory drugs, and following rapid withdrawal of certain antidepressants and benzodiazepines. It can be exacerbated by caffeine, induced by fasting and can develop as a result of emotional shock. It is more likely to occur in highly charged environments. People appear more likely to dissociate in response to flickering lights (such as candles or strobes), when exposed to monotonous chanting or drumming, and when trying to divide their attention between two or more sources. This list appears very wide-ranging with considerable variation from person to person, and so precipitating factors for dissociation are best explored on an individual basis. Once this information is gathered, the sufferer can take steps to avoid situations and environments in which a dissociative state is most likely to develop. This will take time to achieve; in the short-term a person trying not to self-injure might consider avoiding all known potential precipitants.

It is impossible to avoid all cues, but it may be worth trying to avoid the main ones or, perhaps even better, allowing oneself to experience the cues in circumstances when dissociation can be inhibited such as when in the company of trusted friends or helpers. There may sometimes be a prodromal phase before the dissociation develops when a person feels strange or altered but not completely so, and analysis of diary entries can be helpful in exploring this if it occurs.

Psycho-education

The concept of dissociation is frequently unfamiliar to clients, and an uncomplicated explanation about dissociative symptoms and dissociative processes is often well received. Many sufferers find themselves acutely aware of their dissociative experiences and are disturbed by them. They may worry that they are 'going mad', or that they are being taken over in some way, or that they are progressively losing all control.

Psycho-education seeks to explain the nature of dissociation, its possible functions, how it is normal to have some level of dissociative experience, and the ways in which the more profound dissociative phenomena are experienced by other people. The advantages and disadvantages of dissociating every time one comes under stress are explored. Importantly, psycho-education aims to normalize the detachment experience, to reduce shame associated with 'freezing' or with feeling one is viewed by others as behaving as if mad, and to teach that each person can exert control over their dissociative symptoms. This helps reduce the notion that the sufferer is powerless. The term 'psycho-education' implies a structured approach to imparting knowledge, but this may be more successful if done informally in small chunks rather than in a single formal session. Having printed material that the client can take away and which summarizes the key learning points is invaluable, and the use of clear, simple figures and diagrams can be particularly helpful.

Self-help versus professional help

Self-directed methods (such as diary keeping and monitoring for triggers) are useful when trying to avoid the more obvious precipitants, but can be less helpful when trying to monitor and address dissociative episodes. Here a combination of self-help and professional help is generally advisable, for although many of the established techniques for managing dissociation can be read about in a relevant book or leaflet (see Appendix) and can be practised alone, dissociative experience by its very nature introduces blind spots.

Input from a professional may be essential if someone is to recognize his or her own dissociative responses, or to learn what is effective as he or she enters into a dissociative state. Professional input is also useful when trying to build up a picture of how dissociation may fit into an individual's cycle of self-injury, and when trying initially to learn some of the various cognitive techniques (described below) which are claimed to help manage the dissociative process. There is also the possibility that some techniques and interventions will be iatrogenic, and will unintentionally strengthen or deepen a dissociative episode. If the client is the only witness to this, he or she may remain unaware that the treatment is making the situation worse.

Working together, client and professional can agree on a list of things the client can do at the time to prevent dissociation developing and deepening. Such a list might include making contact with others, looking at photographs of family or friends, using a guided imagery technique and specific distraction tasks tailored to suit the individual.

Cognitive techniques

In recent years, a range of cognitive-based techniques have been developed and refined to deal with dissociation and unwelcome flashbacks. These techniques (see Kennerley, 1996; Grame 1993; Benham, 1995) seek to provide people with skills to recognize and terminate a dissociative episode, and to help them reduce their tendency to dissociate (see Text Box 8.1).

Text Box 8.1   Cognitive-based techniques to moderate dissociation
■ Image restructuring/modification (recall with affect, then change scenario)   ■ Graded exposure to feared situations (audio tape, then self-directed exposure)   ■ Awareness of cognitive distortions (educate; continuum work)   ■ Monitoring of automatic negative thoughts   ■ Trigger management (planned avoidance; programme of exposure & response prevention)   ■ Behavioural experiments   ■ Conflict handling techniques   ■ Attention & concentration training   ■ Enhancing self-soothing skills   ■ Grounding techniques (image, word, phrase, object, action and 'safe place')   ■ Refocusing techniques (concentrating on object's colour or texture)

A cognitive therapist may choose to match the therapy not only to the individual but also to the type of dissociation that the therapy aims to address. For example, treatment for dissociation that is predominantly of the 'detachment' type might centre on the prevention of triggering and on terminating the dissociation once it has been triggered; this could include graded exposure to feared situations, attention training, task concentration training and behavioural experiments. On the other hand, treatment for dissociation that is predominantly of the 'compartmentalization' type might centre on reactivation and reintegration of the compartmentalized elements (where appropriate); this could include work to modify catastrophic cognitions, and to modify inappropriate behaviour that maintains symptoms (Holmes et al., 2005).

Many of these techniques appear relatively simple, and there is often the temptation for unskilled staff to 'try them out' with clients. This can certainly produce a satisfactory outcome, but there is always a risk that a specific technique will make matters worse. To take one example, some staff like to encourage a client who talks about wanting to cut to first visualize an image of self-cutting and then, in their imagination, to fade this image out and replace it with an alternative. In many cases this either helps or simply has no effect, but for some unfortunate individuals the initial image of self-cutting gets 'fixed' and subsequently acts to reinforce rather than distract from their craving to self-injure. A skilled cognitive therapist may be able to suggest solutions to this difficulty, and might even have been able to detect in the initial assessment that the client was at risk of reacting in this way.

More recently, various elements from this list (grounding, distraction, refocusing and psycho-education) have been included within a cognitive behavioural therapy protocol termed 'Cognitive processing therapy' for treating adult survivors of childhood sexual abuse. Based on information processing, developmental and self-trauma theories, the protocol describes a 26-session intervention which combines group and individual therapy. Clients are asked to write about their traumatic experiences, and explore their various beliefs (adaptive, schema congruent and discrepant) that they developed during and after the abuse. Chard (2005) describes a well-designed randomized controlled trial comparing the effectiveness of cognitive processing therapy for sexual abuse survivors with a wait-list control group. Analysis suggested that the treatment was more effective for reducing trauma-related symptoms – including dissociation – compared to the control condition and these results were maintained after a one year follow-up interval.

Other techniques
In our view, any treatment for self-injury should include teaching clients other ways of coping with strong feelings without completely dissociating from them. As we have seen, some interventions achieve this by specifically targeting the dissociative process, but others can also help with dissociation, albeit indirectly. One such intervention is individual interpersonal therapy.

Clients can also learn how to cope with difficult feelings without resorting to dissociation within group therapy, and here both trauma-focused and psychodynamic approaches appear to be effective (e.g. Classen et al., 2001). Positive outcomes (including reduced dissociation) are also reported for behavioural therapy in some dissociative conditions (e.g. Moene et al., 1998); for body-orientated therapy on dissociative symptoms in sexual abuse survivors (Price, 2006); for eye movement desensitization and reprocessing (EMDR) on specific dissociative symptoms associated with PTSD (e.g. Silver et al., 1995); for trauma-focused group therapy for PTSD (Lubin et al., 1998); and for affect-management group therapy for survivors of sexual abuse (Zlotnick et al., 1997). Dialectical behaviour therapy (DBT) is discussed below.

To date, no specific medication has emerged that might qualify as a treatment of choice for dissociation or, for that matter, self-injury. Serotonergic functioning may be impaired in depersonalization suggesting a role for some of the SSRI antidepressants (Khazaal et al., 2005) although a recent randomized trial found fluoxetine not to be effective in treating depersonalization disorder (Sierra et al., 2003). The opiate antagonists have been shown to reduce dissociative symptoms; naltrexone on dissociative symptoms in BPD (Bohus et al., 1999); nalmefene on flashbacks in PTSD (Glover, 1993); and naloxone on acute dissociative states in BPD (Philipsen et al., 2004a). In one randomized trial, clonidine (a noradrenergic suppressant) was effective in reducing inner tension, dissociative symptoms and urge to self-injure in a small sample of women with borderline personality disorder (Philipsen et al., 2004b).

Dialectical behaviour therapy

The originator of dialectical behaviour therapy (DBT) – Marsha Linehan – proposes that several different treatment elements are necessary for the effective treatment of people diagnosed with borderline personality disorder. These are (a) 'capability enhancement', which involves training in mindfulness, interpersonal skills and conflict management, emotional regulation, distress tolerance and self management; (b) 'motivational enhancement' which involves weekly sessions of individual therapy – which appears to be similar to other individual therapies used in the field – with an emphasis on cognitive methods, and 'enhancing generalization' through phone contact between sessions; (c) 'structuring the environment' by organizing meetings with family members or other involved professionals; and (d) therapist support and supervision (Linehan, 1993). Three of these seem in our clinical experience to be particular important in the treatment of dissociation in particular, and of addiction to self-injury in general, and we will consider these in more detail.

In one study of DBT (Lieb et al., 2004), the largest effect of change from pre- to post-treatment was obtained, not for repeated self-harm, hopelessness, depression or anxiety, but for dissociation and borderline personality disorder criteria (of which dissociative phenomena are an important component) (Koons et al., 2001). This appears to suggest that the efficacy of this treatment lies in its effectiveness in reducing dissociation rather than any other specific therapeutic efficacy. However, DBT is a multimodal, intensive therapy and it is not at the moment clear which of its various elements are effective in reducing dissociation. There is some doubt whether or not it will turn out to be an improvement on good quality 'treatment as usual', especially where that treatment as usual involves the same emphasis on active outreach to keep clients in therapy that are used by DBT practitioners (Binks et al., 2006).

SOCIAL CONNECTIONS

One reason that the technique that Linehan calls 'structuring the environment' may be effective in the treatment of dissociation is that a lack of connectedness between different manifestations of agency may be mirrored in a functional disconnection. This disconnection can be within the brain, between the prefrontal area and the temporal lobes. There can also be a functional disconnection between different parts of a person's social relationships that arises from being part of several distinct social networks. One of us has argued that the prefrontal part of the brain may be under the influence of social networks mediated by the flux of nonverbal communication that passes between people. Most people would not be surprised to learn that living separate lives and showing different identities to different groups of people might lead to disconnection between brain areas that rely on communication with other brains for effective working. It seems reasonable also that these two kinds of disconnection may result in a predisposition for mental functions to become disconnected, too.

Helping clients to establish communication between split off networks of social relationships may sometimes involve family or systemic therapy with a professional therapist. However, therapy in this type of situation is fraught with danger – secrets may come out, warded off feelings may be aired, while both positive and negative feelings are likely to be aroused. If the client is committed to this approach, if the combined social network is basically supportive, and if bad feelings can be contained, this can indeed be a powerful approach in our experience. But it is rare that these conditions are met.

A similar outcome may be obtained by working in group psychotherapy where members of the group – who will initially be strangers – may come to stand for members of the client's own social network. Group psychotherapy has been shown to be effective in young people who have harmed themselves, and also in reducing dissociation in older, abused women (Wallis, 2002).

LEARNING TO ATTEND IN A DIFFERENT WAY

Group therapy addresses dissociated attention as it is displayed in communication with others. Attention may be distributed across many domains of conscious activity, including monitoring internal processes as well as monitoring interactions with individual others. One useful metaphor for attention – the so-called 'top down model' – is that it is like a searchlight that plays across a scene, bringing one aspect or another into visibility. If we take this metaphor further, the illumination of, let us say, a theatre stage by a spotlight only makes sense to us if the lighting engineer controlling it selects what to illuminate. If the lighting engineer is to keep his job, it is important that the sequence of scenes that the audience sees lit by the spotlight make up an integrated whole. We could imagine that a spotlight that went on and off, illuminating now here, and now there, would leave a fragmented impression of unrelated parts. This would be a visual equivalent of dissociation, and the audience would feel lost and confused. But who is behind the light?

This is of course a meaningless question in brain terms. However, it does seem that all the influences that direct the spotlight of attention pass through one specific region – the cingulated cortex in the forebrain. This is intriguing for two reasons. First, because the cingulated cortex seems to be where emotional influences on decision making come together with reflective thought. Second, because the cingulate cortex is an area whose function seems to be disrupted in post-traumatic stress disorder, which is itself associated with dissociation.

Does this have any practical significance? Commonsense suggests that focussing attention under conscious control might be one way of reducing the splitting of attention that leads to dissociation. This cannot be achieved simply by concentrating hard on something because it is almost inevitable that attention is simply divided differently. The likely result is that most attention goes on the task and less goes on monitoring the environment or the self, and this state of affairs is in fact a kind of dissociation. However, there are an increasing number of meditative and other techniques designed to increase 'mindfulness'. They aim to collect up aggregate attention so that many different processes can be monitored without attention ever getting diverted fully on to any one of them, and so becoming divided. Many of these meditative techniques do alter brain activity, with particular effect on the cingulate cortex (Cahn & Polich, 2006) and might be expected therefore to be of value in dissociation. Some of our patients confirm this, and there are also some published case reports (Waelde, 2004), but to date we have found no systematic study or review that has been undertaken.

Meditation is not a simple intervention. Zen meditation, for example, has two effects: increasing internalized attention and increasing 'mindfulness'. Furthermore, the two effects may be antagonistic (Takahashi et al., 2005) with one acting to counteract some of the effects of the other. Another potential problem is exemplified by relaxation. Relaxation may reduce cingulate over-activity (Lazar et al., 2000), and many health care staff would see it as an appropriate intervention for self-injury clients who commonly report feeling tense and 'wound-up'. However, as we have described in Chapter 4, relaxation can be viewed as very unhelpful by some clients who regularly self-harm (Huband & Tantam, 1999). One reason is that relaxation as prescribed in the UK is rarely a focussed activity. Relaxers are often advised to clear their minds, an inevitable consequence of which is that preoccupations flood in and, for people who are prone to injure themselves, these preoccupations are usually ruminations about some bad or hurtful thing that has happened to them. In fact, as we have already suggested, clearing the mind may actually increase the desire to self-harm. Furthermore, relaxation 'sessions' commonly take place in silence (except for the therapist who speaks instructions) with participants expected to 'relax' with their eyes closed – a situation that raises many difficulties for the client who is over-sensitive to criticism, to being 'observed' and to 'getting things wrong'. Thus the relaxation procedure may (quite unintentionally) induce performance anxiety for some participants. Meditative techniques which involve focussing on a mantra – like transcendental meditation (Yamamoto et al., 2006) – or the act of breathing (like Hatha yoga) may well be more effective.

EMOTIONAL REGULATION AND DYSREGULATION

One persuasive, although unproven, explanation of why dissociation increases in people who become addicted to self-injury is that it provides an escape (like self-injury itself) from irresoluble but distressing feelings.

There is considerable evidence from clinical and nowadays functional imaging studies that there are emotion sequences that are worked through, and emotion sequences that are not resoluble and therefore persist as an emotional residue. People who are 'traumatized' and who experience an irresoluble emotion can be shown to have much more widespread brain activation than people who are not traumatized, but who are left with an emotional residue. It is as if (we say 'as if' because brain function may not be translatable directly into mental function) being traumatized involves having more and more of one's mental life dominated by emotions that never seem to get sorted out, but reverberate around in one's mind.

Under these circumstances, dissociation (or cutting off awareness from the emotional turmoil) may be the only way that a person can continue to function. Both clinicians and dissociators are only too aware that there is a large cost to this. A person cannot dissociate from just one emotion, or from a feeling evoked by just one particular situation or by just one person. A person in turmoil cannot dissociate from one emotion without cutting themselves off from other emotions, too, sometimes to the extent that the person experiences a feeling of being 'on auto-pilot' or 'acting like a robot'. Cutting oneself off from emotions means losing skills that require emotional understanding – for example empathy and consequently interpersonal skills like persuasiveness and charm. It also means that emotionally informed problem solving or conflict resolution is impaired. This leads to worsening of any ability to resolve the kind of problem that might have led to the emotional turmoil in the first place.

Therapeutic techniques that focus on emotional regulation as a first step towards emotional resolution have been developed to try to overcome this disability. We can cite two examples. The first is a group intervention developed by Gratz and Gunderson (Gratz & Gunderson, 2006). The second is termed 'Systems Training for Emotional Predictability and Problem Solving' (STEPPS), a programme which originated in the Netherlands (Van Wel et al., 2006) and is widely available to staff wishing for training. Both techniques have shown promise in reducing self-harm.

Emerging models

Psychological research is beginning to develop greater specificity about the factors that influence when and how we experience an emotion (see Figure 8.1). These more detailed models can help to see better what might go wrong for people who injure themselves, and how they can change. For example, the pathway shown in the figure makes clear that each of us can influence how our emotions have built up, and once they have built up, what happens to the energy that the emotions have created. People who injure themselves often try to suppress their emotions. In fact, the more that a person self-injures, the more likely they are to try to suppress emotions (Chapman et al., 2005). But suppression not only has health consequences – it increases blood pressure – but it also increases cognitive load and therefore reduces cognitive reserves available for memory, and decreases the potential for positive social interaction

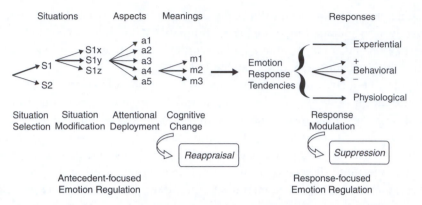

Figure 8.1 States in the development of an emotional response (reproduced from Gross, 2001)

(Gross, 2001). This means that people who suppress their emotions less often benefit from positive input from other people, and are less able to remember any help that they did receive.

The particular challenge arises from experiencing or remembering emotive life-events that cannot be altered. In people who are at risk of dissociation or emotional instability, these can lead to much wider activation of the brain (Beblo et al., 2006) and it is this which probably leads to the experience of feeling that one's head is bursting with overwhelming feelings and that no other thought or mental activity is possible until the emotion has been dealt with. Attempting to suppress this kind of emotion has negative consequences. As we have suggested, forcible suppression of one's feelings leads to further winding of the spring and sooner or later the tension will overwhelm any resolution, however firmly made.

There is, however, a process that can lead to a more positive outcome. Reappraising the emotion is an alternative method which, according to Gross (2001) does not increase blood pressure, and takes less away from mental energy so that people are more able to learn coping strategies for the next time. Learning specific techniques for dealing with overwhelming emotions such as reappraisal rather than suppression is a lynch-pin of both the group training of Gratz and Gunderson (Gratz & Gunderson, 2006) and of the STEPPS programme (Van Wel et al., 2006); we would recommend that this would be a valuable addition to the therapy of anyone who repeatedly self-injures, too.

Reappraisal as a technique for dealing with overwhelming emotions
The following example illustrates how reappraisal can work in practice, and contrasts this with (less healthy) suppression.

Amy was a bit late for her appointment with her regular therapist, and this distressed her because she had a lot to talk about. She had cut herself badly a few days before, and her partner had been unusually critical. In fact, she had threatened to move out. Amy was distraught to be told that the therapist was herself late, because there had been an emergency which she had been called away to deal with. Amy felt her head getting heavy, like there was a hammer beating on her head, and she wondered if she would be able to hang on before cutting herself, which she knew would make her feel better physically, if only for a while. The receptionist encouraged her to stay but she wanted to run out.

After 30 minutes, her therapist did arrive but Amy no longer felt she wanted to see her. Once they were in the meeting room, the therapist apologized but explained that her own lateness had been unavoidable. Amy said ...

(Suppression scenario) ... that it was fine. She quite understood, but as she had a really bad headache, she would rather go home and make another appointment. The therapist who was feeling frazzled herself said this was OK, and that she quite understood. Amy went into the toilets on the way out and cut herself rather messily. She had to be taken to the casualty department to be stitched immediately.

(Reappraisal scenario) ... that she felt really bad, but she could not say why. She had been telling herself that she should just swallow her feelings as she was sure that the therapist could not help being late – and anyway, someone else obviously needed the therapist a lot more than she (Amy) did. The therapist said, 'is that what you expect? That whenever you want something a lot, someone will always stop you getting it?' Amy started to cry and said that she agreed. Then Amy said that (after she had thought about it) the reason that she felt bad was more to do with her assumption that the therapist was going to punish her than that the therapist was 30 minutes late. After all, a 30-minute delay was nothing so long as she knew that she would get the help she needed from the therapist eventually. After realizing this, Amy said that she started to feel less like running out the room and, in fact, that she was starting to feel better altogether. She had successfully reappraised her emotions as being a throwback to the past, which she could replace with a more valid appraisal of the present.

SELF-HELP

Self-help, according to the British Association for Behavioural and Cognitive Psychotherapies, is using material either alone or with limited professional assistance to teach skills and to treat a problem. As with every intervention, however, there are both advantages and disadvantages.

The positive aspects of self-help are its low cost (especially compared to private counselling or therapy if one has to pay for it oneself), and the ability to learn in one's own time and at one's own pace (particularly useful at times when concentration is poor). Once acquired, the self-help material remains available and can be re-visited if memory fails or if a problem that seemed to have been overcome returns unexpectedly. Sometimes the material includes a list of reasons for giving up self-injury (often sourced from other people in a similar position) and reading though this can be a useful way of diverting negative thoughts and stimulating a feeling of hopefulness.

The disadvantages are that the quality of self-help material is often quite variable, and it is not always clear exactly what one is getting or whether others have found it helpful. Concentrating solely on self-help methods may result in professional assessment being bypassed, and this is a further disadvantage. Some types of self-help material are only useful if they match correctly to a clearly defined diagnosis or difficulty, and this often requires input from a professional. As we have already noted, everyone has blind spots.

Books, tapes and other reading material

Over the last decade, a considerable number of booklets and leaflets on self-harm have become available from voluntary organizations, mental health trusts, charities, professional groups, youth organizations and women's groups. All will include sections that cover self-injury. Some are aimed at the sufferer, some at parents and others at partners or close friends who want to learn more about self-injury and what they can do to support someone who does it. Many of these booklets are free, and those that are not are usually quite cheap. Some can be read through in ten minutes or less, whereas others are quite comprehensive and constitute a self-help package in their own right. The more comprehensive booklets are likely to include sections advising on self-care, understanding and enhancing one's relationships with others, looking at what self-injury means to the individual reader, ideas for coping with flashbacks and urges to self-harm, sources of professional and informal support as well as wound care. There are also several very comprehensive, structured packages (some including audiotapes or a DVD) which are designed to be accessed regularly and which aim to teach skills such as distress tolerance, anxiety management and problem solving. A number of examples are given in the Appendix.

Self-help and support groups

Self-help and support groups have become increasingly common over recent years and may have displaced some of the more traditional therapeutic groups with an inter- or intra-personal focus (Horne, 1999). Reasons for this move away from more traditional group format include an increased desire among members for empowerment and control, dissatisfaction with health services and changes in society whereby information is increasingly valued. A typical support group is one which consists of between 4 and 12 members sitting in a circle, where attendance is valued and which is facilitated by a trained leader (Horne, 1999). Self-help groups differ from support groups by having an emphasis on education and information gathering, shared leadership and often a degree of estrangement from social norms (Gazda, 1989), although issues of empowerment and mutual aid are common to both types of group.

Both types of group are available for people who self-harm. They offer the person who self-injures the chance to engage with others who are unlikely to judge or criticize their appearance or preferred means of coping with difficulty. Both types of group have the advantage of providing support and company, plus the opportunity to learn from the experiences of others. Perhaps the biggest disadvantage is that continued membership of such groups allows the person who self-injures to at last feel that he or she 'has a place'. This apparently positive aspect can, unfortunately, become a negative characteristic if the person then starts to develop the identity of a 'self-injurer' and perhaps comes to feel that they can only remain within the supportive group if they continue to self-injure.

Support and self-help via the Internet

The Internet is an increasingly popular medium for communication, education and mutual support, and many people who self-injure now use it for advice and information. Formats include *bulletin boards* – where email messages are sent ('posted') for public display, *chat rooms* – where anyone who is logged in can view email exchanges between members as they occur and *listserv facilities* – where every contribution made over a period of time is sent periodically to each member. Some groups operate in more than one format. For example, a bulletin board for people who self-injure may offer an additional service that periodically emails a summary of all messages that have been posted to it. In this way each member has access to a full history of all postings and so can be sure they will never miss a message of interest to them.

A considerable number of groups offer support specifically to those who self-injure. Many are open with few membership restrictions, and so are available to anyone with access to a computer and a telephone line. Others are closed and require a new member to make an application which must be approved by the group itself, or else its facilitator, before access is permitted. Some groups operate relatively informally; members agree on joining to abide by a few key ground rules, and there is no central facilitator. Other groups run with a facilitator (or 'moderator') who monitors the discourse, provides occasional input and draws attention to situations where a ground rule appears to be violated. Moderators usually reserve the right to terminate the membership of any contributor who is disruptive or who posts messages that are disrespectful to other members.

Some information is available about the ways in which Internet-based support groups function (e.g. Davidson, 1998). Typically there will be perhaps 7 or 8 contributors active at any one time, similar to the conventional 'small group' format, but with many more members reading the group's discourse and perhaps contributing themselves at a later time. Characteristics of Internet group functioning include interwoven threads of discourse, a shared need for safety, a tendency for sub-groups to form and the occasional scapegoating through projective identification. These dynamics are similar to those described by Kreeger (1994) for a classic 'large group' and Davidson suggests that individuals communicating on the Internet may act as a rare example of a healthy, functioning large group.

Obtaining help and support via Internet-based groups offers certain advantages. The communication is text-based rather than verbal, which is helpful to those who struggle with talking to others face-to-face. The user can be sure they are not being judged on physical appearance, or on their race, age, or gender unless they choose to disclose such information. There are also advantages for those with shame issues, with social phobia and for those whose traumatic past makes conventional communication with strangers difficult. The process of writing down emotional material has been shown to help reduce anxiety and depressive symptoms and is also valuable in crisis support – the Samaritans in Britain have used email for this purpose since 1994. The asynchronous nature of any communication requires the user to exercise some patience in waiting for a response, but this also permits them a delay in responding, allowing pause for thought. This may be particularly beneficial for someone who has trouble ordering their thoughts in the moment or who regularly experiences dissociative phenomena. The absence of conventional boundaries of space also confers advantages; there are fewer physical barriers to attendance in groups and participation is easier for those living in remote areas, the housebound and the physically impaired (Morrissey, 1997).

Disadvantages of text-based communication include a dis-inhibition effect, a tendency for messages to appear colder than the author intended and the lack of visual or audible clues. Members have only limited information about other correspondents, which may be a disadvantage when trying to form opinions about others and could interfere with establishing trust with a therapist or with members of a peer group at some later point. Other disadvantages are the requirement that the user be reasonably literate and able use a keyboard, and that some people are more comfortable with the spoken rather than the written word. Although individuals gain freedom from not having to attend sessions or meetings at pre-determined times and places, this can be a disadvantage for clients who benefit from the structure such appointments provide.

The number of sites offering information to people who self-injure appears to be increasing steadily and some examples are given in the Appendix. Many provide ideas of way to cope with distress, advice for choosing a therapy or therapist, ways of managing wounds and scars, details of organizations and links to other relevant web pages. Advantages include ease of access to a vast amount of information, and the ability to select websites that provide information in a format that suits the individual. A recent survey on using the Internet as a source of self-help for people who self-harm concluded that most of the information available was about self-injury (rather than self-poisoning) and that many individuals and organizations regarded Internet information about self-harm as a valuable service (Prasad & Owens, 2001). Disadvantages are that many sites are unregulated and it is hard to be sure of the accuracy of the information. There is also the possibility of accessing (intentionally or accidentally) one of the increasing numbers of websites which provide infor-mation about how to commit suicide (Alao et al., 1999).

DEALING WITH ABUSE

Cohen and colleagues (Cohen et al., 2003) have recently reviewed treatments for borderline personality and substance abuse disorder in adolescents, and their recommendations seem to us also to be very relevant to older people who injure themselves repeatedly. They identify ten key elements, the first of which is the establishment of a consistent, trusting relationship. The authors suggest that this relationship should have structure, but needs also to be sufficiently flexible for the number of sessions available for each treatment component to be adjusted as needed. Change to the order in which the different components are introduced may also be required.

The other elements identified are: providing psycho-education; enhancing stress management, problem-solving and social skills; utilizing exposure tech-niques to help create a narrative of past traumatic experiences; addressing inaccurate cognitions which contribute to negative affect or self-destructive behaviour; and improving the ability to manage negative emotions. Involving carers or partners in treatment and offering adjunctive medications are also advocated, where appropriate.

Perhaps the single most important element of this long list is to treat each person according to their particular needs, experiences, strengths and weaknesses. It is also important to use a collaborative approach based on providing information and explanations to clients about what is being proposed, and why. If there is any single therapeutic manoeuvre, it is to assist clients to be able to tolerate or contain bad thoughts without feeling impelled to act to get rid of them by self-injury (Chapman et al., 2005).

COPING WITH TENSION AND THE WINDING SPRING

The 'switch' pathway appears to become increasingly important in people the more they self-injure. However, as discussed in Chapter 3, self-injury frequently results from the sufferer experiencing a 'spring' of tension winding up to a level of intolerability. This mechanism – which we have called the spring pathway – is of importance for anyone who self-injures, including those who sometimes follow the 'switch' pathway to self-harm.

Techniques to help people to cope with this type of rising tension in the short-term have been discussed in the previous chapter and include distraction and substitution activities such as snapping an elastic band against the wrist. Interventions which seek to help people cope with the winding spring of tension in the longer-term need to focus on two important areas. The first is helping the sufferer to be able to recognize the tension in the spring before it has wound up to discharge point, and our experience is that some clients find this extremely difficult. The second is to help the individual to recognize what winds him or her up in the first place; many clients find this an easier task (at least initially), since most are already able to identify two or three trigger situations. Both techniques will be as important for people seeking to overcome repeated self-injury as for people who have only injured themselves a few times.

One starting point to this might be to ask the client if there are any signs that they recognize of getting tense: perhaps they start to sleep less well, or smoke, eat or drink more. Perhaps they become snappier, or look more at their wrists, or concentrate less well. Listing first all the possible 'early warning' signs and subsequently working through and keeping that list easily available can help someone to be more aware of getting wound-up at a time when they can still do something about it. It can sometimes be difficult carrying out this type of work in a reliable way simply by reviewing it after the event in a one-to-one therapy session. Clients sometimes have difficulty remembering accurately the emotional and situational precipitants for a cut or burn that occurred several days before unless these seemed particularly significant at the time. Writing down thoughts and feelings close to the time they are experienced can enhance many aspects of psychotherapeutic work. In this case keeping such a diary can be particularly useful in helping people be more aware of which events wind them up. Some clients prefer initially to write their diary in conventional 'essay' form, although having a (separate) blank table to complete can help in keeping a focus for this specific task. The table takes the form of a simple chronological record of 'situations', their associated 'thoughts' and any 'early warning signs'. Reviewing the table entries week by week will help the client and the therapist, working together, to begin to categorize the situations that are most likely to push the client towards self-injury. Once this is known, the client can begin to work out what feelings come from these situations, and therefore what feelings wind their particular spring. We have considered these in some detail in Chapter 3 where we saw that the commonest feelings are of abandonment, helplessness or impotence, but it is important that the client and the therapist are able to list the specific, personal emotions linked with self-injury and not just rely on a generalized list that applies to many people.

Once some of the key emotions and situations have been established, strategies can be devised to deal with them. As conflict is often a particular factor contributing to the tension that winds the spring, conflict management methods will often be relevant, particularly if they can be taught by professionals who are able to stay in the company of people who self-injure without displaying strong emotions, either of criticism or sympathy. Most people who repeatedly self-injure tend to avoid conflict, just as they try to suppress emotion. Their second line is to fall back on control or coercion. Negotiation is usually the most successful method of conflict resolution, but is much less often chosen by people who self-injure, perhaps because their own experience has so often been that differences are not accepted but have to be either hidden or removed. It may be this approach to conflict that makes people sometimes say that people who repeatedly self-injure are usually 'black and white thinkers' and that their attitude to other people is either they are all good, or all bad, but that there is no in between.

A FRAMEWORK FOR PROFESSIONAL INTERVENTION

Dealing with repeated self-injury means finding new ways with emotions, and with habitual ways of dealing with emotions. We have considered some of these in detail in this chapter. The information about emotional processing available to professionals is expanding, and what we have said has used some of this up-to-date knowledge. We think that it is important that professionals working with people who self-injure, particularly those who do so repeatedly, maintain their theoretical knowledge about the psychology and sociology of emotion so that they can apply new ideas to their practice as they come along. However, we do not think that it is sufficient for professionals to keep this knowledge to themselves and apply it to their clients without engaging them in the process. Working with clients is a collaborative venture because that's the way it works best. Knowledge needs to be shared as well as the decision-making about the goals and methods of the work.

Let's therefore consider how this might translate into actual client work. Many people and institutions that work with people who injure themselves like to start with a therapeutic contract. So let's start there. We would prefer to call this a memorandum of agreement; not a document that any party signs, nor one that pretends to have some quasi-legal force, but an explication of what both sides will do, and what they expect of each other. This is different from the conventional 'No Self-Harm Contract' which usually makes very clear what is required of the client while saying little about what commitments are made by the professionals involved in his or her care. The memorandum of agreement referred to here considers the expectations and commitments of all parties to an equal degree. Its content should be the result of collaborative discussion, its wording should be agreed by both client and professional, and it should be specific to that particular individual. It should not be a 'standardised' photocopied pro-forma of the type sometimes used in busy institutions where every client needs to be seen to have a 'care plan' in their notes.

A MEMORANDUM OF AGREEMENT

The memorandum of agreement results from initial discussions. We think that these are essential in working with people who self-injure, and yet they are often avoided. This may be because self-injury seems to demand urgent intervention, and so seems to push everyone into jumping in to treatment 'at the deep end'. In retrospect it can seem less benign, amounting to a recapitulation by professionals of the traumatizing relationships that so many people who self-injure have previously experienced. One useful way of considering the preliminary negotiations has been provided by Prochaska and colleagues (Prochaska & Velicer, 1997), and it can be very useful to have copies of a card on which the various stages are described for use in the sessions and for the client to take away with them for reference. Prochaska and DiClimente's stage method (summarized in Text Box 4.1) is often linked to motivational interviewing (Miller, 2000) which is not, as is sometimes assumed, a method of 'motivating' people to undertake therapy. It is, in fact, a method of understanding people's motives or rather what they want to change about themselves, and also what they want to remain the same if that is possible. Motivational interviewing can change motives when the discussion about what people want to stay the same demonstrates to them either that change is inevitable or that change might bring more benefits than has been apparent previously.

The context in which negotiation takes place also affects the memorandum of agreement. An offender who wants to make an impression on the parole board will have different motives to an employed person living alone, and he or she will have different motives to a young person living at home with parents, or to someone living with a partner or with children. It may be useful for the preliminary negotiations to have representation from the third parties involved, providing of course that the client agrees. However, it is important to remember that people who injure themselves have often done so to re-establish some degree of autonomy in the face of control by others. Respect for autonomy – already a fundamental ethical duty for counsellors, psychotherapists and other healthcare professionals – not only has to be observed, but seen to be observed. It may sometimes be more ethical not to include one or more third parties in this stage of the therapeutic process.

People who injure themselves repeatedly may need assessment after a crisis as we described in Chapter 7, and there are rare circumstances when compulsion may be justified. Outside these rare crisis situations, we think that compulsory treatment is rarely, if ever, justified. But this does not mean that professionals should be complacent about people who injure themselves repeatedly and then drop out of treatment. A considerable amount of evidence has accumulated to show that people with relationship problems of all kinds – and we include people who self-injure here – drop out of treatment not because they are getting better, but because they are not getting helped. Follow up shows that the outcome of people who drop out is worse than those who continue with treatment for many different treatment modalities. So if someone declines an intervention now, it is important to leave the door open for reconsideration in the future. This may be achieved by giving the person the opportunity to have a review in 6 or 12 months time; by providing them with reliable and easy to apply information about making a new appointment; or by providing sufficient information to a primary care team to expedite re-referral.

THE CONTEXT OF CARE

Many people who repeatedly self-injure seem much to prefer having contact with the same therapist or key worker over time and to dislike frequent changes in the staff who are involved in their care. This is perhaps unsurprising given the difficulty that many self-injurers have in forming trusting relationships with others. In our own small study, being able to have a long-term relationship with the same key worker was one of the most highly valued therapeutic factors (Huband & Tantam, 2004). The recent UK guidelines on the treatment of self-harm came down in favour of changing therapists, but this was based on one study of people who have recently self-harmed, and not longer-term treatment of repeated self-harming. One point about changing therapist is clearly important. There is chemistry between people that has to be respected: clients and therapists must have some choice in who they work with.

We have slipped into writing about one-to-one work with a professional as if that is the only pattern of care for self-injury. We do think that long-term care is important, and that the main kind of care is likely to be one-to-one, but there are other possibilities. Peer support, family support, a relationship with a partner, group therapy and joining a church or other faith group are all valid alternatives. Professional help may contribute to the success of these, for example by providing psycho-education to families or partners, or by providing mediation and conflict resolution to families, couples or organizations. It is useful to specify which methods are to be used in the memorandum of agreement, and to involve the third parties in the negotiations over the memorandum, too, wherever this is appropriate.

CHANGING IDENTITY

Identifying oneself as a self-injurer can be both hard and reassuring: hard, because it is an identity that may not be acceptable to family, friends or workmates; reassuring because it provides entry into a new and largely supportive world. A person who injures themselves repeatedly gets to know fellow inhabitants of this new world in the waiting rooms and wards of hospitals and clinics, as well as through the Internet. Few professionals visit this world, and none live in it. So its influence over the outcome of self-injury is unknown, although we suspect that it is growing.

There is no reason to doubt that the inhabitants of the self-injury world are as kind and well-meaning as the inhabitants of any other world. In fact, that might be its greatest danger. Giving up self-injury means leaving this world to find another where one can feel completely at home, and this threat to identity may be enough to maintain self-injury and honorary citizenship of the self-injury world.

THE PLACE OF PSYCHOTHERAPY AND COUNSELLING

We began this chapter with a consideration of the specifics of working with people who are trying to overcome self-injury. We suggested that doing this involved learning what to change, and how to change it, but also learning from the experience of trying to change in practice. This kind of learning is sometimes called 'learning by doing', experiential learning or deep learning. It is the kind of learning that involves learning new habits as well as new facts, and it is a kind of learning that changes the way the learner feels about themselves and their world, too.

In the second part of this chapter we considered the context in which learning had to take place, with particular consideration that it should be one that calls for new responses to situations and provides the support to foster them.

Finally, we considered the developmental context of change, which is how the context might itself change as the person who is giving up self-injury changes. As we saw in Chapter 6, repeated self-injury provides an identity that must be replaced by something new and more fulfilling if the self-injury is to be abandoned.

We summarize these steps in the order in which they might be taken in an actual treatment package in Text Box 8.2.

Text Box 8.2   Steps in professional intervention

- Conducting an initial interview
- Negotiating a memorandum of agreement
- Agreeing responsibilities of professionals, clients and any third parties
- Delivering treatment intervention
- Providing a psycho-education package (if not already a component of the intervention)
- Dealing with cravings
- Dealing with dissociation in the short-term
- Identifying triggers to switching
- Reducing dissociative tendencies in the longer-term
- Dealing with problems of abuse, if any
- Addressing emotional regulation
- Detecting the tension in the spring
- Exploring techniques to prevent tension building
- Finding alternative interpersonal strategies
- Strengthening identity change

This might all seem rather complicated, and so we end this chapter on a note of simplicity. All of these very different activities can be subsumed within the longer-term counselling or psychotherapy provided by experienced, trained professionals.

We think that the training provided to therapeutic counsellors or psycho-therapists makes them ideally suited to help people who injure themselves repeatedly, so long as they have the right temperament (for example, the ability to accept risk with equanimity and not to become too controlling in uncertain situations) and so long as they have experience of what it is like to become addicted to self-injury. It will sometimes be the case that people have acquired this experience having been self-injurers themselves. Most often they will have acquired it vicariously through working with and listening to people who self-injure. This requires an immersion in the lives and experiences of people who injure themselves that can only be provided by getting to know an adequate number of different people who do so, usually by being attached to a service dedicated to this group.

Chapter 9

Summary and Conclusions

INTRODUCTION

Not all readers have the time or inclination to read a book of this type from cover to cover. Some will prefer instead to use the index and the table of contents to direct them to a specific topic of interest. This can be an efficient use of time, but it carries with it the risk of failing to understand (or even misinterpreting) an important concept that has been explained earlier but is now referred to only by name.

This chapter aims to avoid such a difficulty by providing a short summary of the various ideas developed within the book. It is placed at the book's end, but could be read first as a concise overview. A number of cross-references are included so that the reader can rapidly locate where an idea was originally explained or an argument developed, and where more detail can be found.

> Private self-injury is usually a secretive activity done to change how a person feels

We have used the term 'private self-injury' for the type of self-harm that is the focus of this book. It can be seen as problematic because it is not socially sanctioned in Western society. It has been described in some detail in Chapter 1, the key points of which are summarized in the following paragraphs.

Private self-injury can be defined as self-inflicted tissue damage that is usually performed in secret, and in which the creation of the wound is an end in itself. Significant anatomical change is not sought. It is usually performed without the assistance of others, and without clear suicidal intent. The injury itself and the scars that result are hidden as being a source of shame (page 2). The arms and legs seem the most common targets (page 11), perhaps simply because of convenience. Estimates of incidence and prevalence vary (page 4), but at least 1 in 600 adults injure themselves sufficiently to receive hospital treatment – and rates appear to be increasing. Both men and women are affected. It is possible that as many men and boys injure themselves as do women and girls, although the relative prevalence rates are uncertain (page 4), partly because women are more likely to seek help and so their self-injury is more likely to be recorded.

Self-injury is more common in people with eating disorders – particularly bulimia and substance misuse (page 9) – and there is also an association with certain mood disorders (page 7) as well as with other forms of self-harm. Self-injury is especially common in prisons, with female prisoners more likely to injure themselves than male inmates. People who are socially or financially disadvantaged (page 7), or who experience significant adversity in childhood (page 6) seem to be particularly at risk. There is a clear associa-tion with youth (page 5), possibly because the behaviour gets performed as a type of self-healing during a difficult developmental phase, or in a struggle to establish an identity. The ability to dissociate is generally more common in the young, and this too may be a factor since self-injury and dissociation are closely linked.

Skin cutting and burning appear as the commonest forms, with cutting the most prevalent. A dysphoric state usually precedes self-injury, and relief usually follows it but with reluctance to seek medical care (page 12). The act is anticipated, either with craving for its effects (pages 17, 40), or with mount-ing tension associated with a struggle to avoid self-harm (pages 26, 40). Any thoughts of the consequences are usually dismissed when the wound is made, as is the case with most addictive behaviours. Some people feel little pain at the time they self-injure, whereas others report that the pain they experience is one of the reasons they do it (page 27).

Self-injury is usually repeated because it is a means of changing how a person feels. It is usually carried out to relieve 'bad' feelings that cannot be dealt with in any other way (page 39). It can occur while in a dissociated state so that the person is not aware of what they are doing until after it has happened (page 52). It is not, however, a response to command hallucinations or psychotic delusions.

People who injure themselves tend to have experienced more than average adversity, either in childhood or in their more recent past. Many have rather poor ability to manage everyday stresses. For them, self-injury becomes a type of coping strategy in which the self-created wound is the goal. This can lead to repetition, and repeated self-injury often becomes addictive and extremely hard to give up once it becomes entrenched (page 21).

The long-term outcome cannot easily be predicted for any particular individual. For some, the pattern is one of a time-limited disorder that begins in early adolescence and remits spontaneously in middle age. For others, regular repetition results in chronicity, an over-reliance on self-injury as a means of coping and a tendency for it to gradually become less effective at relieving difficult feelings. Longer-term consequences include frequent breakdown of close relationships, deterioration of other coping resources, increased isolation, loss of self-confidence, difficulties arising from scarring and physical disability as well as an increased risk of mortality (page 12).

We conclude that self-injury is a complex, private and often shameful activity. There seems little doubt that people who self-injure do so in an attempt to make themselves feel better, and that the creation of a wound is remarkably effective at achieving this speedily and, in the early days, quite reliably. We find it unsurprising that self-injury becomes a kind of 'self-help treatment of choice' for those that do it, that it gets repeated when that person again feels distress, and that it has addictive qualities. But we are also aware that there can be considerable variation among those who harm themselves in this way, and that it is necessary to consider each person individually when attempting to provide help.

> Self-injury exerts a powerful emotional impact on others because of the 'safety-catch' against injury that we all share

We introduced in Chapter 3 the idea of an automatic resistance that all human beings have to getting hurt or injured, and called this the 'safety-catch' (page 31). All people have an in-built mechanism ensuring they minimize the risk of injury to themselves, and so the default position for this safety-catch is 'on'.

We believe that the biggest single problem associated with self-injury is its emotional impact. This is an important theme, and one that runs throughout the book. The concept of the safety-catch can be used to help explain why self-injury exerts such a powerful and personal impact, and why it is so disturbing to witness someone self-injure (page 33). We have also found the idea useful in helping to understand why some people find it easier to self-injure than do others, and to explain why self-injury should not necessarily be seen as an extreme behaviour. The concept is easily understood by clients and so might usefully be introduced into clinical work with someone who wants to reduce their self-injury.

The safety-catch can be explained as a type of automatic protection that causes people to react strongly against anything that is likely to result in their physical injury (such as grasping a carving knife by its blade, or pouring boiling water over the skin). This self-protective function is either innate or else acquired from early caregivers (page 32). We suggest three factors that maintain such resistance – disgust, fear and pain.

One interesting feature of the safety-catch is that it must be by-passed for someone to be able to cut or burn their skin (page 33). It is significant that most people struggle at first to imagine how this might be achieved, for the safety-catch seems like a common-sense instinct and one that would be difficult to turn off. It is particularly hard to imagine neutralizing it to the point where we could slash at our own arm with a razor blade. We think this is partly because the safety-catch operates at the level of the individual. Although common to all human beings, it is very personal in the way it works. We automatically think 'I could never do that to myself', even when there is no hint of a suggestion that we should or would.

It appears, however, that the safety-catch is subverted quite easily if the conditions are right, and that society actually provides directions about the circumstances in which this can happen. Chapter 3 has provided examples of how the safety-catch can become temporarily turned off by prevailing social norms (page 36), as well as by emotional shock (page 35), following intoxication (page 35), during religious, spiritual or audio-visual experiences (page 34) as well as in response to the behaviour of public figures (page 38). The safety-catch can also be subverted with practice, leading to habituation (page 38). This has clear relevance to those who repeatedly self-injure since, in theory, they will become progressively more accomplished at suspending their own safety-catch with each new self-inflicted injury.

Considering the factors that maintain the safety-catch helps explain why witnessing accidental injury often gives rise to strong emotional reaction. Such experiences resonate awkwardly with our own automatic resistance to being harmed. But in cases where the skin cutting is intentional and self-inflicted, catching sight of someone's self-inflicted wounds (or, worse still, catching sight of someone in the process of self-injuring) evokes this disgust or horror at the person who has done the cutting, and not just at the wounds.

This, we suggest, provides clues as to why people who self-injure are often marginalized by those who do not. The difficulty here is that being in the company of someone who has self-injured can engage one's own safety-catch. Personal reactions in such a situation are often quite strong. They may be strong enough to prevent carers dealing with the resulting wounds (or the person who has self-injured) with the diligence and compassion they would normally offer to someone injured in, say, a car crash. We believe that a common reaction is to try to rationalize this defensively. One way is to view self-injury as a very disturbed behaviour, or to view the person doing it as a very disturbed individual. Awareness of the possibility of such a reaction is important not only when attempting to provide care and support, but also when formulating one's own opinions about self-injury.

> People who repeatedly self-injure commonly experience a cycle of increasing tension which the injury relieves

It is possible to view self-injury as analogous to scratching angrily at an itch that has become unbearable. In actual self-injury, however, the focus is not on an itch but on emotional discomfort. We see this discomfort as the emotional trigger for self-injury (pages 26, 41). We used the analogy of a water-pistol in Chapter 3 to illustrate how the emotional trigger often has to be re-applied frequently before someone finally resorts to cutting or burning their skin (page 26). We suggested that whereas the first few experiences of triggering emotion seem to have little effect (as with the first few squeezes on the trigger of a water pistol), they act progressively to build up the internal pressure. Put another way, they are like the trigger on a water pistol that pumps up the pressure in the water until something has to be released.

Those affected find that the more tense they get, the more wound-up they feel. It is as if there is a spring of tension winding inside them. Many report an inner struggle during which they make considerable efforts to avoid self-injury until, finally, they are no longer able to hold the tension inside. A wound is then made which leads to rapid reduction in tension and an improvement in mood. We termed this the 'spring' pathway to self-injury, but it is often know as the 'tension reduction model' (page 40). Ultimately, it is the cut or burn that provides relief. But the relief is only temporary, and can soon be replaced by feelings of shame and even self-disgust at having injured again. This may of itself be sufficient to re-start the cycle, especially as shame is a strong emotion that seems to be able to act as both trigger and consequence.

It is not entirely clear why the skin should provide a way of discharging these unpleasant feelings so effectively. Self-injury may be an extreme form of self-grooming since both can act as distractors, both offer similar benefits and both seem to have a direct (if unclear) effect on neurochemistry (page 44). We also noted that grooming can be used to compensate for negative feelings arising from contact with others and to compensate for the effects of social isolation – and it seems as though self-injury has a similar potential.

The fact that self-injury can improve mood is not enough to explain why a person might consider doing it in the first place. Some people may begin cutting or burning their skin simply as a result of experimenting, but the presence of the safety-catch makes this unlikely in most cases. It can begin by copying others directly, through hearing or reading about others who do it, or as a development of hitting oneself in frustration. But we also think that injuring the skin can appeal as a kind of enactment (pages 45, 61), perhaps in parallel with the recent increase in the popularity of tattooing and body piercing. Self-injury may improve mood via such enactment as a way of re-establishing ownership of one's skin. Skin cutting is one means of regaining possession of an area of skin that has come to feel alien following earlier abuse (page 61). It may also be used as re-enactment of previously experienced trauma in an attempt to re-assert control of the situation in a symbolic way (page 61).

There are certain types of emotion that commonly act as triggers. Some will be particularly distressing because of past experiences. Feelings of powerlessness, self-dislike, suffering, resentment, shame and fear are commonly experienced prior to self-injury (pages 42, 63). We find it interesting that these are emotions that are hard to express, and that are often suppressed. They are also feelings that people tend to dwell on and ruminate about, and we think this ties in with our assertion that cognitive rehearsal of past experience can play a significant part in the build up to a self-inflicted injury.

> It is not always possible to pin down in words the clear function or meaning of self-injury

The puzzling and upsetting nature of the behaviour can lead both professional and lay carers striving to find a single, neat explanation as to why a particular person self-injures and what purpose it serves for him or her. Various psychological, psychoanalytical and behavioural theories have been suggested that seek to explain the functions served by self-injury (page 28) as well as the factors that maintain it (page 30). We conclude, however, that searching for one single cause or purpose is usually fruitless because, like other addictive behaviours, self-injury is over-determined and so can serve more than one function simultaneously. It may be more productive to work with clients individually to explore whether there are certain functions that seem particularly relevant for them.

We have observed that self-injury can be viewed both as a behaviour (which implies that it may be intrinsic or learned or conditioned) and as an action (which implies it has a meaning or meanings). But it is not obviously either (page 15). We believe it is preferable to keep both approaches in mind rather than choosing one over the other, and that this is particularly important when searching for a purpose or a theoretical explanation. Taking self-injury purely as a behaviour suggests that it is not chosen, and so it is difficult to hold the person responsible for it, but as a behaviour it is also has no meaning. On the other hand, taking it purely as an action implies that the person could stop doing so if he or she chose to do so, but as an action it has meaning. It is also the case that actions like self-injury do not have fixed meanings, but are open to interpretation and re-interpretation.

We find that becoming familiar with these various theories is useful if it is done with the aim of increasing awareness and broadening one's thinking. Attempting to match a particular theoretical explanation to a specific individual or to a particular act or pattern of self-injury is likely to be considerably less productive.

> Repeated self-injury can be addictive

A person's experience before, during and after self-injury can become addictive surprisingly quickly. In our view, self-injury carries with it an emotional flavour which becomes so effective in absorbing unpleasant feelings, and even changing them into something more palatable, that the person feels drawn more and more to it (page 70).

Cravings for further self-injury occur, and these are often intense. As with other addictions, the person rapidly becomes dependent on cutting or burning their skin if they feel that is the only way they can deal with feelings or situations that they find difficult. As with other addictions, a tolerance develops with time so that the behaviour becomes less effective as a coping mechanism.

> Some people who repeatedly self-injure can switch into a different state of consciousness in which they find that they have injured themselves

We have found it helpful to consider a second – and often misunderstood – route to self-injury which we term the 'switch' pathway (page 56). This occurs when a person who has no thoughts of self-harm, and feels little desire or craving to do so, suddenly switches into injuring themselves. Here the cut or burn is made almost without thinking, which is in contrast to the 'spring' pathway where there is a progressive build-up of tension. We see this alternative pathway involving the person switching into a different state of mind or consciousness – and this new state is one that makes self-injury very likely to recur in someone who regularly does it.

There is some evidence that people who experience this type of switching are often those who have been injuring themselves over a longer period, or who self-injure more frequently or more deeply, compared to those who experience only the 'spring' path (page 40). They also seem more prone to dissociation and more likely to experience the addictive features of self-injury that include craving for its repetition.

One difficulty with this switch pathway is that it is so unpredictable. People who experience it are usually also very familiar with the spring path, and so are surprised when they suddenly realize they have cut or burnt their skin again. This unpredictability is confusing for carers, too, and can lead to misunderstandings over how much effort a person is really making to resist their urge to self-harm.

The trigger for this switching process seems to be different from the emotional trigger that winds up and eventually releases the spring of tension. It often takes the form of some reminder of previous self-injury, like suddenly finding a razor blade in a drawer. We have used the concept of emotional flavour to explain how this type of trigger works (page 55). For people who cut themselves often, for example, the blade can become associated with the emotions they experienced before previous cutting episodes and, importantly, the relief they regularly experience after having cut their skin.

We have suggested this 'switch' pathway based on our research findings and on our clinical experience with people who self-injure. Others may prefer instead to see this type of self-injury as an example of impulsive self-harm, but we have tried to avoid invoking the notion of impulsivity in this context because impulsivity is such a broad concept. Recent research has shown that impulsivity is not solely a trait driven by biological processes but one that is also influenced by life experiences. Also that it is not just one trait, but several. Viewing self-injury as an essentially impulsive act makes it difficult to account for times when there is a protracted struggle to resist. Furthermore, it does not fit well with the type of person who sometimes cuts suddenly and unexpectedly, but who otherwise is not at all impulsive. These difficulties can be circumvented, we think, by introducing the idea that there are two different pathways to self-injury, and that it is not unusual for a person to have experience of both. There is also the advantage that the concept of a switch pathway is fairly easily understood by clients and can form a useful starting point for discussions about how a person who self-injures can reduce the tendency to dissociate and increase their awareness of potential triggers.

Dissociation plays an important role in repeated self-injury

Dissociation can be seen as a loss of awareness of an action or perception. As such, people who experience significant dissociation can sometimes appear to others to be acting with full awareness and yet have little or no awareness themselves.

Dissociation and self-injury are closely linked. People who self-injure tend to dissociate more than those who do not, particularly if they do so frequently. People whose self-injury has become repetitive can find themselves switching between emotional states that have become dissociated or separated from each other. This can result in a potentially dangerous form of self-injury that is performed without premeditation and outside of the person's awareness.

It is possible to discern three distinct types of dissociation. One form ('absorption') is generally viewed as normal and controllable (page 51). It involves a person concentrating their attention to the point that he or she is completely absorbed in what they are thinking or doing. It is something that most of us have experienced.

There is a second type which can usefully be termed 'dissociative detachment' (page 51). A key feature is a loss of emotional meaning, and the detachment presents itself as the experience of feeling unreal, feeling 'spaced out' or feeling numb. It includes depersonalization and derealization states. It is often suggested that is that self-injury has a powerful ability to terminate this type of unpleasant dissociation and that this is one reason why people injure themselves. We agree that the overall effect of cutting or burning the skin can be very effective in terminating unwelcome dissociative states, but we suggest that self-injury probably does not have a direct effect on dissociative detachment. It seems more likely that it relieves the tension and anxiety that were maintaining the dissociation, and may even have initiated it (page 53).

The third type is termed 'compartmentalisation' (pages 51, 53). Here an internal separation develops between, for example, the thoughts, actions and feelings that a person feels they own and control and those that are disavowed or repressed. One consequence is that memory becomes fragmented. Someone who experiences this type of dissociation may not recall cutting or burning their skin, and find they sometimes self-injure as if on 'automatic pilot'. Factors that increase the risk of this fragmentation include repeated self-deception, previous sexual abuse, and the experience of feeling threatened or controlled by others.

Dissociation tends to become easier the more a person does it (page 54). This has clinical significance. People who regularly self-injure can become quite proficient at dissociating which in turn weakens the safety-catch and so makes further self-harm yet more likely. This suggests that clinical interventions with people who self-injure should educate about dissociation in general, as well as addressing how triggers for dissociation may be avoided on an individual basis.

> Giving up self-injury requires considerable determination, but just trying hard is not enough

Any intervention that focuses on getting someone to stop self-injury makes very good sense to the outside observer who may be struggling with the idea that a person they care about has become addicted to cutting or burning their skin. Professionals too can fall into the trap of desperately wanting to 'make it stop'. However, not everyone who self-injures will have reached the point where they want to give it up. Some are unwilling even to consider any reduction at present, although they may still welcome help with other issues that trouble them. Others may have been considering stopping, but are yet only at the stage of preparation and are not yet ready to take action. For both groups, exerting pressure to stop may actually increase their self-harm. The notion of a 'treatment for self-injury' sits awkwardly in these circumstances. We prefer to think in terms of an 'intervention for people who self-injure', since this throws the focus onto the person rather than the behaviour.

There is a third group who are ready to take action and who want to change. Members of this group invariably report that giving up self-injury is hard to do and requires considerable determination. Their desire for change arises from recognition of the adverse long-term consequences of self-injury, but their main difficulty arises because of the significance of the short-term rewards.

Determination can be weakened by several factors (page 68). It will, for example, be undermined by circumstances that increase the trigger emotions, and any relapse is likely to have a significant effect since the shame in feeling one has failed again itself constitutes a powerful trigger. It is also weakened by repetition, since the more the person falls back on self-injury as a way of changing emotional experience, the more irresistible it becomes. Finally, trying desperately to force oneself to change can, somewhat paradoxically, itself weaken determination. This usually results in strong feelings being suppressed, which in turn further winds the spring of inner tension that so often precedes self-injury.

> Self-injury may be driven by a wish to change identity and self-image

We have suggested that self-injury is frequently linked to a failure to establish a satisfactory identity (page 74). Difficult negative emotions tend to dominate when a person is uncertain about who they are, or when in transition from one identity to another. Self-injury often takes place at such times, possibly because it is so effective at providing a temporary way of managing difficult emotions. If psychotherapeutic intervention is then sought, we believe it should not focus solely, or even mainly, on the person's self-injury, but rather on assisting that person to establish a solid identity that feels comfortable to them.

One fundamental component of identity – the body image – has been considered in some detail in Chapter 4. People who self-injure can feel as though their skin has disappeared from their body image. We also think that their body image can become fissured by new internal boundaries. Self-deception and dissociation are examples of such boundaries, and shame can help create them. The body image is changed by the addition of these new internal boundaries so that it cracks or becomes fragmented or twisted. This is an awkward rearrangement, and some characteristics that are crucial to identity get left out or misplaced. As a result, the person feels uncertain about who they are (page 77). Outside observers also are puzzled by apparent inconsistencies in the way the person talks and acts.

The boundary of the self-image is a key element of personal identity, and it seems that people who self-injure often cut their skin as if to break through barrier and so feel whole again. In effect, the skin becomes a testing ground for the boundary. But self-injury is only a temporary solution. It soon becomes a trap because the shame and secrecy that it engenders actually cause these internal boundaries to strengthen, and it becomes more difficult for a person's identity to grow as they become stronger. Here again, self-injury acts as a double-edged sword for it relieves the boundary problem in the short-term while strengthening it in the long-term.

> Establishing a new identity is difficult, but possible

It is possible to identify three factors that are needed for an identity to develop (page 85). The first is its potential final form. As this component is not easily altered it may be more useful to spend time in defining a potential new identity that is realistic, rather than focusing on one that will be almost impossible to achieve.

The second is the energy the person has available to fill that potential and so 'inflate' a new identity. This is sometimes called vital energy, self-efficacy or determination (page 85) and has been shown to be weaker for people who self-injure and for those who have experienced abuse. It is also depleted by the type of negative emotions that trigger self-injury. This can make establishing a new identity particularly difficult for someone who repeatedly cuts or burns their skin. Finding better ways to manage these triggering emotions should be of considerable benefit to someone who wants to develop their sense of identity, but who struggles to find the inner energy to do so.

The third is the nature of the social environment that determines what space is available for an identity to develop. We have found it convenient to see this as a social 'mould' (page 87). The mould can be constricting when other people deny the person the space into which his or her ideal form can develop, and so may need to be broken to allow a new identity to grow. It is possible to break the mould and so move forward, although to do this often means a complete change of one's social environment. In some cases this can mean relocation to a different area and leaving old acquaintances behind. There can also be side effects since it can take some time to readjust to the loss of any care or control that the original mould provided.

Finally, self-injury can of itself lead to development of a new identity – such as that of being a 'cutter' – but when this happens the identity it creates is a secret one that can bring as many snags as it can solutions (page 188).

We conclude that it is quite possible for someone who self-injures to create a new identity and to make it stick. Special attention needs to be paid to ensure that the proposed new identity is realistic, that the person has sufficient reserves of inner energy to achieve it, and that he or she can break out of a constricting social environment if necessary.

> The strength of other people's reactions to self-injury should not be under-estimated

---

Self-injury has a strong emotional impact on other people, particularly for those closely involved such as partners, friends and family members. Professional carers are not immune either (page 109). Reactions to this impact are not easily predicted, but they seem more often to be negative than positive. Negative reactions are generally unhelpful if they lead to the person feeling punished or blamed since these particular feelings are quite likely to have contributed to the creation of the wound in the first place.

Taking time to consider one's own attitudes and reactions can, we think, be as important as considering the reactions of others. Professional staff may, if they are honest, be able to admit that working with people who self-injure challenge their views about their own skills, their role and even their autonomy (page 104). Non-professionals may be able to recognize times when they feel anger and disgust towards someone they care deeply about, and fury at the position they so often find themselves in when trying to deal with yet another self-inflicted injury. The person who self-injures and seeks help may be able to appreciate not only the emotional impact on their friends and family, but also of how that impact might influence their relationship with professionals.

One solution is first to identify the extreme positions, and then to attempt to steer a middle course between them. A carer might consider striking a balance between, for example, being judgemental and colluding, or between over-reacting and being unmoved. The person who self-injures might consider a balanced position between expecting all mental health staff to be knowledgeable about wound care, and expecting them all to be ignorant and squeamish.

The potential for a team of carers to split into groups with strongly contrasting views about how best to manage their more challenging patients is well documented. This type of polarization is usually damaging to all parties (page 110). There are many possible lines of cleavage, but we have found that a common split is between those who prefer a 'firmer' management style (who are less tolerant and see the patient as more in control) and those with a 'softer' style (who are more tolerant and see the patient as less in control). How such divisions come about is the subject of some conjecture. Some professionals view certain of their patients as having the ability to split care teams, perhaps by evoking complex counter-transference reactions. We have found (as have others) that the splits that commonly occur within care teams are often along lines of cleavage that already exist, and that mildly polarized views can easily become more extreme when strong emotions are experienced by individual members of the team. Holding regular discussions between team members in attempt to find a middle ground is the usual attempt at a solution. We suggest this is helpful if it leads to inter-personal conflicts being resolved, but unhelpful if the conflicts fester or the two groups are unable to tolerate each other's views.

Dealing with the uncomfortable feeling that one does not know who the person who self-injures really is can be another difficulty. People who self-injure often seem as though they do not have a properly developed identity. They often seem unstable and behave inconsistently. This unpredictability leads to others experiencing frustration, distrust and even fear (page 115). Coping with that frustration by blaming or avoiding the self-injuring person is, however, more likely to exacerbate the situation than help it.

The last section of Chapter 6 considers issues of safety and protection. Making a decision about when it is appropriate for one adult to take responsibility over another is never straightforward, particularly when considering people who injure themselves without clear suicidal intent. The law offers only limited guidance, and views about what constitutes a person's safety vary between professional groups and care agencies (page 127). Compulsory admission to hospital for treatment is only possible under certain specific circumstances which include that the person be suffering from a diagnosable mental disorder, is currently a danger to him/herself or others, and that treatment is likely to improve his/her condition. In the case of self-injury, compulsory admission may, in fact, take responsibility away from the person and thus lead to an increase rather than a decrease in self-harm (page 128).

We conclude that the threat of further self-injury is not, of itself, sufficient to justify restraint or compulsory treatment. There needs to be additional, significant evidence that the person is unable to take responsibility for his or her actions, or a definite increased risk of suicide, or a real risk that further self-injury will result in permanent disfiguring mutilation.

> Immediate challenges for professional carers include assessing risk, deciding about safety and offering short-term coping strategies

Professional health care staff often have difficulty knowing how best to respond to someone who has just self-injured. Unfortunately, there is currently little research evidence to indicate the most effective ways of managing people who self-injure in the short-term.

Care staff will need to address the risk both of suicide and of further self-injury, but many find that carrying out this type of assessment is not straightforward. An essential first step is to establish a relationship with the self-injuring person and to build a rapport. Focusing solely on his or her injury is usually not the best way to achieve this (page 136). There is a need to strike a balance between acknowledging the person, acknowledging their injuries and acknowledging one's own reaction to both. Establishing such a balance is necessary because this type of risk assessment involves carefully questioning the person, unlike some medical assessments which concentrate on physiological indicators. This is a point that is sometimes missed by staff working in busy casualty units.

Chapter 7 has provided a summary of the main risk factors for suicide after self-harm (page 138). This risk is increased where there has been previous self-harm, where the injury is serious, when the client reports that self-injury no longer relieves dysphoria and where there is profound hopelessness. Suicide also appears more likely if there is a recent pattern of increased self-injury, addiction to alcohol or drugs or concurrent serious mental illness. These potential indicators are derived statistically from observations of large groups of people, however. The clinician will need to be aware that their predictive ability may be poor at the individual level.

The likelihood of repetition may also need to be assessed (page 144). Here the main risk factor is the number previous acts of self-harm, so that someone who has already cut themselves many times is very likely to do so again. The presence of substance misuse, unemployment, younger age and hopelessness also appear as significant factors. We suggest that it is also relevant to ask the person how addictive they feel their self-injury has become, as well as to question them about cravings, how frequently they experience 'switching' suddenly into self-injury, and how often they have dissociative experiences.

In cases where a significant risk of suicide or serious further self-harm is apparent, health care staff need to decide if coercion is justified in an attempt to avert a possible tragedy (page 151). We conclude that coercion can only be justified if one can show clearly that the person is irrational. Here we find that the presence of severe depression or other serious mental illness can be sufficient, but that the presence of personality disorder alone is not. Coercion may also be justified where there is a clear indication of intent to commit suicide, particularly where there is concurrent hopelessness and isolation. Compulsory admission to hospital requires very careful consideration, however, since it may be more likely to make self-injury worse.

A more common situation is one where the risk of further serious harm is relatively low, but where a person presents in distress and asks for immediate help to help them avoid self-harming. This can be particularly challenging for both formal and informal carers who then feel they are 'put on the spot' to deliver some effective short-term intervention that will help alleviate the crisis (page 153). Unfortunately, again, the current research literature offers no conclusive evidence of any intervention being effective in such situations. We suggest there is value in working with the client to develop a portfolio of short-term coping strategies since these can become useful self-help techniques that are at their most valuable when professional help is unavailable (page 154). Examples provided in Chapter 7 include distraction techniques, strategies that substitute for some of the effects of self-injury (page 158), methods to express emotion and to manage flashbacks as well as dissociative episodes (page 157).

> Longer-term interventions for people who self-injure need to be multi-facetted

Self-injury can become a trap in the long-term when a person has become addicted to it, or when it seems the only way that they can cope with unpleasant and overwhelming feelings. It also happens when the self-injury itself becomes a component of that person's identity. People who self-injure repeatedly may eventually decide they want to get out of this trap, and look around for a professionally-delivered intervention to help them achieve this.

To date, however, we can find no convincing evidence of any intervention specifically designed for people who self-injure – of even, more broadly, for people who self-harm – being consistently effective. This can seem disappointing at first. It is however worth recalling that self-injury is a behaviour that can serve many functions, and that to focus solely on a treatment to extinguish it may be to pay insufficient attention to the problems and issues that give rise to the feelings that it temporarily moderates. The interventions that are available tend either to address specific difficulties, or to help groups of people with particular patterns of difficulty. An example of the latter is dialectical behaviour therapy (page 173) which is a promising multi-modal therapy originally developed for people diagnosed with borderline personality disorder and which addresses self-harm in the context of the other characteristics commonly associated with that diagnosis. This includes difficulty in regulating emotions and tolerating stress. Certain components of this approach seem to be particularly relevant to people who self-injure and the therapy has been shown to lead to reduced self-harm in some trials, although this change has not always been statistically significant.

We conclude that any approach to helping someone who wants to give up self-injury will need to be multi-facetted if it is to be effective. Psychological interventions currently appear to show more promise that pharmacological ones, although a combination of the two is often helpful. The overall framework should facilitate the setting of goals that are realistic and obtainable within a reasonable time period (page 186). It is often preferable to focus on one day at a time, as with other addictive behaviours. Clients can be helped to identify any clear triggers and to learn to avoid, where practical, the types of situation that give rise to them (page 184). Specific techniques may then be considered for managing the various elements that we now know contribute to persistence of self-injury. These include craving, dissociation and switching as well as emotional dysregulation.

Cravings are not easily weakened (page 167), but can diminish with time if they are not acted upon. Learning to oppose a craving with some strong alternative positive reward can be more effective, although it is not always easy to find such an alternative for a person whose life seems full of problems and crises. Certain medications (for example, the dopamine agonists) have a theoretical potential to help reduce craving, but none have yet shown to have any consistent beneficial effect. Psychotherapy can also help, but tends to require that the person must first have made a firm decision to change.

Reduction in the frequency and intensity of switching and transient dissociative episodes can usually be achieved with practice. This can be addressed directly though psycho-education, cue identification and avoidance as well as specific cognitive interventions (page 171). Other techniques increase 'mindfulness' as way of focusing attention under conscious control and so may reduce the tendency to dissociate (page 175). Dialectical behaviour therapy also appears to reduce dissociation, although it remains unclear which of its therapeutic components are responsible.

Learning to deal with difficult emotions without dissociating from them has obvious potential. Research is beginning to provide useful information about how emotions are processed and group-based programmes have been developed for reappraising – rather than suppressing – difficult emotions (page 178). Cognitive therapy can help a person to change their assumptions about self-injury as the only method of coping with difficult emotions. In the longer-term, the person may also need assistance in learning to replace the identity of being a self-injurer, and to be able to live without self-injury but with the inevitable long-term effects of the scars.

We conclude that counselling and psychotherapy can play a key role in helping people who self-injure, particularly when the contact can be sustained over a reasonable time period. There are advantages if this can be combined with appropriate self-help techniques. It seems to us essential to establish a collaborative agreement with the client from the start and to be able to work consistently towards increasing his or her sense of autonomy. We also think it valuable that each person has some choice in who they work with, and in the modality of any psychological treatment they undergo.

A look to the future

It has been encouraging to see how awareness of the problems faced by people who self-injure has improved in the last few years. With this has come a significant increase in the provision of dedicated self-harm teams and in the number mental health liaison staff available to assess patients who attend casualty departments after self-harming. Self-harm is a topic now included in most training programmes for those seeking a professional clinical qualification, and is regularly addressed through short in-service courses run by care service providers. Staff who work in agencies other than mental health are also becoming more aware of the issues in managing people who self-poison and self-injure, and this will be valuable if it helps weaken the somewhat artificial divide between physical and mental health care.

We believe there can, however, be disadvantages in taking too general an approach to self-harm, and advantages to considering self-injury in its own right. We have suggested that the process that leads to a self-inflicted injury is not necessarily the same as that which leads to an overdose, although more research is needed to confirm the circumstances in which the two differ.

Research is also needed to identify factors that both weaken and strengthen the safety-catch. One possible factor is the history of how well a person's skin has been cared for, although this needs substantiating. Learning how the safety-catch can be strengthened would be of particular clinical value, especially as experience suggests that people who self-injure often try to find ways of doing this for themselves when struggling to avoid cutting. Investigation is also needed to discern why some people experience a pattern of self-injury that becomes chronic over time, whereas others appear more resilient. If factors that differentiate these two groups can be identified, additional help and support might be offered to those more likely to be vulnerable.

There is scope for further work to improve our understanding of dissociation in the context of self-injury. Existing cognitive techniques that can help a person reduce their tendency to dissociate might be refined so as to be more easily matched to a particular presentation, and documented so that they can be offered to clients in a consistent way.

Further investigation into the role played by shame in self-injury is, we suggest, likely to be particularly fruitful. Shame is an exceptionally powerful emotion; it appears to be predictive of self-harm (page 63), can act as an emotional trigger in the spring pathway to self-injury, is able to destroy a person's sense of identity and often emerges directly as a consequence of skin cutting (page 18). It reduces the ability to form and maintain relationships since the action tendency associated with shame is to hide (page 47), and the secrecy that ensues may promote dissociation as well as reducing the person's potential to get help from others. Any intervention that is able to reduce shame is likely to have a very significant positive impact on the life of someone who self-injures.

Appendix – Self-Help Resources

BOOKS AND PAMPHLETS

A wide variety of books, booklets and pamphlets that focus on self-harm are available from booksellers, voluntary organizations, charities, mental health trusts, professional associations, youth organizations and women's groups. Most have sections that cover self-injury, although not all provide much in the way of self-help material. The following list contains some of those that do:

- *Life After Self-Harm: a guide to the future* is a book written by Ulrike Schmidt and Kate Davidson specifically for individuals who have harmed themselves. It takes the form of a self-help manual and aims to teach a number of skills such as how to keep safe in a crisis, how to develop coping strategies and how to deal with seemingly insolvable problems. It is published in the UK by Brunner-Routledge (2004).
- *The Hurt Yourself Less Workbook* is a comprehensive manual written for people who self-harm by people who self-harm. It offers a wide range of practical self-help exercises. The workbook is available from the National Self-Harm Network, PO Box 7264, Nottingham, NG1 6WJ, UK (1998). Website: www.nshn.co.uk/
- *Women and Self-Harm* is a book written by Gerrilyn Smith, Dee Cox and Jacqui Saradjian. The authors devote a full chapter to self-help. It is published by The Women's Press, London, UK (1998).
- *The Scarred Soul* is a book written by Tracy Alderman as a self-help guide. It is designed for people who experience 'self-inflicted violence' and covers a broad range of topics including advice on dealing with dissociation, finding appropriate support and beginning therapy. It is published by New Harbinger, Oakland, California (1997).

■ *Understanding Self-Injury: a workbook for adults* is written by Kristy Trautmann and Robin Connors. It too offers a wide range of practical self-help exercises and can be ordered from Pittsburgh Action Against Rape at 81 South 19th Street, Pittsburgh, PA 15203.

■ *The Rainbow Journal* is a colourful newsletter produced by Bristol Crisis Service for Women specifically for young people who self-injure. The Service also produces a series of well-written and inexpensive booklets on various aspects of self-harm including *Self-help for Self-Injury* and *Women and Self-Injury: Information for Family and Friends* (both by Lois Arnold). Details are available from the Bristol Crisis Service for Women, PO Box 654, Bristol BS99 1XH, UK. Website: www.users.zetnet.co.uk/BCSW/publications.htm.

■ *The Cutting Edge* is a newsletter for women living with self-inflicted violence and is available from The Cutting Edge, PO Box 20819, Cleveland, Ohio 44120, USA.

■ The Basement Project (www.basementproject.co.uk/) produces a number of books and resource packs that contain self-help material. The range includes *The Self-Harm Help Book* written by Lois Arnold and Anne Magill for people who want to help themselves or others in their struggle with self-harm. It is available from: Green Leaf Bookshop, 82 Colston St, Bristol BS1 5BB, UK. Tel: 0117 921 1369.

■ *Healing the Hurt Within* is written by Jan Sutton and includes sections on self-help. The book seeks to improve understanding about self-injury and self-harm and is aimed both at sufferers and staff that care for them. It is published by How To Books Ltd, Oxford, UK (2005).

WEBSITES

There are currently a considerable number of websites offering resources to people who self-injure. The following short list illustrates the range. Some sites offer online support through discussion forums and bulletin boards. Most offer self-help materials and ideas, links to other sources of online support, advice on getting professional help as well as information for friends and family. There are many other sites available.

www.palace.net/~llama/psych/injury.html
www.selfharm.org/
www.siari.co.uk/
www.shsanctuary.com/forum/index.php

www.recoveryourlife.com/

www.psyke.org/

www.self-injury.net/

www.mirror-mirror.org/selfinj.htm

www.users.zetnet.co.uk/BCSW/

www.mosaicminds.org/safe-ground-new.shtml

ORGANIZATIONS AND CHARITIES

- MIND, 15–19 Broadway, London E15 4BQ, UK. Tel: 020 8519 2122. Website: www.mind.org.uk/
- YoungMinds, 48–50 St John Street, London EC1M 4DG, UK. Tel: 020 7336 8445. Website: www.youngminds.org.uk/
- Mental Health Foundation, 9th Floor, Sea Containers House, 20 Upper Ground, London, SE1 9QB, UK. Website: www.mentalhealth.org.uk/
- National Self Harm Network, PO Box 7264, Nottingham, NG1 6WJ, UK. Website: www.nshn.co.uk/
- Eating Disorders Association, Sackville Place, 44 Magdalen Street, Norwich NR3 1JU, UK. Tel: 01603 619090. Website: www.edauk.com/
- International Society for the Study of Trauma and Dissociation, 8201 Greensboro Drive, Suite 300, McLean, VA 22102 USA. Tel: 703/610-9037. Website: http://www.isst-d.org/
- First Person Plural, PO Box 2537, Wolverhampton, WV4 4ZL, UK. Website: www.firstpersonplural.org.uk/
- The Basement Project, PO Box 5, Abergavenny NP7 5XW, UK. Tel: 01873 856524. Website: www.basementproject.co.uk/
- Bristol Crisis Service for Women, PO Box 654, Bristol BS99 1XH, UK. Tel: 0117 925 1119. Website: www.users.zetnet.co.uk/BCSW/
- National Children's Bureau. Self-Harm website: www.selfharm.org.uk/default.aspa
- NHS Direct. Tel: 0845 4647. Website: www.nhsdirect.nhs.uk/
- Samaritans: Tel: 08457 909090. Website: www.samaritans.org.uk/
- ChildLine: Tel: 0800 1111. Website: www.childline.org.uk/

Notes

1 THE BASIC FACTS ABOUT SELF-INJURY

1. Readers who are interested in self-injury that is valued rather than condemned by society, or the self-injury which is an incidental consequence of deliberate bodily modification, can read our review of these and other kinds of self-injury at www.reconciliation.org.uk.

2 UNDERSTANDING THE PERSON WHO SELF-INJURES

1. We provide a more broadly based anthropological review of self-injury in the supplementary chapter that is freely available at www.reconciliation.org.uk.

7 FIRST PROFESSIONAL RESPONSES TO SELF-INJURY

1. From 'Youth and self-harm: Perspectives'. A summary of research commissioned by Samaritans and carried out by the Centre for Suicide Research, University of Oxford.
2. In comparison with non-repeaters.

References

Adams J, Rodham K & Gavin J (2005). Investigating the 'self' in deliberate self-harm. *Qualitative Health Research*, 15, 1293–1309.

Agargun M Y, Tekeoglu I, Kara H, Adak B & Ercan M (1998). Hypnotizability, pain threshold, and dissociative experiences. *Biological Psychiatry*, 44(1), 69–71.

Alao A, Yolles J C & Armenta W (1999). Cybersuicide: the Internet and suicide. *American Journal of Psychiatry*, 156, 1836–7.

Alexius B, Berg K & Aberg-Wistedt A (2002). Psychiatrists' perception of psychiatric commitment. *International Journal of Law and Psychiatry*, 25, 109–17.

Allen C (1995). Helping with deliberate self-harm: some practical guidelines. *Journal of Mental Health*, 4, 243–50.

Amis M (1989). *London Fields*. London: Jonathan Cape.

Anon (2004). Australian and New Zealand clinical practice guidelines for the management of adult deliberate self-harm. *Australian and New Zealand Journal of Psychiatry*, 38(11–12), 868–84.

Antonowicz J L, Taylor L H, Showalter P E, Farrell K J & Berg S (1997). Profiles and treatment of attempted suicide by self-immolation. *Gen Hosp Psychiatry*, 19(1), 51–5.

Anzieu D (1989). *The Skin Ego: A Psychoanalytical Approach to the Self* (translated by Chris Turner). New Haven: Yale University Press.

Arango V, Huang Y Y, Underwood M D & Mann J J (2003). Genetics of the serotonergic system in suicidal behavior. *Journal of Psychiatric Research*, 37(5), 375–86.

Armel K C & Ramachandran V S (2003). Projecting sensations to external objects: evidence from skin conductance response. *Proceedings: Biological Sciences / The Royal Society*, 270, 1499–506.

Arnold L (1995). *Women and Self-Injury: a survey of 76 women*. Bristol: Bristol Crisis Service for Women.

Arnold L & Magill A (1996). *Working with Self-Injury*. Bristol: The Basement Project.

Arnold L & Magill A (2000). *Making Sense of Self-Harm*. Abergavenny: The Basement Project.

Ayton A, Rasool H & Cottrell D (2003). Deliberate self-harm in children and adolescents: association with social deprivation. *European Child and Adolescent Psychiatry*, 12(6), 303–7.

Babiker G & Arnold L (1997). *The Language of Injury: comprehending self-mutilation.* Leicester: BPS Books.

Bales R F (1955). Adaptive and integrative changes as sources of strain in social systems. In: *Small Groups* (eds A P Hare, E F Borgatta & R F Bales), pp. 127–31. New York: Alfred A.Knopf.

Balsam K F, Beauchaine T P, Mickey R M & Rothblum E D (2005). Mental health of lesbian, gay, bisexual, and heterosexual siblings: effects of gender, sexual orientation, and family. *Journal of Abnormal Psychology*, 114, 471–6.

Barabasz A (1984). Enhancing hypnotic response with isolation. *Harvard Medical Area Focus* (1984, 4 January).

Beblo T, Driessen M, Mertens M, Wingenfeld K, Piefke M, Rullkoetter N, Silva-Saavedra A, Mensebach C, Reddemann L, Rau H, Markowitsch H J, Wulff H, Lange W, Berea, C, Ollech I & Woermann F G (2006). Functional MRI correlates of the recall of unresolved life events in borderline personality disorder. *Psychological Medicine*, 36, 845–56.

Benham E (1995). Coping strategies: a psychoeducational approach to post-traumatic symptomatology. *Journal of Psychosocial Nursing and Mental Health Services*, 33(6), 30–5.

Bernstein E M & Putnam F W (1986). Development, reliability and validity of a dissociation scale. *Journal of Nervous and Mental Disease*, 174(12), 727–34.

Biddle L, Gunnell D, Sharp D & Donovan J L (2004). Factors influencing help seeking in mentally distressed young adults: a cross-sectional survey. *British Journal of General Practice*, 54(501), 248–53.

Bierer L M, Yehuda R, Schmeidler J, Mitropoulou V, New A S, Silverman J M & Siever L J (2003). Abuse and neglect in childhood: relationship to personality disorder diagnoses. *CNS Spectrums*, 8, 737–54.

Binks C A, Fenton M, McCarthy L, Lee T, Adams C E & Duggan C (2006). Psychological therapies for people with borderline personality disorder. *Cochrane Database of Systematic Reviews* 2006, Issue 1. Art. No.: CD005652. DOI: 10.1002/14651858. CD005652.

Bohus M, Limberger M, Ebner U, Glocker F X, Schwarz B, Wernz M & Lieb K (2000). Pain perception during self-reported distress and calmness in patients with borderline personality disorder and self-mutilating behavior. *Psychiatry Research*, 95(3), 251–60.

Bohus M J, Landwehrmeyer G B, Stiglmayr C E, Limberger M F, Bohme R & Schmahl CG (1999). Naltrexone in the treatment of dissociative symptoms in patients with borderline personality disorder: an open-label trial. *Journal of Clinical Psychiatry*, 60(9), 598–603.

Bornovalova M A, Lejuez C W, Daughters S B, Zachary R M & Lynch T R (2005). Impulsivity as a common process across borderline personality and substance use disorders. *Clinical Psychology Review*, 25, 790–812.

Boyle A, Jones P & Lloyd S (2006). The association between domestic violence and self harm in emergency medicine patients. *Emergency Medicine Journal*, 23(8), 604–7.

Brain K L, Haines J & Williams C L (1998). The psychophysiology of self-mutilation: evidence of tension reduction. *Archives of Suicide Research*, 4, 227–42.

Breeze J A & Repper J (1998). Struggling for control: the care experiences of 'difficult' patients in mental health services. *Journal of Advanced Nursing*, 28(6), 1301–11.

Briere J & Gil E (1998). Self-Mutilation in clinical and general population samples: prevalence, correlates and functions. *American Journal of Orthopsychiatry*, 68(4), 609–20.

Briere J & Runtz M (1993). Childhood sexual abuse: long-term sequelae and implications for psychological assessment. *Journal of Interpersonal Violence*, 8(3), 312–30.

Brodsky B S, Cloitre M & Dulit R A (1995). Relationship of dissociation to self-mutilation and childhood abuse in borderline personality disorder. *American Journal of Psychiatry*, 152(12), 1788–92.

Brown G K, Beck A T, Steer R A & Grisham J R (2000). Risk factors for suicide in psychiatric outpatients: a 20-year prospective study. *Journal of Consulting Clinical Psychology*, 68, 371–7.

Brown M, Levensky E & Linehan M M (1997). The relationship between shame and parasuicide in borderline personality disorder. *Proc. Ann. Conv. Conf. Association for Advancement of Behavior Therapy (Nov 1997)*. Florida: Miami Beach.

Brundle J (1995). Dissociation among self-mutilating and non-self-mutilating female adolescents on an inpatient psychiatric hospital ward. *Dissertation Abstracts International: Section B: The Sciences & Engineering*, 56(6-B), 3434.

Burnham D L (1966). The special-problem patient: victim or agent of spitting. *Psychiatry*, 29, 105–22.

Butler L D, Duran R E, Jasiukaitis P, Koopman C & Spiegel D (1996). Hypnotizability and traumatic experience: a diathesis-stress model of dissociative symptomatology. *American Journal of Psychiatry*, 153(7), 42–63.

Cahn B R & Polich J (2006). Meditation states and traits: EEG, ERP, and neuroimaging studies. *Psychological Bulletin*, 132, 180–211.

Castillo R J (1990). Depersonalization and meditation. *Psychiatry*, 53, 158–68.

Cavanaugh R M (2002). Self-Mutilation as a manifestation of sexual abuse in adolescent girls. *Journal of Pediatric and Adolescent Gynecology*, 15, 97–100.

Cedereke M & Ojehagen A (2005). Prediction of repeated parasuicide after 1–12 months. *European Psychiatry*, 20, 101–9.

Chapman A L, Specht M W & Cellucci T (2005). Borderline personality disorder and deliberate self-harm: does experiential avoidance play a role? *Suicide and Life Threatening Behavior*, 35, 388–99.

Chard K M (2005). An evaluation of cognitive processing therapy for the treatment of PTSD related to childhood sexual abuse. *Journal of Consulting & Clinical Psychology*, 73(5), 965–71.

Chew G C, Bashir C & Chantler K (2002). South Asian women, psychological distress and self-harm: lessons for primary care trusts. *Health & Social Care in the Community*, 10(5), 339–47.

Chu J A, Frey L M, Ganzel B L & Matthews J A (1999). Memories of childhood abuse: dissociation, amnesia, and corroboration. *American Journal of Psychiatry*, 156, 749–55.

Classen C, Koopman C, Nevill-Manning K & Spiegel D (2001). A preliminary report comparing trauma-focused and present-focused group therapy against a wait-listed condition among childhood sexual abuse survivors with PTSD. *Journal of Aggression, Maltreatment & Trauma*, 4(2), 265–88.

Cohen J A, Mannarino A P, Zhitova A C & Capone M E (2003). Treating child abuse-related posttraumatic stress and comorbid substance abuse in adolescents. *Child Abuse & Neglect*, 27, 1345–65.

Colman I, Newman S C, Schopflocher D, Bland R C & Dyck R J (2004). A multivariate study of predictors of repeat parasuicide. *Acta Psychiatrica Scandinavica*, 109, 306–12.

Connors R E (1996). Self injury in trauma survivors. 1: functions and meanings. *American Journal of Orthopsychiatry*, 66(2), 197–206.

Connors R E (2000). Self-Injury: psychotherapy with people who engage in self-inflicted violence. New Jersey: Jason Aronson Inc.

Conterio K, Lader W & Bloom J K (1998). Bodily harm: the breakthrough healing program for self-injurers. New York: Hyperion.

Crowe M J (1997). Deliberate self-harm. In: *Troublesome Disguises: undiagnosed psychiatric syndromes* (eds D Bhugra & A Munro), pp. 206–25. London: Blackwell Science.

Crowell S E, Beauchaine T P, McCauley E, Smith C J, Vasilev C A & Stevens A L (2008). Parent–Child interactions, peripheral serotonin, and self-inflicted injury in adolescents. *Journal of Consulting & Clinical Psychology Special Section: Suicide and Nonsuicidal Self-Injury*, 76, 15–21.

Cullen J E (1985). Prediction and treatment of self-injury by female young offenders. In: *Prediction in Criminology* (eds D P Tarrington & R Tarling), pp. 135–48. Albany: State University of New York Press.

Curtis V, Aunger R & Rabie T (2004). Evidence that disgust evolved to protect from risk of disease. *Proceedings: Biological Sciences / The Royal Society*, 271, Suppl. 4, S131–3.

Daldin H J (1988). A contribution to the understanding of self-mutilating behaviour in adolescence. *Journal of Child Psychotherapy*, 14, 61–6.

Dallam S J (1997). The identification and management of self-mutilating patients in primary care. *The Nurse Practitioner*, 22, 151–8.

Darche M A (1990). Psychological factors differentiating self-mutilating and non-self-mutilating adolescent in-patient females. *Psychiatric Hospital*, 21, 31–5.

Davidson B (1998). The Internet and the large group. *Group Analysis*, 31, 457–71.

Davison K (1964). Episodic depersonalization: observations on 7 patients. *British Journal of Psychiatry*, 110, 505–13.

De Leo D, Scocco P, Marietta P, Schmidtke A, Bille-Brahe U, Kerkhof A J, Lonnqvist J, Crepet P, Salander-Renberg E, Wasserman D, Michel K & Bjerke T (1999). Physical illness and parasuicide: evidence from the European Parasuicide Study Interview Schedule (EPSIS/WHO-EURO). *International Journal of Psychiatry in Medicine*, 29, 149–63.

De Lissoroy V (1961). Head banging in early childhood: a study of incidence. *Journal of Pediatrics*, 58, 803–5.

De Young M (1982). Self-Injurious behaviour in incest victims: a research note. *Child Welfare*, 61, 577–84.

Deiter P J, Nicholls S S & Pearlman L A (2000). Self-Injury and self capacities: assisting an individual in crisis. *Journal of Clinical Psychology*, 56, 1173–91.

Demitrack M A, Putnam F W, Brewerton T D, Brandt H A & Gold P W (1990). Relation of clinical variables to dissociative phenomena in eating disorders. *American Journal of Psychiatry*, 147(9), 1184–8.

Dennis M, Beach M, Evans P A, Winston A & Friedman T (1997). An examination of the accident and emergency management of deliberate self-harm. *Journal of Accident & Emergency Medicine*, 14, 311–15.

Desai M (1997). Self-Harm in South Asian women. *Proc. 50th Anniv. Conf. Henderson Hospital: Managing Self-Harm*. London: St George's Hospital Medical School.

Deurzen E V (1994). Existential therapy. In: *Individual psychotherapy in Britain* (ed. W Dryden), pp. 120–30. Milton Keynes: Open University Press.

DiClemente R J, Ponton L E & Hartley D (1991). Prevalence and correlates of cutting behavior: risk for SIV transmission. *Journal of the American Academy of Child and Adolescent Psychiatry*, 30, 735–9.

Dong J Y, Ho T P & Kan C K (2005). A case-control study of 92 cases of in-patient suicides. *Journal of Affective Disorders*, 87, 91–9.

Donnellan C (ed.) (2000). *Issues Volume 51: Self-Harm and Suicide*. Cambridge: Independence Educational Publishers.

Draijer N & Langeland W (1999). Childhood trauma and perceived parental dysfunction in the etiology of dissociative symptoms in psychiatric inpatients. *American Journal of Psychiatry*, 156, 379–85.

Drew B L (2001). Self-Harm behavior and no-suicide contracting in psychiatric inpatient settings. *Archives of Psychiatric Nursing*, 15, 99–106.

Drug and Crimes Prevention Committee (2002). *Inquiry into the Inhalation of Volatile Substances: discussion document*. Melbourne: Victorian Government Printer. http://www.parliament.vic.gov.au/dcpc/Reports%20in%20PDF/Volatile_Substances_discuss_paper.pdf.

Dube S (2001). Childhood abuse, household dysfunction, and the risk of attempted suicide throughout the life span: findings from the adverse childhood experiences study. *JAMA*, 3089–96.

Dubrow-Eichel L & Dubrow-Eichel S (1985). The manipulation of spiritual experience: unethical hypnosis in destructive cults (Parts I, II and III). *Hypnosis Reports*, pp. 1–2 (July), pp. 3–4 (August), pp. 2–3 (September).

Dunbar R I M (2004). Gossip in evolutionary perspective. *Review of General Psychology*, 8, 100–10.

Durkheim E (1970). *Suicide: a study in sociology.* London: Routledge and Kegan Paul.

Evans J, Battersby S, Ogilvie A D, Smith C A, Harmar A J, Nutt D J & Goodwin G M (1997). Association of short alleles of a VNTR of the serotonin transporter gene with anxiety symptoms in patients presenting after deliberate self harm. *Neuropharmacology,* 36(4–5), 439–43.

Favazza A R (1996). *Bodies Under Siege: self-mutilation in culture and psychiatry* (2nd edition) Baltimore: Johns Hopkins University Press.

Favazza A R & Conterio K (1989). Female habitual self-mutilators. *Acta Psychiatrica Scandinavica,* 79, 283–9.

Fewtrell WD (1984). Relaxation and depersonalisation. *British Journal of Psychiatry,* 145, 217.

Fitzgerald S G & Gonzalez E (1994). Dissociated states induced by relaxation training in a PTSD combat veteran: failure to identify trigger mechanisms. *Journal of Traumatic Stress,* 7(1), 111–15.

Fontenot M B, Padgett E E, Dupuy A M, Lynch C R, De Petrillo P B & Higley J D (2005). The effects of fluoxetine and buspirone on self-injurious and stereotypic behavior in adult male rhesus macaques. *Comprehensive Medicine,* 55, 67–74.

Freud S (1914). *The History of the Psychoanalytic Movement.* Translation by A. A. Brill (1917). German original first published in the Jahrbuch der Psychoanalyse, 4.

Friedman T, Newton C, Coggan C, Hooley S, Patel R, Pickard M & Mitchell A J (2006). Predictors of A&E staff attitudes to self-harm patients who use self-laceration: influence of previous training and experience. *Journal of Psychosomatic Research,* 60(3), 273–7.

Frischholz E J, Lipman L S, Braun B G & Sachs R G (1992). Psychopathology, hypnotizability, and dissociation. *American Journal of Psychiatry,* 149(11), 1521–5.

Gabbard G O (1989). Splitting in hospital treatment. *American Journal of Psychiatry,* 146, 444–51.

Galdas P M, Cheater F & Marshall P (2005). Men and help-seeking behaviour: literature review. *Journal of Advance Nursing,* 49 (6), 616–23.

Gardner D L & Cowdry M D (1985a). Suicidal and para-suicidal behaviour in borderline personality disorder. *Psychiatric Clinics of North America,* 8(2), 389–403.

Gardner D L & Cowdry M D (1985b). Alprazolam-induced dyscontrol in borderline personality disorder. *American Journal of Psychiatry,* 142, 98–100.

Gardner F (2001). *Self-Harm: a psychotherapeutic approach.* East Sussex, UK: Brunner-Routledge.

Garrick J (2006). The humor of trauma survivors: its application in a therapeutic milieu. *Journal of Aggression, Maltreatment & Trauma,* 12(1–2), 169–82.

Gazda G (1989). *Group Counseling: a developmental approach.* (4th edition) Englewood Cliffs, NJ: Prentice Hall.

Gershuny B S & Thayer J F (1999). Relations among psychological trauma, dissociative phenomena, and trauma-related distress: a review and integration. *Clinical Psychology Review,* 19, 631–57.

Gilbert P, Pehl J & Allan S (1994). The phenomenology of shame and guilt: an empirical investigation. *British Journal of Medical Psychology*, 67(1), 23–36.

Gilbody S, House A & Owens D (1997). The early repetition of deliberate self harm. *Journal of the Royal College of Physicians of London*, 31, 171–2.

Glover H (1993). A preliminary trial of nalmefene for the treatment of emotional numbing in combat veterans with post-traumatic stress disorder. *Israel Journal of Psychiatry and Related Sciences*, 30(4), 255–63.

Grame C J (1993). Internal containment in the treatment of patients with dissociative disorders. *Bulletin of the Menninger Clinic*, 57, 3, 355–61.

Gratz K L & Gunderson J G (2006). Preliminary data on an acceptance-based emotion regulation group intervention for deliberate self-harm among women with borderline personality disorder. *Behavior Therapy*, 37, 25–35.

Graumann C F (2002). The phenomenological approach to people-environment studies. In: *Handbook of Environmental Psychology* (eds R B Bechtel & A Churchman.), pp. 95–113. John Wiley & Sons: New York.

Greenspan G S & Samuel S E (1989). Self-Cutting after rape. *American Journal of Psychiatry*, 146, 789–90.

Gross J (2001). Emotional regulation in adulthood: timing is everything. *Current Directions in Psychological Science*, 10(6), 214–19.

Gupta M A, Gupta A K & Johnson A M (2004). Cutaneous body image: empirical validation of a dermatologic construct. *Journal of Investigative Dermatology*, 123, 405–6.

Gutierrez P M, Rodriguez P J & Garcia P (2001). Suicide risk factors for young adults: testing a model across ethnicities. *Death Studies*, 25, 319–40.

Haas B & Popp F (2006). Why do people injure themselves? *Psychopathology*, 39(1),10–18.

Harcourt Assessment (2006). *Beck Hopelessness Scale*. Texas: San Antonio.

Hawton K (2000). Sex and suicide: gender differences in suicidal behaviour. *British Journal of Psychiatry*, 177, 484–5.

Hawton K & Catalan J (1987). *Attempted Suicide: a practical guide to its nature and management.* (2nd edition). Oxford: Oxford University Press.

Hawton K, Fagg J & Simkin S (1996). Deliberate self-poisoning and self-injury in children and adolescents under 16 years of age in Oxford, 1976–1993. *British Journal of Psychiatry*, 169, 202–8.

Hawton K, Harriss L, Simkin S, Juszczak E, Appleby L, McDonnell R, Amos T, Kiernan K & Parrott H (2000). Effect of death of Diana, Princess of Wales on suicide and deliberate self-harm, *British Journal of Psychiatry*, 177, 463–6.

Hawton K, Harriss L, Hodder K, Simkin S & Gunnell D (2001). The influence of the economic and social environment on deliberate self-harm and suicide: an ecological and person-based study. *Psychological Medicine*, 31, 827–36.

Hawton K, Rodham K, Evans E & Weatherall R (2002). Deliberate self-harm in adolescents: self-report survey in schools in England. *British Medical Journal*, 325, 1207–11.

Hawton K, Harriss L, Hall S, Simkin S, Bale E & Bond A (2003). Deliberate self-harm in Oxford, 1990–2000: a time of change in patient characteristics. *Psychological Medicine*, 33, 987–95.

Hayman R (1983). *Kafka, a biography.* Oxford: Oxford University Press.

Herman J L (1992). Trauma and recovery: from domestic abuse to political terror. London: Pandora.

Herpertz S, Sass H & Favazza A (1997). Impulsivity in self-mutilative behavior: psychometric and biological findings. *Journal of Psychiatric Research*, 31(4), 451–65.

Himber J (1994). Blood rituals: self-cutting in female psychiatric inpatients. *Psychotherapy: Theory, Research, Practice, Training*, 31(4), 620–31.

Hintz K J, Yount G L, Kadar I, Schwartz G, Hammerschlag R & Lin S (2003) Bioenergy definitions and research guidelines. *Alternative Therapies in Health and Medicine*, 9 (suppl. 3), A13–A30.

Hollander J E & Singer A J (1999). Laceration management. *Annals of Emergency Medicine*, 34(3), 356–67.

Holmes E A, Brown R J, Mansell W, Fearon R P, Hunter E C, Frasquilho F & Oakley D A (2005). Are there two qualitatively distinct forms of dissociation? A review and some clinical implications. *Clinical Psychology Review*, 25, 1–23.

Horne S (1999). From coping to creative change: the evolution of women's groups. *Journal for Specialists in Group Work*, 24(3), 231–45.

Horrocks J, Price S, House A & Owens D (2003). Self-Injury attendances in the accident and emergency department. *British Journal of Psychiatry*, 183, 34–9.

Howard League (1999). *Scratching the Surface: the hidden problem of self-harm in prisons.* London: Howard League for Penal Reform.

Howard League (2003). *Suicide and Self-Harm Prevention: the management of self-injury in prisons.* London: Howard League for Penal Reform.

Huband N & Tantam D (1999). Clinical management of women who self-wound: a survey of Mental Health professionals' preferred strategies. *Journal of Mental Health*, 8(5), 473–87.

Huband N & Tantam D (2000). Attitudes to self-wounding within a group of mental health staff. *British Journal of Medical Psychology*, 73, 495–504.

Huband N & Tantam D (2004). Repeated self-wounding: women's recollection of pathways to cutting and of the value of different interventions. *Psychology & Psychotherapy*, 77, 413–28.

Ivanoff A, Linehan M M & Brown M (2001). Dialectical behavior therapy for impulsive self-injurious behaviors. In: *Self-Injurious Behaviours: assessment and treatment* (eds D Simeon & E Hollander), pp. 149–73. Washington, DC: American Psychiatric Publishing Inc.

Jacobs B W & Isaacs S (1986). Pre-pubertal anorexia nervosa. *Journal of Child Psychology and Psychiatry*, 27, 237–50.

Jang K L, Paris J, Zweig-Frank H & Livesley W J (1998). Twin study of dissociative experience. *Journal of Nervous & Mental Disease*, 186(6), 345–51.

Janoff-Bulman R (1992). Shattered assumptions: towards a new psychology of trauma. New York: The Free Press.

Johnson F G, Frankel B G, Ferrence R G, Jarvis G K & Whitehead P C (1975). Self-Injury in London, Canada: a prospective study. *Canadian Journal of Public Health*, 66, 307–16.

Jones I H (1982). Self-Injury: towards a biological basis. *Perspectives in Biology and Medicine*, 26, 137–50.

Kamphuis J H, Ruyling S B & Reijntjes A H (2007). Testing the emotion regulation hypothesis among self-injuring females: evidence for differences across mood states. *J Nerv Ment Disease*, 195(11), 912–18.

Kapur N (2005). Management of self-harm in adults: which way now? *British Journal of Psychiatry*, 187, 497–9.

Kashani J H, Canfield L A, Borduin C M, Soltys S M & Reid J C (1994). Perceived family and social support: impact on children. *Journal of the American Academy of Child and Adolescent Psychiatry*, 33, 819–23.

Kelly J B (2000). Children's adjustment in conflicted marriage and divorce: a decade review of research. *Journal of the American Academy of Child & Adolescent Psychiatry*, 39, 963–73.

Kemperman I, Russ M J & Shearin E (1997). Self-Injurious behavior and mood regulation in borderline patients. *Journal of Personality Disorders*, 11, 146–57.

Kennerley H (1996). Cognitive therapy of dissociative symptoms associated with trauma. *British Journal of Clinical Psychology*, 35, 325–40.

Khantzian E J & Mack J E (1983). Self-Preservation and the care of the self: ego instincts reconsidered. *Psychoanalytic Study of the Child*, 38, 209–32.

Khazaal Y, Zimmermann G & Zullino D F (2005). Depersonalization: current data. *Canadian Journal of Psychiatry*, 50(2), 101–7.

Kleindienst N, Bohus M, Ludäscher P, Limberger M F, Kuenkele K, Ebner-Priemer U W, Chapman A L, Reicherzer M, Stieglitz R D & Schmahl C (2008). Motives for nonsuicidal self-injury among women with borderline personality disorder. *J Nerv Ment Disease*, 196(3), 230–6.

Klonsky E D (2007). The functions of deliberate self-injury: a review of the evidence. *Clinical Psychology Review*, 27(2), 226–39.

Klonsky E D, Oltmanns T F & Turkheimer E (2003). Deliberate self-harm in a nonclinical population: prevalence and psychological correlates. *American Journal of Psychiatry*, 160, 1501–8.

Koons, C R, Robins C J, Tweed J L, Lynch T R, Gonzalez A M, Morse J Q, Bishop G K, Butterfield M I & Bastian L A (2001). Efficacy of dialectical behavior therapy in women veterans with borderline personality disorder. *Behavior Therapy*, 32, 371–90.

Korte S M, Koolhaas J M, Wingfield J C & McEwen B S (2005). The Darwinian concept of stress: benefits of allostasis and costs of allostatic load and the trade-offs in health and disease. *Neuroscience & Biobehavioral Reviews*, 29, 3–38.

Kreeger L (ed.) (1994). *The Large Group: dynamics and therapy*. London: Kamac.

Lacey J H & Evans C D H (1986). The impulsivist: a multi-impulsive personality disorder. *British Journal of Addiction*, 81, 641–9.

Laloe V (2004). Patterns of deliberate self-burning in various parts of the world: a review. *Burns*, 30, 207–15.

Langeland W, Draijer N & van den Brink W (2002). Trauma and dissociation in treatment-seeking alcoholics: towards a resolution of inconsistent findings. *Comprehensive Psychiatry*, 43(3), 195–203.

Lazar S W, Bush G, Gollub R L, Fricchione G L, Khalsa G & Benson H (2000). Functional brain mapping of the relaxation response and meditation. *Neuroreport*, 11(7), 1581–5.

L'Hermitte J & Tchehrazi E (1937). L'image du moi corporel et ses déformations pathologiques. *L'Encephale*, 32, 1–24.

Lieb K, Zanarini M C, Schmahl C, Linehan M M & Bohus M (2004). Borderline personality disorder. *The Lancet*, 364, 453–61.

Liebenluft E, Gardner D L & Cowdry R W (1987). The inner experience of the borderline self-mutilator. *Journal of Personality Disorders*, 1(4), 317–24.

Liebling A (1998). Young women and self-injury in prisons. In: *Working with Young People in Custody – Training Pack*. London: Trust for the Study of Adolescence.

Linehan M (1993). *Cognitive Behavioural Treatment of Borderline Personality Disorder*. New York: The Guildford Press.

Lipschitz D S, Kaplan M L, Sorkenn J, Chorney P & Asnis G M (1996). Childhood abuse, adult assault, and dissociation. *Comprehensive Psychiatry*, 37(4), 261–6.

Low G, Jones D, MacLeod A, Power M & Duggan C (2000). Childhood trauma, dissociation and self-harming behaviour: a pilot study. *British Journal of Medical Psychology*, 73(2), 269–78.

Lubin H, Loris M, Burt J & Johnson D R (1998). Efficacy of psychoeducational group therapy in reducing symptoms of posttraumatic stress disorder among multiply traumatized women. *American Journal of Psychiatry*, 155(9), 1172–7.

Main T F (1957). The ailment. *British Journal of Medical Psychology*, 30(3), 129–45.

Major B & O'Brien L T (2005). The social psychology of stigma. *Annual Review of Psychology*, 56, 393–421.

Manuskiatti W & Fitzpatrick R E (2002). Treatment response of keloidal and hypertrophic sternotomy scars: comparison among intralesional corticosteroid, 5-fluorouracil, and 585-nm flashlamp-pumped pulsed-dye laser treatments. *Archives of Dermatology*, 138(9), 1149–55.

Markowitz P I & Coccaro E F (1995). Biological studies of impulsivity, aggression and suicidal behaviour. In: *Impulsivity and Aggression* (eds E Hollander & D J Stein), pp. 71–91. New York: John Wiley.

Marks I (1988). Blood-injury phobia: a review. *American Journal of Psychiatry*, 145(10), 1207–13.

Marriott R, Horrocks J, House A & Owens D (2003). Assessment and management of self-harm in older adults attending accidents and emergency: a comparative cross-sectional study. *International Journal of Geriatric Psychiatry*, 18(7), 645–52.

Martin G, Rozanes P, Pearce C & Allison S (1995). Adolescent suicide, depression and family dysfunction. *Acta Psychiatrica Scandinavica*, 92, 336–44.

Martin G & Waite S (1994). Parental bonding and vulnerability to adolescent suicide. *Acta Psychiatrica Scandinavica*, 89(4), 246–54.

Matsumoto T, Yamaguchi A, Chiba Y, Asami T, Iseki E & Hirayasu Y (2004). Patterns of self-cutting: a preliminary study on differences in clinical implications between wrist- and arm-cutting using a Japanese juvenile detention center sample. *Psychiatry and Clinical Neurosciences*, 58(4), 377–82.

Matsumoto T, Yamaguchi A, Chiba Y, Asami T, Iseki E & Hirayasu Y (2005). Self-burning versus self-cutting: patterns and implications of self-mutilation: a preliminary study of differences between self-cutting and self-burning in a Japanese juvenile detention center. *Psychiatry and Clinical Neurosciences*, 59 (1), 62–9.

Matthew R J, Wilson W H, Humphreys D, Lowe J V & Weithe K E (1993). Depersonalization after marijuana smoking. *Biological Psychiatry*, 33, 431–41.

McCarthy G & Taylor A (1999). Avoidant/ambivalent attachment style as a mediator between abusive childhood experiences and adult relationship difficulties. *Journal of Child Psychology and Psychiatry and Allied Disciplines*, 40, 465–77.

McDonagh-Coyle A, McHugo G J, Friedman M J, Schnurr P P, Zayfert C & Descamps M (2001). Psychophysiological reactivity in female sexual abuse survivors. *Journal of Traumatic Stress*, 14, 667–83.

Medford N, Baker D, Hunter E, Sierra M, Lawrence E, Phillips M L & David A S (2003). Chronic depersonalization following illicit drug use: a controlled analysis of 40 cases. *Addiction*, 98(12), 1731–6.

Melzer H, Jenkins R, Singleton N, Charton J & Yar M (1999). *Non-Fatal Suicidal Behaviour among Prisoners*. London: ONS.

Melzer H, Lader K, Corbin T, Singleton N, Jenkins R & Brugha T (2002). *Non-fatal Suicidal Behaviour among Adults Aged 16 to 74 in Great Britain*. London: The Stationary Office.

Menninger K (1935). A psychoanalytical study of the significance of self-mutilation. *Psychoanalytic Quarterly*, 4, 408–66.

Meyer J (1984). Intentional self-cutting and borderline personality disorder. Unpublished dissertation. Los Angeles: California School of Professional Psychology.

Miller D (1994). *Women Who Hurt Themselves*. New York: Basic Books.

Miller W (2000). Motivational interviewing: IV. Some parallels with horse whispering. *Behavioural and Cognitive Psychotherapy*, 28, 285–92.

Mitchell A J & Dennis M (2006). Self harm and attempted suicide in adults: 10 practical questions and answers for emergency department staff. *Emergency Medicine Journal*, 23, 251–5.

Mitchell J E, Boutacoff L I & Hatsukami O (1986). Laxative abuse as a variant of bulimia. *Journal of Nervous and Mental Disease*, 171, 174–6.

Moene F C, Hoogduin K A & Van Dyck R (1998). The inpatient treatment of patients suffering from (motor) conversion symptoms: a description of eight cases. *International Journal of Clinical & Experimental Hypnosis*, 46(2), 171–90.

Morgan C J A, Riccelli M, Maitland C H & Currant H V (2004). Long-Term effects of ketamine: evidence for a persisting impairment of source memory in recreational users. *Drug & Alcohol Dependence*, 75(3), 301–8.

Morgan H & Owen J (1990). *Persons at Risk of Suicide: guidelines on good clinical practice*. Nottingham: Boots.

Morgan J & Hawton K (2004). Self-Reported suicidal behavior in juvenile offenders in custody: prevalence and associated factors. *Crisis*, 25, 8–11.

Morrissey M (1997). NBCC webcounseling standards unleash intense debate. *Counseling Today*, 40(6), 8–12.

Morton A (1997). *Diana: her true story in her own words*. London: Simon & Schuster.

Mourad I, Lejoyeux M & Ades J (1998). Prospective evaluation of antidepressant discontinuation. *Encephale*, 24(3), 215–22.

Nada-Raja S, Morrison D & Skegg K (2003). A population-based study of help-seeking for self-harm in young adults, *Australian and New Zealand Journal of Psychiatry*, 37, 600–5.

National Self-Harm Network (1998). *Hurt Yourself Less Workbook*. Nottingham: National Self-Harm Network.

Neeleman J, de Graaf R & Vollebergh W (2004). The suicidal process: prospective comparison between early and later stages. *Journal of Affective Disorders*, 82, 43–52.

Negro P, Palladino-Negro P & Louza M (2002). Do religious mediumship dissociative experiences conform to the sociocognitive theory of dissociation? *Journal of Trauma and Dissociation*, 3, 51–73.

Nelson S & Grunebaum H (1971). A follow-up study of wrist slashers. *American Journal of Psychiatry*, 128, 1345–9.

NICE (2004). Self-Harm. The short-term physical and psychological management and secondary prevention of self-harm in primary and secondary care. London: National Institute for Clinical Excellence.

Noshpitz J D (1994). Self-Destructiveness in adolescence. *American Journal of Psychotherapy*, 48, 330–46.

Novak M A (2003). Self-Injurious behavior in rhesus monkeys: new insights into its etiology, physiology, and treatment. *American Journal of Primatology*, 59, 3–19.

Noyes R Jr, Hoenk P R, Kuperman S & Slymen D J (1977). Depersonalization in accident victims and psychiatric patients. *J Nerv Ment Dis.*, 164(6), 401–7.

ONS (1997). Psychiatric Morbidity among Prisoners in England and Wales. London: Office for National Statistics.

Owens D, Horrocks J & House A (2002). Fatal and non-fatal repetition of self-harm: systematic review. *British Journal of Psychiatry*, 181, 193–9.

Page A C (2003). The role of disgust in faintness elicited by blood and injection stimuli. *Journal of Anxiety Disorders*, 17, 45–58.

Paivio S & McCulloch C (2004). Alexithymia as a mediator between childhood trauma and self-injurious behaviors, *Child Abuse and Neglect*, 28, 339–54.

Patton G C, Harris R, Carlin J B, Hibbert M, Coffey C, Scwartz M & Bowers G (1997). Adolescent suicidal behaviors: a population-based study of risk. *Psychological Medicine*, 27, 715–24.

Philipsen A, Schmahl C & Lieb K (2004a). Naloxone in the treatment of acute dissociative states in female patients with borderline personality disorder. *Pharmacopsychiatry*, 37(5), 196–9.

Philipsen A, Richter H, Schmahl C, Peters J, Rusch N, Bohus M & Lieb K (2004b). Clonidine in acute aversive inner tension and self-injurious behavior in female patients with borderline personality disorder. *Journal of Clinical Psychiatry*, 65(10), 1414–19.

Pitman R K (1990). Self-Mutilation in combat-related PTSD. *American Journal of Psychiatry*, 147, 123–4.

Polk E & Liss M (2007). Psychological characteristics of self-injurious behavior. *Personality and Individual Differences*, 43, 567–77.

Pooley E C, Houston K, Hawton K & Harrison P J (2003). Deliberate self-harm is associated with allelic variation in the tryptophan hydroxylase gene (TPH A779C), but not with polymorphisms in five other serotonergic genes. *Psychological Medicine*, 33(5), 775–83.

Prasad V & Owens D (2001). Using the Internet as a source of self-help for people who self-harm. *Psychiatric Bulletin*, 25, 222–5.

Price C (2006). Body-Oriented therapy in sexual abuse recovery: a pilot test comparison. *Journal of Bodywork and Movement Therapies*, 10(1), 58–64.

Prochaska J O & DiClemente C C (1983). Stages and processes of self-change of smoking: toward an integrative model of change. *Journal of Consulting and Clinical Psychology*, 51(3), 390–5.

Prochaska J O & Velicer W F (1997). The transtheoretical model of health behavior change. *American Journal of Health Promotion*, 12, 38–48.

Psychology Today (2006). http://www.medicinenet.com/script/main/art.asp?articlekey= 34778 (accessed 5 June 06).

Putman F W, Guroff J J, Silberman E K, Barban L & Post R M (1986). The clinical phenomenology of MPD: review of 100 cases. *Journal of Clinical Psychiatry*, 47, 285–93.

Radkowsky M & Siegel L J (1997). The gay adolescent: stressors, adaptations, and psychosocial interventions. *Clinical Psychology Review*, 17, 191–216.

Raleigh V S (1996). Suicide patterns and trends in people of Indian subcontinent and Caribbean origin in England and Wales. *Ethnicity and Health*, 1, 55–63.

Rashid A & Gowar J P (2004). A review of the trends of self-inflicted burns. *Burns*, 30, 573–6.

Rayner G C, Allen S L & Johnson M (2005). Countertransference and self-injury: a cognitive behavioural cycle. *Journal of Advanced Nursing*, 50(1), 12–9.

Reilly S P (1983). A study of self-mutilation and prognosis in personality disorder. MSc Thesis, University of Manchester.

Robinson A & Duffy J (1989). A comparison of self-injury and self-poisoning from the Regional Poisoning Treatment Centre, Edinburgh. *Acta Psychiatrica Scandinavica*, 80, 272–9.

Rodham K, Hawton K & Evans E (2004). Reasons for deliberate self-harm: comparison of self-poisoners and self-cutters in a community sample of adolescents, *Journal of the American Academy of Child and Adolescent Psychiatry*, 43, 80–7.

Rosen P M & Heard K V (1995). A method for reporting self-harm according to level of injury and location on the body. *Suicide and Life-Threatening Behavior*, 25(3), 381–5.

Ross C A, Ryan L, Anderson G & Ross D (1989). Dissociative experiences in adolescents and college students. *Dissociation: Progress in the Dissociative Disorders*, 2(4), 239–42.

Ross S & Heath N (2002). A study of the frequency of self-mutilation in a community sample of adolescents. *Journal of Youth and Adolescence*, 31(1), 67–77.

Royal College of Psychiatrists (2004). *Assessment following self-harm in adults*. Council report CR 122 2004. London: Royal College of Psychiatrists.

Russ M J, Roth S D, Lerman A, Kakuma T, Harrison K, Shindledecker R D, Hull J & Mattis S (1992). Pain perception in self-injurious patients with borderline personality disorder. *Biological Psychiatry*, 32, 501–11.

Sansone R A & Levitt J L (2002). Self-Harm behaviors among those with eating disorders: an overview. *Eating Disorders: The Journal of Treatment & Prevention (Special Issue: Self-Harm and Eating Disorders)*, 10 (3), 205–13.

Schmidt U & Davidson K (2004). *Life after Self-Harm: a guide to the future*. Hove, UK: Brunner-Routledge.

Schmidtke A, Bille-Brahe U, DeLeo D, Kerkhof A, Bjerke T, Crepet P, Haring C, Hawton K, Lönnqvist J, Michel K, Pommereau X, Querejeta I, Phillipe I, Salander-Renberg E, Temesváry B, Wasserman D, Fricke S, Weinacker B & Sampaio-Faria J G (1996). Attempted suicide in Europe: rates, trends and sociodemographic characteristics of suicide attempters during the period 1989–1992. Results of the WHO/EURO Multicentre Study on Parasuicide, *Acta Psychiatrica Scandinavica*, 93, 327–38.

Schwartz R H, Cohen P, Hoffman N G & Meeks J E (1989). Self-Harm behaviors (carving) in female adolescent drug users. *Clinical Pediatrics*, 28, 340–6.

Seedat S, Stein M B & Forde D R (2003). Prevalence of dissociative experiences in a community sample: relationship to gender, ethnicity, and substance use. *Journal of Nervous and Mental Disease*, 191, 2, 115–20.

Sierra M, Phillips M L, Ivin G, Krystal J & David A S (2003). A placebo-controlled, cross-over trial of lamotrigine in depersonalization disorder. *Journal of Psychopharmacology*, 17(1), 103–5.

Siever L J, Trustman R L & Silverman J M (1992). Validation of personality disorder assessment of biologic and family studies. *Journal of Personality Disorder*, 6, 301–12.

Silver S M, Brookes A & Obenchain J (1995). Treatment of Vietnam war veterans with PTSD: a comparison of eye movement desensitisation and reprocessing, biofeedback and relaxation training. *The Journal of Traumatic Stress*, 8(2), 337–42.

Simeon D, Stanley B, Frances A, Mann J J, Winchel R & Stanley M (1992). Self-Mutilation in personality disorders: psychological and biological correlates. *American Journal of Psychiatry*, 149, 221–6.

Simeon D & Favazza A R (2001). Self-Injurious behaviors: phenomenology and assessment. In: *Self-Injurious Behaviors: Assessment and Treatment* (eds D Simeon & E Hollander), pp. 1–28. Washington: American Psychiatric Publishing.

Simmer E D (1999). A fugue-like state associated with diazepam use. *Military Medicine*, 164(6), 442–3.

Sinclair J & Green J (2005). Understanding resolution of deliberate self harm: qualitative interview study of patients' experiences. *British Medical Journal*, 330, 1112.

Skegg K (2005). Self-Harm. *Lancet*, 28, 1471–83.

Smith G, Cox D & Saradjian J (1998). *Women and Self-Harm*. London: The Women's Press.

Sockalingam S & Stergiopoulos V (2005). Case report: repetitive autocastration secondary to severe personality disorder. *General Hospital Psychiatry*, 27, 453–4.

Sourander A, Aromaa M, Pihlakoski L, Haavisto A, Rautava P, Helenius H & Sillanpää M (2006). Early predictors of deliberate self-harm among adolescents. A prospective follow-up study from age 3 to age 15. *Journal of Affective Disorders*, 93, 87–96.

Sourkes T L (2006). On the energy cost of mental effort. *Journal of the History of the Neurosciences*, 15, 31–47.

Spender Q (2005). Assessment of adolescent self-harm. *Current Paediatrics*, 15, 120–6.

Stein D J & Niehaus D J H (2001). Stereotypic self-injurious behaviors: neurobiology and psychopharmacology. In: *Self-Injurious Behaviors: Assessment and Treatment* (eds D Simeon & E Hollander), pp. 29–48. Washington: American Psychiatric Publishing.

Stein M B & Uhde T W (1989). Depersonalization disorder: effects of caffeine and response to pharmacotherapy. *Biological Psychiatry*, 26 (3), 315–20.

Strong M (1998). *A Bright Red Scream: self-mutilation and the language of pain*. New York: Penguin Group.

Suominen K, Isometsa E, Ostamo A & Lonnqvist J (2004a). Level of suicidal intent predicts overall mortality and suicide after attempted suicide: a 12-year follow-up study. *BMC Psychiatry*, 4, 11.

Suominen K, Isometsa E, Suokas J, Haukka J, Achte K & Lonnqvist J (2004b). Completed suicide after a suicide attempt: a 37-year follow-up study. *American Journal of Psychiatry*, 161, 562–3.

Sutton J (2004). Understanding dissociation and its relationship to self-injury and childhood trauma. *Counselling & Psychotherapy Journal*, April 2004, 24–7.

Suyemoto K L (1998). The functions of self-mutilation. *Clinical Psychology Review*, 18(5), 531–54.

Szmukler G I & Tantam D (1984). Anorexia nervosa: starvation dependence. *British Journal of Medical Psychology*, 57(4), 303–10.

Takahashi T, Murata T, Hamada T, Omori M, Kosaka H, Kikuchi M, Yoshida H & Wada Y (2005). Changes in EEG and autonomic nervous activity during meditation and their association with personality traits. *International Journal of Psychophysiology*, 55, 199–207.

Tang C P, Pang A H & Ungvari G S (1996). Shoplifting and robbery in a fugue state. *Medicine, Science & the Law*, 36(3), 265–8.

Tantam D (1996). Fairbairn. In: *150 Years of British Psychiatry* (eds G Berrios & H Freeman), pp. 549–64. London: Athlone.

Tantam D (1998). Shame and the presentation of emotional disorders. In: *Shame: interpersonal behaviour, psychopathology and culture* (eds P Gilbert & B Andrews), pp. 161–75. Oxford: Oxford University Press.

Tantam D (2002). Reasons and psychological explanation. *International Journal of Psychotherapy*, 7, 165–73

Tantam D (2003). The flavour of emotions. *Psychology and Psychotherapy*, 76(1), 23–45.

Tantam D & Whittaker J (1992). Personality disorder and self-wounding. *British Journal of Psychiatry*, 161, 451–64.

Taylor B (2003). Exploring the perspectives of men who self-harm. *Learning in Health and Social Care*, 2(2), 83–91.

Toch H (1975). *Men in Crisis*. Chicago: Aldine.

Van der Kolk B, Perry C & Herman J L (1991). Childhood origins of self-destructive behavior. *American Journal of Psychiatry*, 148, 1165–73.

Van der Kolk B A (1989). The compulsion to repeat the trauma. Re-enactment, revictimization, and masochism. *Psychiatric Clinics of North America*, 12, 389–411.

Van Wel B, Kockmann I, Blum N, Pfohl B, Black D W & Heesterman W (2006). STEPPS group treatment for borderline personality disorder in the Netherlands. *Annals of Clinical Psychiatry*, 18(1), 63–7.

Waelde L (2004). Dissociation and meditation. *Journal of Trauma and Dissociation*, 5, 147–62.

Wallace A R (1910). *The World of Life: a manifestation of creative power, directive mind and ultimate purpose*. Chapter 19: Is nature cruel? The purpose and limitations of pain. London: Chapman & Hall.

Wallis D A N (2002). Reduction of trauma symptoms following group therapy. *Australian and New Zealand Journal of Psychiatry*, 36, 67–74.

Walsh B W & Rosen P M (1988). *Self-Mutilation: theory, research and treatment*. New York: Guildford Press.

Warren F, Dolan B & Norton K (1998). Bloodletting, bulimia nervosa and borderline personality disorder. *European Eating Disorders Review*, 6(4), 277–85.

Weller A & Feldman R (2003). Emotion regulation and touch in infants: the role of cholecystokinin and opioids. *Peptides*, 24, 779–88.

White V E, Trepal-Wollenzier H & Nolan J M (2002). College students and self-injury: intervention strategies for counselors. *Journal of College Counseling*, 5, 105–13.

Wilkinson-Ryan T & Westen D (2000). Identity disturbance in borderline personality disorder: an empirical investigation. *American Journal of Psychiatry*, 157, 528–41.

Williams J M (1986). Differences in reasons for taking overdoses in high and low hopelessness groups. *British Journal of Medical Psychology*, 59(3), 269–77.

Winnicott D (1945). Primitive emotional development. *International Journal of Psycho-Analysis*, 26, 137–43.

Wodarz N & Boning J (1993). 'Ecstasy'-Induced psychotic depersonalization syndrome. *Nervenarzt*, 64 (7), 478–80.

Yamamoto S, Kitamura Y, Yamada N, Nakashima Y & Kuroda S (2006). Medial prefrontal cortex and anterior cingulate cortex in the generation of alpha activity induced by transcendental meditation: a magnetoencephalographic study. *Acta Medica Okayama*, 60, 51–8.

Yang G H, Phillips M R, Zhou M G, Wang L J, Zhang Y P & Xu D (2005). Understanding the unique characteristics of suicide in China: national psychological autopsy study. *Biomedical and Environmental Sciences*, 18, 379–89.

Yates T M (2004). The developmental psychopathology of self-injurious behavior: compensatory regulation in posttraumatic adaptation. *Clinical Psychology Review*, 24, 35–74.

Yip P S & Cheung Y B (2006). Quick assessment of hopelessness: a cross-sectional study. *Health and Quality of Life Outcomes*, 4, 13.

Young R, Sweeting H & West P (2006). Prevalence of deliberate self harm and attempted suicide within contemporary Goth youth subculture: longitudinal cohort study. *British Medical Journal*, 332, 1058–61.

Zemaitiene N & Zaborskis A (2005). Suicidal tendencies and attitude towards freedom to choose suicide among Lithuanian schoolchildren: results from three cross-sectional studies in 1994, 1998, and 2002. *BMC Public Health*, 5, 83.

Zlotnick C, Shea T, Recupero P, Bidadi K, Pearlstein T & Brown P (1997). Trauma, dissociation, impulsivity, and self-mutilation among substance abuse patients. *American Journal of Orthopsychiatry*, 67(4), 650–4.

Zlotnick C, Mattia J I & Zimmerman M (1999). Clinical correlates of self-mutilation in a sample of general psychiatric patients, *Journal of Nervous and Mental Disease*, 187, 296–301.

Zoroglu S S, Tuzun U, Sar V, Tutkun H, Savacs H A, Ozturk M, Alyanak B & Kora M E (2003). Suicide attempt and self-mutilation among Turkish high school students in relation with abuse, neglect and dissociation, *Psychiatry and Clinical Neurosciences*, 57, 119–26.

Index